Canto is an imprint offering a range of titles, classic and more recent, across a broad spectrum of subject areas and interests. History, literature, biography, archaeology, politics, religion, psychology, philosophy and science are all represented in Canto's specially selected list of titles, which now offers some of the best and most accessible of Cambridge publishing to a wider readership.

Japan's capitalism: creative defeat and beyond

Japan's capitalism: creative defeat and beyond

Shigeto Tsuru

CAMBRIDGE
UNIVERSITY PRESS

Published by the Press Syndicate of the University of Cambridge
The Pitt Building, Trumpington Street, Cambridge CB2 1RP
40 West 20th Street, New York, NY 10011–4211 USA
10 Stamford Road, Oakleigh, Melbourne 3166, Australia

© Cambridge University Press 1993

First published 1993
First paperback edition 1994
Reprinted 1995
Canto edition 1996

Printed in Great Britain at the University Press, Cambridge

A catalogue record for this book is available from the British Library

Library of Congress cataloguing in publication data

Tsuru, Shigeto, 1912–
    Creative defeat and beyond: Japanese capitalism since the war /
Shigeto Tsuru.
        p.   cm. – (Cambridge surveys of economic policies and
institutions)
    Includes index.
    ISBN 0 521 36058 7 (hardback). – ISBN 0 521 57621 0 (paperback)
    1. Japan – Economic conditions – 1945–1989.   2. Japan – Economic
policy – 1945–1989.   3. Capitalism – Japan – History – 20th century.
4. Japan – Economic conditions – 1989–   5. Japan – Economic
policy – 1989–   6. Japan – Foreign economic relations – United States.
7. United States – Foreign economic relations – Japan.   I. Series.
HC462.9.T7627   1992
338.952'009'045 – dc20   92–4607   CIP

ISBN 0 521 36058 7 hardback
ISBN 0 521 57621 0 paperback

Contents

Foreword

JOHN KENNETH GALBRAITH

I have been a friend of Shigeto Tsuru for more than half a century. Our friendship began at Harvard in the years before the Second World War; in one fashion or another, we have maintained a close association ever since.

But more than friendship has been involved. More than anyone else, far more indeed, Shigeto Tsuru has been my instructor on and guide to the Japanese economy and polity for all these years. It is because of this, and not to add to Mark Perlman's excellent biographical note, that I am led to write this prefatory word.

Nothing like this book has been written about the Japanese economy before, and I cannot think of a single volume that covers similarly and so professionally and perceptively the economic development of any other country in these last fifty years. Quite literally, it is all here and in good, economical and persuasive English. We are accustomed to looking to the Japanese for achievement and excellence in other fields; here is achievement and excellence in economic history with a more than comprehensive view of the present scene.

In the marshalling of economic (and political) fact and its organization into a continuing and broadly based account, Tsuru has performed at the very highest level of historiography. One can only admire the way in which historical detail, not excluding the relevant supporting data, has been sought out and brought into continuing service. But there is more.

There is also the author's viewpoint. This involves a calm, detached look at both private achievement and public policy. He sees them both in their strengths, their weaknesses and their pursuit of economic interest and ideology. All this is observed and on occasion criticized. Let me emphasize: the superb and informed scholarship is the major reason to recommend this work.

But it would be a mistake, indeed, to suggest that this is a history of Japanese economic development in the conventional sense. In the later sections Tsuru comes to a scrutiny of Japanese capitalism both in its larger manifestation and in a wealth of detail. The latter ranges from observation on land speculation and neighborhood destruction in the great cities to the issue of privatization of public enterprises to the concept of the mixed economy. Then, in the final chapter, he urges the goals for Japanese economic, political and social development. He deals specifically with national defense, which he sees as best served by the absence of fear that comes from a Japan not oriented in any way toward militarism. He takes up policy toward the poor lands, the preservation of the Japanese landscape, medical development, and much else. All, no reader will doubt, is accomplished with informed good sense.

There is a final and remarkable feature. With many of the matters here described, and from the earliest days of the Occupation after the Second World War, Shigeto Tsuru has himself been intimately involved. Some of this has been by active participation, more, perhaps, because of his role and his leadership in the broad political current of social democracy. Yet no one will seriously suppose that this book is an exercise in personal history. The author's role in great decisions or his view and comment at the time receives at most only passing mention. This history is of Japanese capitalism and the present prospect, not of the author's far from minor role therein. Few who have had such a role are so reticent.

There is more to be said, including reference to the superb documentation that is woven into the text. But these are discoveries for the reader to make. There has been much discussion over the years of the at least mildly impenetrable character of the Japanese culture which is complicated by the defenses imposed by the Japanese language. The early pages of this volume tell of a somewhat overmotivated educational mission from the United States in the days of MacArthur that thought that language reform should be a major objective not only for the benefit of foreigners but also for the Japanese as well. After this book no one with an interest in Japanese economic development, its prospect and the needed course of policy can complain of any problem of access to the Japanese economic scene. And no one who has not read this book can presume to a full knowledge of that development and that prospect. These are strong words. They are strongly meant.

Acknowledgements

The birth of this volume owes much to Professor Mark Perlman who suggested as early as in 1986 that I venture a definitive work on the postwar economic development of Japan. I had published a small volume called *The mainsprings of Japanese growth: a turning point?* for the Atlantic Institute for International Affairs in 1976. Since that time, I have been thinking of expanding and bringing it up to date. Thus Professor Perlman's suggestion was a welcome opportunity.

There are already a large number of books and articles in non-Japanese languages which have dealt with the growth and development of the Japanese economy since the last war. But very few, I thought, have related the subject matter to the evolution of Japanese capitalism in its institutional characteristics. This gap I meant to fill in the present endeavor.

The sub-title chosen for this volume – Creative defeat and beyond – originates from Professor Kenneth Boulding's hypothesis that "very often there is the creative reaction to defeat," except that I chose to add "and beyond" since I consider that what happened after the high growth period in Japan is extremely important from the institutional point of view.

I have published a large number of essays in this field in my native language and naturally I drew upon some of them in the preparation of this volume. I shall not refer to them here. But as for the essays I wrote in English in the past, I should report that certain repetitions can be found here, first, in Chapter 6 where the discussion on the land "price revolution" dwells greatly on what I wrote in the *Festschrift* volume for Professor J.K. Galbraith (1989), and secondly, in Chapter 8 where I map out the programs for future Japan, repeating more or less what I wrote in *Japan Quarterly*, Volume 27, No.4, 1980.

In the preparation of this volume, I have of course benefited greatly from the researches by a number of scholars but, in particular, from those by Professor Yoshikazu Miyazaki, as readers will be able to confirm from the frequency of his appearance in the notes. I am especially grateful to him.

After the original manuscript was completed, I was fortunate in receiving helpful comments from Lord Eric Roll, Professor Martin Bronfenbrenner, Dr. Robert Feldman and a young Canadian graduate student Mr. Owen Griffiths, not to speak of the anonymous referee for publication. Needless to say, whatever inadequacies and faulty interpretations that may still remain are entirely my own. To all these people I express my heartfelt gratitude.

Last but not least, both Mark Perlman and Kenneth Galbraith have kept on encouraging me in my endeavor to complete the volume and in addition contributed embroidering pieces for this book, enhancing, I expect, the interests of readers to brief through the text. I cannot thank them enough for their ever-warm gesture of half a century of friendship.

This volume is my second major attempt to write a book-length treatise in English. My fifty-year-long helpmate, Masako, supported and assisted me in the first endeavor, which was my Ph.D dissertation at Harvard University in 1939–40. On this occasion of fulfilling my second endeavor, I take this opportunity to express my special gratitude to her, whose serious illness happened to coincide with the latter stage of my writing this book and yet who was ever considerate in enabling me to concentrate on the completion of the task. Fortunately, the sun shines on us both as I lay down my pen.

Introduction

"The rise of the Phoenix" may well be an apt phrase for the dramatic renascence of the Japanese economy from the hopelessly prostrated nadir of the immediate postwar period to the top-rank position in per capital GNP within less than a generation. One statistic alone is sufficient in testifying to this soaring performance: with the 1950 level at 100, the index for 1973 of the growth rate of labor productivity in manufacturing was 1412 for Japan, contrasted to 210 for the US and 411 for West Germany. An analysis of how this was possible is part of the task attempted in this volume. But it is, from my point of view, the less important task.

Challenge for affluence was accepted and the accomplishment in terms of GNP growth is beyond doubt. But the pitfalls of affluence are now no less evident, especially as the consequences of "the price revolution" in urban land and of financial euphoria have steeped into the fabric of a society with a prevalent money-oriented psychology. One of the pitfalls came to be exposed in the month of August 1991 as I write this Introduction, i.e., a number of financial scandals involving security houses, banks, credit unions, and some bureaucrats. As *The Economist* wrote: "[these scandals] make the eyes spin like a fruit machine. Add more noughts to the figures, find scams in every financial firm in the land, and no Japanese would any longer be surprised. It is dawning on many in the West, too: Japan is up to its neck in dirt . . . Scandals are sewn into the fabric of Japan's financial system, its corrupt politics and even of its business ways. They are systemic not only in nature but also in the risk that they pose: the world's largest single source of capital and one of its three top financial centres is riddled with crookery, has been supervised by the blind or the complacent, and could be – not is, but could be – facing collapse. Japan's dirt is dangerous stuff."[1]

It is clear enough that the sequel to the "The rise of the Phoenix" story has to deal with the logical and historical connections of such "systemic" scandals to the antecedent events in the Japanese economy as well as to

1

broader background in the international financial world. As readers will see, I have not done this task fully, partly because the revelation of the infamous events came only after I completed the text of this volume. However, I may point out that Chapters 6 and 7 do discuss somewhat longer-range development of the basic aspects of Japanese capitalism which might illuminate the systemic roots of the recent volcanic eruption of financial scandals. For the elucidation of this connection, I propose to add a few paragraphs here, in a hope of providing readers with a perspective of my own longer-range approach to the subject in question.

Schumpeter used to say: "You can ride on a horse, but not on a claim to a horse, whereas a claim to money or to objects of money is as good as money itself." Credit received is a claim to money, involving intertemporal exchange at a price which is called the rate of interest; and in Schumpeter's theoretical structure credit creation was regarded as pivotal in economic development under capitalism. But it is likely that Schumpeter never dreamed of the extent of multiplication of credit instruments in the decades after his death and the emergence of what Peter Drucker calls "symbol economy" – capital movements, exchange rates and credit flows – uncoupled from the "real economy" – the flow of goods and services.[2] It cannot be doubted that "what is essentially new in the present economic situation is that the center and focus of the capitalist economy has shifted from the production of goods and services to the buying, selling, and mutiplication of financial assets."[3]

Statistical confirmation of this trend is patent enough. For the international scene, relevant comparison would be between the volume of international trade in goods and services with the turnover of foreign-exchange transactions in the world's main money centers. As of April 1989 it was reported that the average daily net foreign-exchange transactions in the four world markets (London, New York, Tokyo, and Toronto) amounted to 445.9 billion dollars, or 111 trillion dollars on the annual base.[4] This figure, be it noted, is about 22 times the total annual world trade of approximately 5 trillion dollars in 1989. The trend was also significantly shown by the fact that the foreign-exchange transactions in the four markets increased by 116 percent from March 1986 to April 1989, while external trade in goods and services of the four countries (UK, the USA, Japan and Canada) expanded by 56 percent between the first quarter of 1986 and the first quarter of 1989. The gap in question was definitely widening in recent years.

Turning our attention to Japan's domestic scene, we observe, as described in Chapter 6, that due to the urban land-price revolution capital gains in landed property in one single year, in 1987 for example, amounted to 416 trillion yen – an amount exceeding Japan's GNP of that year (343 trillion yen) by more than 20 percent. A clear enough evidence of excessive overgrowth of claims to money as against productive activities!

Thus in both respects, that is, in the international financial activities and in the domestic monetary transactions, Japanese capitalism has come to develop a structure top-heavy with multi-layered financial claims on the basis of "the real economy", naturally enlarging the scope of mercenary and speculative activities among the men in "the symbol economy" echelon structure. One after another of revelations in the nature of financial scandals in Japan as the decade of the 1990s opened, involving security houses, banks, a "nod and wink"-prone Ministry of Finance, and even gangster groups, are of one piece with the pitfalls of affluence which set great store by money-making among the general public in the era of corporate capitalism. Galbraith has warned recently that "there is the possibility, even the likelihood, of self-approving and extravagantly error-prone behavior on the part of those closely associated with money."[5] This in itself is true enough. But more than the personal behavior pattern of individuals is at issue. The systemic roots of the type of excesses in "the symbol economy", so admirably analyzed by Anglietta and Orléan in their *La Violence de la Monnaie*,[6] are the problems challenging political economists of today to wrestle with.

Social consequences of the land-price revolution are discussed in Chapter 6 of the text; but broader ramifications of the financial euphoria in the various aspects of the present-day Japan are not dealt with here. Therefore, I may relate one piece of evidence in this regard, which has far-reaching significance for the future of Japan.

A recent opinion survey of high-school students[7] showed that more than 50 percent of them responded affirmatively to the statement that "the present-day Japan sets too much store by money and material objects and makes little of warmth of heart." Further, on the question: "Which color do you choose to characterize the future of Japan?", their response was "grey" 38.8 percent, "black" 15.7 percent, and "rose-color" 3.1 per cent. The survey suggests clearly that the younger generation in Japan is groping for concrete guiding principles for themselves, living as they do in the money-contaminated materialistic society of today. It is ironic that when small boys are asked if they know what a beetle is like the most commonly received answer is: "Yes, I know. That's what I can buy with a hundred yen coin."

It is certainly high time, I believe, that a generation like mine, which has gone through Japan's vicissitudes of war and peace, hardship and affluence, fulfils its responsibility of transmitting the lessons learned and of bringing out in bold concrete visions for the future of the country, so that hopefully at least 30 percent of the high-school students and not a mere 3.1

percent will be able to see "rose-color" prospect for themselves. This is what I have tried to do in the concluding chapter.

There is one other matter which I should like to explain by way of offering an excuse for my not applying a commonly used growth accounting approach in the discussion of Japan's growth performance in the postwar period.

The so-called "fundamental equation of growth accounting" is given, e.g. by Samuelson and Nordhaus,[8] as:

$$\% \text{ Q growth} = \tfrac{3}{4}(\% \text{ L growth}) + \tfrac{1}{4}(\% \text{ K growth}) + \text{T.C.}$$

where Q stands for output, L for labor, K for capital and T.C. for technical change (or total factor productivity) that raises productivity, and where $\tfrac{3}{4}$ and $\tfrac{1}{4}$ are the relative contributions of each input to economic growth, given by their relative shares of national income. Since, however, technical change cannot be measured directly, it is calculated as a residual, thus:

$$\text{T.C.} = \% \text{ Q growth} - \tfrac{3}{4}(\% \text{ L growth}) - \tfrac{1}{4}(\% \text{ K growth})$$

On the basis of this equation, Samuelson and Nordhaus calculated, substituting numbers for the period 1900–86 in the US, the contributions of technical change to be 1.85 percent per year against the 2.1 percent per year increase in output per worker, capital deepening accounting for the remaining 0.25 percent. More recent statistical studies for the US do not attribute such a big share to technical change in the growth accounting.

A natural question arises: What were the respective contributions of labor, capital and technical change to the 10 percent annual growth rate period of postwar Japan? It should be most interesting if we could compare the results with other countries and other periods. And we do have studies carried out by Japanese economists applying the above growth accounting approach. Readers will be able to find the answers in the Annual Economic Report of the Economic Planning Agency, giving the figures, for example, for the period 1970–89, of 4.8 percent for output, 2.9 percent for capital, 0.3 percent for labor, and 1.5 percent for technical change.

One wonders how useful these figures are. As for myself, I have been skeptical of this growth accounting approach ever since the idea was first formulated by Robert Solow in 1957; and I wrote a critical essay on the subject in 1965.[9] I take up this problem here because it is concerned with a basic methodological stand which lies behind my thinking as a political economist.

Readers will note that I make a peripheral reference to the distinction between "the real-wealth aspect" (or the *real* aspect) and "the socio-institutional aspect" (or the *value* aspect) as I discuss the role played by technological progress.[10] There, my thesis is that technological progress, which belongs to the realm of the real-wealth aspect, does impinge upon the mode of production, or the socio-institutional aspect, in such a way that this latter undergoes qualitative changes often of major dimensions. Methodological significance of this distinction between the real aspect and the value aspect, as well as the need for integrating the two, is quite far-reaching in the historical analysis of institutional development; and I dwelled on this problem quite extensively in my Mattioli Lectures of 1985.[11]

More specifically, the basic difficulty with the growth accounting approach is: whereas technical change belongs in the realm of the real aspect, factors of production, capital in particular, are essentially value concepts. In order that the Cobb–Douglas function, on which the accounting is based, be applicable, both capital and labor have to be identifiable in homogeneous physical units. But, for a dynamic economy, the choice of units for both labor and capital presents a formidable problem. For example, one cannot escape from the *value* implication of capital as affected by the rate of interest, the time pattern of wage rate changes, the interaction effects, etc., unless we assume a radically simplified economy with one-type of machine and no technological change. A great many refinements have been made on the technique of growth accounting by E. Denison and others over the last three decades; but the doubt still remains as to the practical significance of this approach, which does not go beyond a common-sense statement for Japan like: "the very high 1953–71 Japanese growth rate was not ascribable to any single determinant."[12]

The problem of units, I believe, remains unsolved. Economists like Keynes and Harrod, who performed a pioneering role in the development of modern macroeconomic theory, were, in their own way, aware of the peculiar difficulty which presented itself in the matter of the choice of units – the difficulty which stemmed from the double character (the value and the physical) of the production process, especially of the economic system as a whole. Keynes' solution was, as is well known, to adopt the labor-unit and/ or the wage-unit. Harrod, too, wrestled with a similar problem when he posed the question of whether neutral technical progress required new investment and answered that it was a question of definition – that the answer depended on whether a labor standard of value is chosen or a goods standard of value. The distinction between a labor standard or a goods standard corresponds to that of the value aspect and the real or physical aspect. Whereas microeconomics for a capitalist society can navigate almost entirely in the world of values, macroeconomics, especially of the dynamic type, finds it difficult to dissociate itself from the real or physical aspect of the subject matter. In this sense, the fact that Keynes, who was interested more in the short-run problem with no technological change, chose a labor standard and Harrod, who was concerned with a dynamic economics, chose a goods standard is easily understandable.

I hope that the foregoing is sufficient to convey my methodological inclination, while at the same time giving an explanation for my not using the growth accounting approach in the text.

1   The defeat and the Occupation reforms

This opening chapter is intended to serve as factual background for my analysis, in later chapters, of the vicissitudes of Japanese capitalism in the postwar period. Thus, I tried to be as objective as possible in following the relevant events, refraining from interweaving the accounts with my personal involvement in the affairs of the state. The chapter begins with the summary of the consequences of the defeat in the war, followed by a somewhat textbook style account of what the occupying authorities, essentially led by the US government, attempted to achieve by way of reforming Japan. Probably the most important among the reform programs were the land reform and the revision of the Constitution, both of which have had long-lasting impact on Japanese society, most likely because they found solid backing in the minds of Japanese people themselves. Since the subject matter dealt with in this chapter is a well-trodden ground, I felt that I could fulfil the task in a condensed manner, relying on the fact that interested readers could consult the fuller accounts given in the bibliographical references cited at the end of the book.

1. Consequences of the defeat in the war

The postwar history of Japan has to begin with the account of losses and damages as consequences of the defeat in their manifold aspects – territorial, material, human and organizational.

Territorially, the partition of the erstwhile Japanese empire involved, first by the terms of the Cairo Declaration of December 1943, the "stripping of all the islands in the Pacific which Japan has seized or occupied since the beginning of the first World War in 1914, and restoring to the Republic of China all the territories Japan had stolen from the Chinese, such as Manchuria, Formosa, and the Pescadores," and also the promise that "in due course Korea shall become free and independent"; and, second, by the terms of the Yalta Agreement of February 1945, the cession to the Soviet

Union of the southern half of Sakhalien (Karafuto) and the Kurile Islands. In addition, by the terms of Japan's surrender, a large part of peripheral islands, such as Ryūkyū (including Okinawa), Bonin, Izu, Iwō, and Marcus, were relegated to the trusteeship of the United States. In other words, Japan at the end of the war was shrunk essentially to four main islands of Hokkaido, Honshū, Shikoku, and Kyūshū.

Related to the loss of territories was the severe restriction of fishing grounds imposed by the Allied Powers. Before the war, Japan was the world's foremost fishing country, with an annual catch of almost one million tons. But the catch declined to 360 thousand tons by 1950.

Material losses and damages might have been far greater were it not for the fact that the fighting was terminated without a last ditch stand on the main islands. Thus a statement by Ambassador Edwin W. Pauley, head of the US Reparations Mission to Japan, in December 1945, as follows:

Despite all the destruction, Japan still retains, in workable condition, more plant and equipment than its rulers ever allowed to be used for civilian supply and consumption even in peaceful years. That surplus must be taken out. To complete the demilitarization of Japan by taking it out will not mean the complete deindustrialization of Japan. I want to be very emphatic on that point. Figures concerning one key industry will show what I mean. In steel, and in machine tools and other machinery made from steel, Japan's own figures show that she still has, in workable condition, more than twice the facilities that she had when she invaded Manchuria in 1931.[1]

Still, the extent of losses and damages was severe enough through the bombings from air, bombardment from warships and submarine attacks; and it is generally agreed that of the total national man-made material wealth which would have been in existence in 1945 in the absence of wartime damage roughly one-quarter was gone.[2] This meant that the amount of damage was approximately equal to the net addition to such national wealth over the decade of 1935 to 1945, leaving the remaining total equivalent to the amount existing in 1935.

Naturally, damage was quite uneven among different categories of material wealth. Most severely hit were commercial ships. There were six million tons of such ships before the war, and four million tons were built during the war. But 8.6 million tons of them were sunk in the war, leaving approximately 1.5 million tons of which two-thirds required major repairs.

The major damage, other than plant and equipment closely related to war activities, was in residential houses, most of which in Japan, being of wooden construction, were highly vulnerable to incendiary bombs during air attack. It is estimated that 2.1 million units were destroyed through bombing, and in addition 550,000 units were lost through removal and demolition, creating a shortage to the amount of 4.5 million units at the end of the war, taking into consideration the net increase of demand by repatriates and also the needed catch-up construction to fill the gap of absolute shortage during the war.

In a number of industries what is called "indirect damage" has to be taken into account, that is to say, loss of capacity performance due to insufficient repairs and up-keep caused by lack of component materials and speeded-up production – an inevitable consequence of the war-time effort. The extent of loss in this regard is not easy to estimate in terms of stocks, but can be guessed at in terms of flows of subsequent production. The government report earlier cited gives the figure of stock-equivalent loss of a little less than one-third of the "direct damage" loss; but the accuracy of this estimate is somewhat questionable.

The overall effect of the war on *man-power* supply is rather complex. On the one hand, the number of those who died in battle or from diseases contracted at the front was fairly accurately counted inasmuch as their relatives had to be officially notified of their death. Official figures of such death, estimated as of 1948, were:

1,140,429	Army
414,879	Navy
1,555,308	Total

This total, however, was the minimum figure since it did not include (a) those who were "missing," numbering 240,000 as of 1948, (b) the heavily wounded persons who subsequently died, and (c) those who died in non-official duties on the battle ground. On the other hand, the number of civilian deaths through bombing (including atomic bombs) is far more uncertain, although official figures (as of May 1948) showed:

299,485	deaths
24,010	"missing"
146,204	seriously wounded
469,699	Total

This total, however, does not include the civilian deaths in Okinawa, which are variously estimated as being within the range of 100,000 to 200,000. Thus, the total fatal war casualties may be roughly estimated to be anywhere around two and a half million.

Against this negative population effect we have to take into consideration the positive addition to domestic population in the form of returnees from mainland China and other Asiatic regions after the end of the war, numbering some six million, a large part of whom was technically qualified personnel. For example, in the category of railroad workers alone the forced returnees from China numbered close to 200,000. Most of such returnees entered the employment market, willing to work at lower wage-rates than their qualifications warranted.

Thus, the net effect of the defeat in the war upon the manpower situation could be considered positive from the standpoint of needed economic reconstruction within the shrunken territory of postwar Japan.

Organizationally, consequences of the defeat in war subsequent to the extreme strains for the war effort were, to say the least, considerable. The normal distribution system was naturally slow to recover after commandeering for military purposes was terminated and the dire shortage of basic consumers' goods continued in the atmosphere of popular resistance against war-time rationing. A natural consequence was the hoarding of any stocks which promised price rises on the one hand and the mushroom growth of black-market dealers on the other. As the defeat in the war became obvious to everyone through the Emperor's broadcast on August 15, 1945, or even before this day of unconditional surrender, since through the years of 1944 and the spring of 1945 defeat appeared inevitable, the national sense of manifest destiny, instigated by the war-time leaders, started to wane very rapidly; and this had the necessary effect on the established mores of social discipline as regards respecting of boundaries of propriety. The lid was lifted by natural force, so to speak, from sundry restraints that had been imposed by the war-time government. The obvious, overall consequence was that the general price rise was further stimulated by the wanton disbursement of the budgetary war fund, immediately subsequent to the unconditional surrender, for the liquidation of war-time contracts and for lump-sum retirement grants to the military personnel.[3]

The best indication of the general price rise was the trend of the official producers' price of rice, which was set on September 18, 1941 at 49.00 yen per *koku* (180 liters), raised on April 30, 1945 to 92.50 yen per *koku*, and then again raised in March 1946 to 300.00 yen per *koku* – the price which was applied retroactively to the rice harvested in 1945. It can be seen from this trend that whereas the percentage rise during the Pacific War was 89 percent, the end of the war precipitated the rise to 224 percent.

The organizational disruption brought about in the realm of corporate management was serious enough, although the disruptive effect was destined to become more intense as the mandatory reparation removals, the dissolution of the *zaibatsu*, and the purge orders against war-time business leaders loomed on the horizon. Inevitably, the recovery of production in the manufacturing sector took longer time than otherwise would have been the case.

2. The initial occupation policy of the US

The Japanese government decided to accept the terms of unconditional surrender specified in the Potsdam Declaration (July 26, 1945) of the Allied Powers on August 9, 1945 – the day the second atomic bomb was dropped on Nagasaki; and the Emperor broadcast over the radio the historic message of the termination of the war on August 15, 1945. The occupation of Japan began on 2 September with the signing of the surrender document on the US battleship *Missouri* in the Tokyo Bay.

The Occupation authorities, headed by General MacArthur, the Supreme Commander for the Allied Powers (SCAP), were confronted with an economy in collapse; but the original Presidential Policy Statement on Japan (made public on September 22, 1945) clearly stated that the responsibility for economic reconstruction was to be left primarily in the hands of the Japanese people and their government, saying in part that "the plight of Japan is the direct outcome of its own behavior, and the Allies will not undertake the burden of repairing the damage." It was further stated in the Basic Initial Post-Surrender Directive to SCAP for the Occupation and Control of Japan (November 8, 1945) that "you will make it clear to the Japanese people that you assume no obligation to maintain any particular standard of living in Japan." This particular point was made more specific by the Pauley Reparation Mission in November 1945 to the effect that the Allied Powers "should take no action to assist Japan in maintaining a standard of living *higher than* that of neighboring Asiatic countries injured by Japanese aggression" (italics added). No doubt this statement was intended to create scope for squeezing out greater reparations, but it was an extremely severe condition in the light of the multiple differentials which had existed in the standards of living between Indonesia, for example, and Japan. The lack of realism in the Pauley statement was soon recognized by the Allied Powers and in January 1947 the Far Eastern Commission, the eleven-nation commission meeting in Washington, DC with the responsibility for formulating policies for Japan, issued a directive declaring that "the peaceful needs of the Japanese people should be defined as being substantially the standard of living prevailing in Japan during the period of 1930–34." Originally, the target date for the attainment of this objective was 1950, but it soon became apparent that this was unrealistic and the Occupation authorities felt increasingly constrained by the fact that they had to be involved in the task of the economic reconstruction of Japan.

Thus it was that General MacArthur, becoming impatient of the sluggish, ineffectual manner in which the Japanese government was tackling the urgent problem of economic reconstruction, sent a severe letter of admonition to Prime Minister Yoshida on March 22, 1947, which said in part:

The Allied Powers, of course, are under no obligation to maintain or to have maintained any particular standard of living in Japan, nor is there any responsibility to import foodstuffs to meet deficits arising from the failure of Japan to assure the just and efficient distribution of its own food supplies . . . What is required is an integrated approach across the entire economic front. Accordingly, it is essential that the Japanese Government, through the Economic Stabilization Board which was created for this purpose, take early and vigorous steps to develop and implement the integrated series of economic and financial controls which the current situation demands . . . The social and economic welfare of Japan will depend largely on Japan's own efforts in the redirection of its human and natural resources to peaceful living and upon competent public administration of democratic and effective economic controls. Aid to Japan cannot be expected upon a scale sufficiently great to overcome maldistribution and inflation within Japan. Outside assistance is contingent upon full utilization of indigenous resources, which is entirely a responsibility of the Japanese Government.[4]

Following this letter, SCAP ordered the strengthening of the powers of the Economic Stabilization Board (ESB), to the extent of giving it some judicial and prosecuting powers and also of transferring to it a part of the budgetary powers of the Ministry of Finance. The renovated ESB came into existence under the Katayama Cabinet in June 1947 – a coalition cabinet with a socialist as Prime Minister.

It seems that the Occupation authorities were in a quandary as to whether to take a greater responsibility in assisting the economic recovery of Japan or to let the Japanese themselves muddle through and take the consequences. A sober appraisal of the situation by a resources expert, Dr Edward A. Ackerman, who made an intensive investigation of Japan's natural resources as a special adviser to the Occupation in the immediate postwar years, was rather pessimistic, as can be seen from the following concluding remarks in his Report to General Headquarters in 1948:

In the light of an analysis of its resources, the Japan of the next three decades appears likely to have one of two aspects if its population continues to grow to 100 million or more. (1) It may have a standard of living equivalent to that of 1930–34 if foreign financial assistance is continued indefinitely. (2) It may be "self-supporting," but with internal political, economic and social distress and a standard of living gradually approaching the bare subsistence level. Either of these alternatives seems more likely than that of a Japan which will have made itself self-supporting at a 1930–34 standard through foreign trade and improved resources utilization.[5]

In those early postwar years the pessimistic atmosphere was fairly prevalent especially because of the reparation issues which were in the background. The Japanese people at the time were keenly aware of the historical examples not only of the German reparation cataclysm subsequent to the First World War but also of the cold-blooded manner in which Japan extorted reparations from China after the Sino-Japanese War of 1894–95. Besides demanding, and obtaining, on that occasion, the cession of Formosa and the Liantung Peninsula and bringing Korea effectively under Japanese rule, Japan exacted the monetary reparation in species and pound sterling from China to the amount of 364 million yen – equivalent to one-third of Japan's national income at the time or four times the annual total imports of Japan. If Japan were to pay reparations to China after 1945 to the amount comparable to this, it would have meant at least twenty billion dollars, or about seven times the value of Japan's annual export at the time. Of course, the damage inflicted by Japan on China in human and material terms this time was incomparably greater than whatever damage was caused by China in the earlier war. Moreover, there were several other countries, like the Philippines, Burma, etc., which could claim restitution from Japan.

The Japanese were forewarned of the inevitable reparation burdens by the Potsdam Declaration of July 26, 1945, which, under Section 11, stated that "Japan shall be permitted to maintain such industries as will sustain her economy and permit the exaction of just reparations *in kind*, but not those which would enable her to re-arm for war" (italics added). Why "in kind"? The reasons were: (1) monetary reparations would necessitate the earning of foreign exchange, which would mean the encouragement of Japan's exports; (2) reparations by sending of Japanese workers abroad would lead to undesirable competition in labor markets of receiving countries which in fact were suffering from over-supply of unskilled labor; and (3) by the same token, reparations in the form of manufactured products, though "in kind," had to be avoided because they would help the reconstruction of Japanese manufacturing industries. Following this basic orientation, the initial reparation statement by Mr Pauley, cited earlier, giving specific scope for dismantling of durable producers' goods for the reparation purpose, was released on December 7, 1945.

This statement, starting in a tone thick with dramatic effect, to wit: "Four years ago today Japan attacked Pearl Harbor. America will never forget the attack. Japan will never forget the consequences," went on to recommend "an interim program of removals" of various categories of plant and equipment, as follows:

1 Half the capacity for the manufacture of machine tools.
2 All equipment in all Japanese Army and Navy arsenals, in the entire aircraft industry, in all plants making ball bearings and roller bearings, and in all plants making aircraft engines.

3 All equipment and accessories in 20 shipyards to the extent that it is not needed for the repair of shipping essential to the occupation.

4 All steel working capacity in excess of 2,500,000 tons per year out of the existing capacity of 11,000,000 tons.

5 Half of the coal-burning electric generating plants in Japan.

6 All contact-process sulphuric acid plants, except those necessary to recover waste gases from zinc, lead, copper and other heavy metal smelters; the most modern of Japan's four large solvay process soda-ash plants, and 20 out of 41 of the most modern large plants for the production of caustic soda.

7 All capacity for producing magnesium and alumina, and for the reduction of alumina to aluminium, except facilities for processing scrap, and all strip mills, rolling mills, extrusion presses, etc., used in finishing magnesium and aluminium.

8 Deprive all Japanese, including the Japanese Government, the Emperor and the Imperial Household, and the *zaibatsu*, of the ownership or control of any assets located outside Japan proper.

9 The bulk of the gold and other precious metals now amassed in Japan should be shipped to the United States Mint in San Francisco, to be held in custody pending decision as to its disposal.

In addition, there was a mandatory instruction in the Pauley recommendation to the effect that the reparation removals should start, first of all, from the assets held by *zaibatsu* groups. Naturally, the publication of the Pauley Report created grave concern in the business world of Japan. But it soon became clear that, first, the dismantling and transfer of plant and equipment to receiving countries would cost quite a lot, and second, they might prove of little or no value to them, and third, as some people argued, the de-industrialization of Japan would leave a void in the Far Eastern economy that would react unfavorably upon all countries, not only on Japan. But the argument most germane to American concerns was that reparations removals from Japan would be in effect paid for by the American taxpayer inasmuch as the Pauley reparations proposals would make it impossible for Japan to become self-supporting and the deficient Japanese economy would remain a semi-permanent burden upon the resources of the United States. Thus it became increasingly clear as the years wore on into 1947–48 that the Pauley proposals would have to be revised. We shall come back to this later.

3. The initial reform ideas on the Japanese side

Considering the radical changes called for after the complete breakdown of the erstwhile national purpose and the unprecedented debacle and disorganization of the socioeconomic structure, one is naturally prompted to ask a question: Did not the Japanese themselves, who had fought against the militarism of their own country and found themselves in the position of playing a positive role in the reforming of Japan, come to the fore to fill the political vacuum after the defeat? What were they doing during the period of 1945 to 1952, when the Occupation technically ended?

On the whole we have to say that the 180 degree reversal of domestic political leadership and the reawakening of liberal and even socialist ideologies, coming out of their hibernation, produced only a meager impact on the process of reform. True, there were some positive ideas advanced by the Japanese themselves during the Occupation. Compared, however, with the Meiji Restoration period of 1868 and thereafter, when a host of reform ideas cropped up and were actually put into practice, the native-born ideas of reform this time were, on the whole, rather stereotyped or weak and did not have the force of imperative necessity. When we realize the magnitude of the problems with which Japan was beset, requiring major transformation in its social and economic structure, we must say, as then was the general comment among the Japanese themselves, that people were on the whole in the state of psychological and/or mental prostration ("kyodatsu").

Representative, probably, of the independent Japanese efforts for formulating reform ideas for postwar Japan was the report[6] of a "Special Survey Committee" organized in the Foreign Office on the eve of surrender with awareness of its inevitability. Actually, the first meeting of this committee was held on August 16, 1945, a day after the termination of the war, and was able to bring together some thirty academics and publicists,[7] almost all of whom were quite eminent in the intellectual world either with anti-war or neutral orientation and many of whom were later to occupy prominent positions in post-Peace-Treaty Japan. These included six presidents of universities, a president of the Japan Science Council, a head of the Federation of Economic Associations, a member of parliament, an editorial writer of a national newspaper and a member of cabinet.

What were the salient features of their positive proposals? A brief summary may be given here, as follows:

1 Especially important from the standpoint of democratization of the economy is the democratization of financial institutions, making them publicly accountable through the participation of representatives of consumers, producers, political parties, etc., in their operation.
2 *Zaibatsu* (multi-industry semi-monopoly groups) may have to be dissolved. However, they for their part have played in the past certain necessary functions – the functions which a newly democratized government will have to take over.

3 Generally speaking, the planning principle should be introduced in the important sectors of the economy, and for some key industries nationalization should be considered.

4 The first step towards democratization of the economy is the modernization of agriculture, for which purpose land reform is urgently called for; also deliberate steps to transfer labor power from farms to manufacturing firms are needed.

5 Japan cannot do without foreign trade; but too much dependence on it carries some dangers. Therefore, energetic development and utilization of domestic resources and the rationalization of consumer activities are absolutely necessary.

6 There are many who point to the population surplus in Japan and urge the need to reduce the population. However, a decrease in the population is a defeatist policy. From a progressive point of view, search for a means to assure survival for a growing population should be the agenda for Japan.

The report concluded with the following statement: "The basic structure of the Japanese economy still retains the factors which may turn the nation again to militarism unless it is reformed completely. Realizing such risks, continuous efforts must be exerted to see that Japan will not follow in the wake of Nazi Germany to lead itself and all the world to a dire disaster."[8]

Though couched somewhat in a compromising language, it was clear that the general direction indicated by the report was reformist in character, emphasizing, in particular, the need for democratization and looking ahead towards a mixed economy type of society.

A propitious occasion came in 1947 through the coming into power of the Socialist Party although in coalition with two conservative parties. This government, headed by Tetsu Katayama, a socialist as well as a Christian, was fully supported by General MacArthur, and started its activities with a fair amount of ambition, publishing the First Economic White Paper, which played an enlightening role in impressing upon public the need for progressive measures in the economic sphere. The government also proposed the nationalization of coal mines, and the enabling law was enacted subsequently in December 1947 with a three-year time limit.

The White Paper referred to was prepared by the Economic Stabilization Board under my guidance rather hastily in about two weeks as a support document for the "Emergency Economic Policy Measures" announced by the Katayama Cabinet on June 11, 1947. Statistical scaffolding was still meager, but it was probably the first time in Japan that macroeconomic analysis was applied in the diagnosis of the economy as a whole. It laid special emphasis on the urgent necessity of eradicating the root causes of the prevalence of black markets in various sectors of the economy. Thus it stated in the concluding paragraphs:

Speaking figuratively, our difficulties are not simply that our fingers have been cut or our legs broken. It may be said that we are suffering from more serious physiological effects such as blood poisoning or disorder of function of the ductless glands. The facts that honest men are quite often fooled and that those who work sincerely suffer from losses testify to the physiological malady of the economic organism of this country . . . In our modern society with its complex organization, it is no easy task to trace out how the result of the labor of each individual is related to the improvement of his own living conditions. It is not so simple a relation as that in which Robinson Crusoe could improve his livelihood through his own effort. When, however, we face an economic crisis, we are forced, willy-nilly, to realize things in their real direct relationships. Indeed we must do so. The stages in which the people, after going through conditions in which the base of reproduction gets more and more restricted, emerge, with hope for the future, into the road to rehabilitation and reconstruction, shall be the stages in which those who work honestly in close relation with each other, will make their livelihood easier through their own effort, though *inevitably they will have to go through a temporary period of hardship of deficiencies, which they should consider as a hardship imposed on them by themselves.* The starting point of a democratic government must mean that we are faced with the question of forming a government of the people, by the people, and for the people. "Government for the people" must be a "government by the people." The Government can succeed, we are convinced, only on the basis of support and encouragement of the people.[9] (Italics added.)

The White Paper was generally well-received by the public; but the italicized phrase in the above quotation was a target of criticism by the left-wing working class who claimed that it denied the importance of class struggle and forced austerity on the oppressed class. And, as could have been expected, Marxist-oriented economists, including those who were members of the Foreign Office "Special Survey Committee" cited earlier, took exception to what they called "the equilibrium doctrine of economics" and also to the emphasis on the normalization of the distribution system as against the imperative of material production.

In retrospect some credit can be given to the Katayama cabinet for directing the Japanese economy towards stabilization; but its tenure of office was too brief (about eight months) to have any lasting impact, what with the dissension unavoidable in a coalition cabinet and what with the coincident shift in the US Occupation policy towards making Japan a bulwark against Chinese communism – which we shall take up later. Furthermore, the Socialist Party itself was cleft between the right wing and the left; and the cabinet crisis came when Mosaburo Suzuki, a left-wing socialist who headed the Budget Committee of the Diet, thrust back to the administration the supplementary budget proposal on a catch-up rate pay raise for civil servants. The cabinet fell on February 10, 1948 and was succeeded by a new coalition headed by Hitoshi Ashida of the conservative Democratic Party. Through this change in the government, the Economic Stabilization Board, once headed by Hiroo Wada and staffed by progressive officials under Katayama, suffered an exodus of men and lost its élan as a force for reform.

4. The Occupation reforms

The agenda for reforms by the Occupation authorities were quite manifold and their intent was far-reaching. In fact, the climate of official American opinion in the year following Japan's surrender was unequivocally of the type that all the roots of Japan's past militaristic tendencies had to be eradicated completely. Not only were the war criminals to be named and tried, but all those who held high positions in war-time Japanese society and also those who were considered to have been sympathetic in their views towards Japan's expansionism were to be purged from responsible posts. Further, Japan's constitution itself had to be revised by MacArthur's office. Major organizational reforms were also to be carried out; and typical in this regard was Pauley's condemnation of the *zaibatsu*, although the specific task he was charged with was the reparation problem. The relevant passage from Pauley's Report is as follows:

Japan's Zaibatsu [literally, "financial clique"] are the comparatively small group of persons, closely integrated both as families and in their corporate organizations, who throughout the modern history of Japan have controlled not only finance, industry and commerce, but also the government. They are the greatest war potential of Japan. It was they who made possible all Japan's conquests and aggressions . . . Not only were the Zaibatsu as responsible for Japan's militarism as the militarists themselves, but they profited immensely by it. Even now, in defeat, they have actually strengthened their monopoly position . . . Unless the Zaibatsu are broken up, the Japanese have little prospect of ever being able to govern themselves as free men.[10]

Thus it was logical that the first item on the agenda for Occupation reforms was the dissolution of the *zaibatsu*.

Zaibatsu *dissolution*

As early as January 1946 the Corwin Edwards Mission was sent by the United States to formulate concrete policies for the dissolution of the *zaibatsu*. Upon arrival in Japan, Edwards emphasized in particular that:

1 The aim of *zaibatsu* dissolution is to destroy Japan's militaristic power both psychologically and as a system, and
2 To enable Japanese workers, who had been exploited by the *zaibatsu* in the past, to obtain higher wages and salaries, thus expanding the domestic market.

This second point was based on the recognition that in the past the narrow domestic market, conditioned by the inordinately unequal distribution of income, had led to a policy of export expansion with imperialistic ambition. On the basis of such analysis, the Edwards Mission set two objectives of (a) the elimination of excessive concentration of economic power and (b) the liquidation of semi-feudalistic remnants in monopoly (or oligopoly) organizations and employment practices.

This was a tall order inasmuch as both of these objectives implied major systemic reformation of economic structure; and Edwards, an experienced corporation analyst, was fully aware that reforms of this kind could not succeed unless they were rooted in the voluntary will of the nation concerned.[11] Still, the Allied Powers gave special priority to this matter; and the US government submitted to the Far Eastern Commission in Washington the so-called "Directive 230" in June 1947, without making it public, so that MacArthur's office in Tokyo could treat the issue as a unilateral order to the Japanese Government. Thus it was that the Law for Elimination of Excessive Concentration of Economic Power was pushed through the Diet in December 1947. This law gave the Holding Company Liquidation Commission (HCLC) the authority to designate "excessive economic concentrations" and to reorganize such combines into independent companies to ensure a reasonable degree of competition and freedom of enterprise. In February 1948, HCLC designated 325 companies as chargeable under the law and issued orders for their deconcentration. But, just as Edwards foresaw, the alien character of the law, in spite of all the pressures exerted by the Occupation authorities, turned out to be its essential weakness. As Eleanor Hadley, who was one of the Occupation officials in charge of this matter, wrote:

In effect it [the law] represented the result of two years of tortuous work involving SCAP and Washington, on the one hand, and Japanese politicians schooled in subterfuge, on the other . . . The pattern of these battles is always the same. First an attempt is made to prevent the antimonopoly legislation from getting on the books; secondly, if legislation cannot be avoided, effort is made to emasculate as far as possible its various provisions; thirdly, and as a last resort, comes sabotage of enforcement.[12]

The fate of the law might have been as Hadley described. But it cannot be denied that the shift in the US Occupation policy, which we shall discuss later, did play a part in ameliorating its impact immediately after the HCLC's designation in early 1948. In fact, even before the law was passed in December 1947, the FEC Directive 230, mentioned earlier, was tabled on the request of an American member in the FEC, though this fact was not public knowledge in Japan.

It was a matter of holy prestige for General MacArthur that a policy which he once adopted and kept on pressurizing the Japanese Government to accept had to be pursued as far as that could be done. Thus it was that in the midst of suspected changes in the basic US policy on Japan, the General declared in his New Year Message of 1948:

Economically, Allied policy has required the breaking up of that system which in the past has permitted the major part of the commerce and industry and natural resources of your country to be owned and controlled by a minority of feudal families and exploited for their exclusive benefit. The world has probably never seen a counterpart to so abnormal an economic system. It permitted exploitation of the many for the sole benefit of the few. The integration of these few with government was complete and their influence upon government policies inordinate, and set the course which ultimately led to war and destruction.[13]

This was almost exactly the repetition of the wording in the Pauley Report quoted earlier. However, the tide was turning quickly; and by July 1, 1948 the HCLC reduced the list of companies to be dissolved to 100 from the initial list of 325. How the reversal in the dissolution issue actually took place, after all the hullabaloo during 1946 and 1947, is a topic to be dealt with in a later section.

The land reform

The Japanese themselves were keenly aware of the need for land reform as was indicated clearly in the report of the Foreign Office "Special Survey Committee," cited earlier; and already in October 1945 Kenzo Matsumura, Minister of Agriculture and Forestry in the Shidehara Cabinet, proposed a reform plan:

1 To change the tenant's rent payment in kind to payment in money;
2 To strengthen measures to increase land-owning, self-cultivating farmers; and
3 To democratize the organization of the Agricultural Land Committees in each region.

A bill was drafted incorporating these measures; but opposition to it was very strong internally, and only after SCAP's memorandum of December 9, 1945, it passed the Diet about three weeks later. The internal opposition was from the landed interest in agricultural regions and also from conservative political leaders who were afraid of radicalism among tenants.

The SCAP memorandum was not a product of careful preparation, but was originally drawn up by Robert A. Fearey, an official of the State Department, who had been transferred to Tokyo only in October 1945. However, his memorandum caught MacArthur's imagination, apparently because of father MacArthur's connection with Philippine land reform at the beginning of the century. And MacArthur, during the congressional hearings in connection with his dismissal later on, referred to the Japanese land reform as the greatest effort in that direction since Gracchus in the days of the Roman Empire.[14]

The first Land Reform Act (December 1945) was defective in a number of respects – for example: (1) the permitted maximum holding of 5 *cho* (5 hectares) was too large; (2) the holdings were defined in terms of individuals and not of households, so that landlords could escape forced disposal by distributing ownership titles among members of their households; and (3) the definition of "absentee landlord" was too vague and would have permitted many evasions.

Thus, opposition arose immediately from progressive wings in Japan itself and also in the discussions in the Allied Council for Japan; in particular, General Derevyanko of the USSR, delegate in the Council, spoke of the reform's paramount importance in view of the fact that "it is well known that one of the main reasons of domination of reactionary chauvinistic military cliques has been the vitality of medieval survivals in the country and especially the presence of feudalistic oppression in the Japanese village." Derevyanko's proposal was very drastic; and a more moderate reform plan was proposed by W. MacMahon-Ball, the British Commonwealth representative in the Council.

With MacMahon-Ball's proposal as a base, and with the addition of an able land-problem specialist, Ladejinsky, to the Occupation staff and also with the willing cooperation of Japanese government officials, the second Land Reform Act was passed in the Diet on October 21, 1946. This act specified that: (1) all the land of absentee owners is to be purchased by the government; (2) all tenanted land owned by resident landowners in excess of one *cho* (2.5 acres),or 4 *cho* in Hokkaido, is to be purchased by the government; and (3) the purchase price, in bonds bearing interest rates of 3.6 percent and redeemable in 30 years, was the same as that finally embodied in the first Land Reform Act, but plus some bonus in cash. The total payment, including the bonus, per one *tan* (one-fourth of an acre) of rice land worked out, on an average, to something less than 1,000 yen. It was estimated at the time (by A.J. Grad) that this price could buy in 1948 only 13 packets of cigarettes or 0.24 tons of coal whereas the price of good rice land in 1939 could buy 3,000 packets of cigarettes or 31 tons of coal.[15] In addition, forestry land was excluded from the Reform Act; and this fact was a cause of great dissatisfaction among those resident landowners who had turned forest land, through their own efforts, into cultivable farm land, especially in view of the fact that forest owners profited greatly as the price level kept on rising in subsequent years.

On the whole, however, it can be said that the Occupation land reform went a long way towards meeting the need which had been keenly felt by the Japanese themselves. The credit for this accomplishment should be shared by both the Occupation authorities and "that body of cautious but enlightened opinion within the Japanese bureaucracy."[16] The appraisal, quoted below, by Wolf Ladejinsky, one of the American experts intimately connected with the reform, may be said to be a judicious summary on apportionment of the credit:

Without underestimating the drive and single-mindedness of the Occupation, it should be noted that its principal role was that of a midwife to a healthy reform which had been in its pre-natal stage. The reform idea was Japanese in origin; it was not a policy imposed by a conqueror on the conquered.[17]

In spite of the basically progressive intent of the Land Reform Act, its implementation process was not plain sailing. One of the knotty problems that arose was its possible conflict with the constitutional clause on property rights. The new Constitution of Japan, clearly a joint product of the Occupation authorities and the Japanese government, which was promulgated on November 3, 1946 (coming into effect on May 3, 1947) rather on the heels of the passing of the Land Reform Act in the Diet, had an article (Article 29) where "the right to own or to hold property is inviolable." It was specified in this article that "private property may be taken for public use upon just compensation therefor." Naturally, questions arose immediately as to whether (1) the government purchase of farm lands was for "public use" and (2) the compensation proposed for such purchase was "just." Both of these points went as far as the Supreme Court for deliberation; and, especially as regards the former, whether the transfer-sale of farm land to erstwhile individual tenants could be interpreted as "for public use," was considered legally contestable. For one thing, many of the Japanese reformists in the field of agricultural economics had been advocating a type of land reform with major emphasis on "the right to cultivation" rather than "the right to ownership." Thus it was contested that the creation of new individual private owners of farm land out of former tenant farmers could not be interpreted as "for public use" to begin with, and, further, that it might leave unreformed various structural problems attendant to private ownership of land in general. The Supreme Court, however, cleared both of the above points in favor of the Land Reform Act.

Labor reforms

A labor movement of any progressive character was generally suppressed and persecuted before the war in Japan. The main legal weapon for this then in the hands of the government was the so-called "Peace Preservation Law" of 1925, which set ideological limits for individuals and organizations and served as a framework for the creation of special techniques for handling "thought criminals" – persons holding ideological positions deemed by the government to be subversive. The target of persecution as defined by this law was "anyone who has organized an association with the objective of altering the *Kokutai* (national polity) or of denying the system of private property." After the passage of this law, independent labor unions were not permitted to exist; and only the labor-front organizations with pro-capital and/or pro-military orientation were allowed. It cannot be denied, however, that a basically progressive labor-movement potential was there, hidden and dormant under suppression during the war years.

Under the Occupation the basic reforms in the field of labor focussed on the emergence of a strong union movement and the achievement of substantial advantages for labor. But the pattern was drawn almost wholly from American practices. In the background was the "FEC 16 Principles"; but before this was finally approved by the Far Eastern Commission (on April 9, 1946), the US government had, by December 28, 1945, already prepared the following set of explicit reform policies:

a Encouragement of the formation of free trade unions.
b Abolition of repressive laws and prohibition of unfair labor practices.
c Freedom of speech, publication, assembly, etc.
d Collective bargaining to be legally approved and an arbitration system for labor disputes to be created.[18]

In addition, there was, significantly enough, a clause saying that any strike directly prejudicial to the Occupation's objectives would be prohibited. Little was it expected that this clause would be invoked in an actual situation during the Occupation.

As we review the Occupation history, we are impressed by the fact that the policies related to labor reform were most expeditiously carried out by MacArthur's office. In fact, immediately after the opening of that office in Tokyo, that is, on October 18, 1945, the release of political prisoners was ordered, liberating a number of old-time labor leaders and, even before the formal decision by the US government on the labor reform program, referred to above, the Occupation authorities pressed the Japanese government to legislate the Trade Union Law of December 1945, which guaranteed the right to organize and to bargain collectively and recognized the right to strike. The said Law was clearly modeled after the US National

Labor Relations Act of 1935. This 1945 law also contained detailed provisions requiring unions to register with the authorities; and a system of Labor Relations Committees on both a national and prefectural level was to be established for the handling of disputes arising under the law.

With this encouragement from the Occupation authorities, the formation of, or actually the resuscitation of, trade unions grew suddenly like "bamboo shoots after a rain," as we say in Japan. Whereas there were, in February 1946, 675 unions with a total membership of 496,000, the movement grew rapidly to 33,940 unions with a membership of 6,637,710, or more than fifteen times by July 1948, i.e., within a little more than two years.

It was almost impossible to arrest the dynamic of this rebirth of the workers' movement in Japan; and, with or without unions, industrial disputes broke out everywhere, often escalating to the workers' seizure of the enterprise, or to what was then called the "production control" by workers. The first example of such production control took place at the Yomiuri Newspaper in October 1945, lasting almost a full year with tangled lessons for the Occupation in dealing with the labor problems of a foreign society.[19] The lesson learned by the Occupation authorities, however, triggered the enactment of the second major piece of labor legislation, the Labor Relations Adjustment Law, which passed the Diet on September 20, 1946.

This law provided the framework for conciliation, mediation or arbitration, as the parties may select, under the auspices of the Labor Relations Committee. Labor did not welcome this law inasmuch as it imposed certain restrictions on the right to strike, in particular the prohibition from striking by general government employees. Also, public utility workers, though permitted to organize, could not strike for thirty days after presentation of an appeal for mediation to the Labor Relations Committees. Not only were transportation, mail, telephone and telegraph, water supply, gas and electricity, and medical, sanitation and public health designated as public utilities, but in addition, the act gave the government the power to extend the scope of public utilities by designating as a public utility any enterprise whose suspension would disturb the public economy or the people's daily livelihood. It was only to be expected that labor would object particularly to such restrictions.

The dynamic of the rebirth of the workers' movement, whetted by the restrictive legislation of the autumn of 1946, began gathering momentum as economic distress deepened in the winter months of that year. The opening salvo was a dispute involving 2.6 million government workers who demanded a wage adjustment to a level comparable to that of private industry workers. But, while the government vacillated in their response, the unions in private industries, numbering 3.4 million in membership, joined their forces; and the movement escalated into a political one of demanding the resignation of the Yoshida cabinet. Finally, a general strike was called for February 1, 1947, involving perhaps two-thirds of all those employed outside the farms, forest and fisheries. If this strike had actually taken place, the country undoubtedly would have been paralyzed; and such militancy on the part of labor provided the first occasion to test the limits of the Occupation's tolerance.

The ten days preceding the fateful projected day of the general strike were the period, probably, of most critical drama in the confrontation of the Occupation authorities with the left-wing leadership of Japanese unions.[20] Although a rather unequivocal strike-ban warning was communicated to labor leaders in the name of General MacArthur on 22 January, a specific instruction was that the labor leaders were not authorized to make this warning statement public. MacArthur apparently wished to avoid an unambiguous public strike-ban, thinking that such an action might be construed as strikebreaking or, at the least, a tacit admission that his democratization of Japan was not working altogether smoothly. The labor leaders took advantage of this reluctance on the part of SCAP and went on disregarding the warning. A general strike appeared to be unavoidable on the morning of January 31, forcing MacArthur to issue a public statement at the last moment, which read:

Under the authority vested in me as the Supreme Commander for the Allied Powers, I have informed the labor leaders whose unions have federated for the purpose of conducting a general strike that I will not permit the use of so deadly a social weapon in the present impoverished and emaciated condition of Japan and have accordingly directed them to desist from the furtherance of such action.

Thus, the drama ended; and Theodore Cohen, a most energetic participant on the Occupation side in this drama, summarized the whole incident as follows:

The general strike that never took place was nevertheless a watershed in the Occupation, particularly in Japan's developing response to the democratization pressures applied by America. It was the high-water mark of extremism. Until then almost anything, no matter how helter-skelter, that promised to "democratize" the country was welcomed. But the traumatic experience of being hustled helplessly to the precipice in the name of the workers and the dramatic last-minute rescue by General MacArthur completely transformed the national mood. Suddenly, the Japanese people again became conscious of the need for limits.[21]

The Occupation's intervention in Japan's postwar labor relations did not end with this "traumatic experience." A year and a half later, when government workers threatened to strike over the issue of pay scale,

General MacArthur wrote to the Japanese Prime Minister, declaring that "no person holding a position by appointment or employment in the public service of Japan, or in any instrumentality thereof, should resort to a strike or engage in delaying or other dispute tactics which tend to impair the efficiency of government operations." This letter, dated July 22, 1948, was of historical significance, marking SCAP's direct intrusion into the *institutional framework* of employment relations of government workers. The Japanese government, emboldened by this SCAP declaration, immediately proceeded to promulgate an ordinance denying government workers not only the right to strike but also the right to collective bargaining. We shall touch on this problem again in the next section in connection with the reform of the civil service system. By this time in 1948, the tide had turned in "the reverse direction," as used to be commented on in the public press in Japan. And, within the Occupation itself, James Killen, the top official in the Labor Division, resigned in protest against this retrogressive move.

Other reforms

There were several other major reforms, involving different degrees of guidance by the Occupation authorities, before Japan regained its autonomy in 1952, in such fields as: the educational system, the civil service system, setting of the single exchange rate, the taxation system, etc. But probably the most important in the sense of having far-reaching consequences was SCAP's attempt to innovate the Meiji Constitution which had been anchored on the supreme power of Emperor. We shall briefly touch on this subject first.

a. The revision of the constitution

In the discussion of Japan's postwar economic development it is not necessary to trace in detail the tortuous process by which the new Constitution of Japan came to be finally promulgated on November 3, 1946. But in retrospect, it is truly remarkable that the Japanese government was so insensitive in the post-surrender period to the need for drastic changes required in the Meiji Constitution of 1889, which, after all, had been the basic framework for that unique concept of "kokutai" (national polity) and also for the expansionism of Imperial Japan.

Both the Higashikuni and the Shidehara cabinets in the immediate postwar period took the position that no basic revision was needed in the constitution and, in particular, maintained that the fundamental principle of the Emperor's power of reign over the country's sovereign rights should be retained. And the first official move for the deliberation of the problem on the Japanese side was taken by Prince Konoe, later designated as a war criminal, after his meeting with General MacArthur on October 4, 1945. From then on, the Japanese government retreated step by step, often with resistance, but subservient in the end, in the face of more or less consistent steerage by the Occupation for an overall revision of the Meiji Constitution. Impatient with the delaying tactics on the Japanese side, the Occupation power prepared a draft constitution for Japan and handed it to the Japanese government on February 13, 1946. According to contemporary accounts, both Shigeru Yoshida, then the Minister of Foreign Affairs, and Jōji Matsumoto, the Minister in charge of Constitutional Problems, were "shocked" by the distance from their own thinking it illustrated. The government hastened to revise their earlier draft more or less in accord with the GHQ draft and drew up what later came to be called the "March 2nd" draft; this became the basis for further negotiation with the Occupation authorities.

Even for our somewhat limited purpose here, it is still important to dwell upon one particular article in MacArthur's draft, which the Japanese government persistently tried to have withdrawn. That was Article 28, which reads:

The ultimate fee to the land and to all natural resources reposes in the State as the collective representative of the people. Land and other natural resources are subject to the right of the State to take them upon just compensation therefor, for the purpose of securing and promoting the conservation, development, utilization and control thereof.

This Article was followed by another, stating that "ownership of property imposes obligations," which expression reminds one immediately of the oft-quoted clause in the West-Germany Constitution (Article 14) to the effect that the property right involves certain obligations.

In the light of what was most likely to happen in a country destined to be highly congested on a meager natural resource base with over six million repatriates coming home from battle areas of the Pacific War, the SCAP proposal that "the ultimate fee to the land and to all natural resources reposes in the State as the collective representative of the people" was remarkably prescient. But the Japanese government, then headed by Yoshida, strongly resisted this SCAP proposal and finally succeeded in replacing it with the wording which we now find in Article 29 of the Constitution, as follows:

The right to own or to hold property is inviolable.
Property rights shall be defined by law, in conformity with the public welfare.
Private property may be taken for public use upon just compensation therefor.

Basically, this clause is identical to Article 27 of the Meiji Constitution except that the third sentence of the 1946 version speaks of "just compensation therefor." The "inviolability" concept goes back to the French Declaration of Human Rights (1789) in which the memorable phrase "un droit inviolable et sacré" appeared – the phrase that has been so often repeated in the capitalist world ever since and had been the basic tenet of prewar Japanese society.

The implication of Article 28 of the MacArthur draft was revolutionary from the standpoint of conservative Japanese at the time; however, forty years later, as we shall see in a subsequent chapter, public opinion in Japan came to realize the long-range wisdom contained in that Article and lamented sorely the short-sighed obstinacy of the Japanese government in 1946.

The unique feature of Japan's new Constitution, one that affects the conduct of economic affairs as well, was Article 9, which reads:

Aspiring sincerely to an international peace based on justice and order, the Japanese people forever renounce war as a sovereign right of the nation and the threat or use of force as a means of settling international disputes.

In order to accomplish the aim of the preceding paragraph, land, sea, and air forces as well as other war potential will never be maintained. The right of belligerency of the State will not be recognized.

The wording was almost exactly the same as in the so-called "MacArthur Note" of February 3, 1946, which apparently was hastily drafted after the so-called "Matsumoto Draft" had been leaked to the press a few days earlier and found to be unsatisfactory from the Occupation's point of view. Thus, in subsequent research on the genesis of this idealistic Article some experts have claimed that it was more or less forced upon the Japanese government by MacArthur's office. But, on the other hand, it is known that Prime Minister Shidehara, in his conference with General MacArthur on January 24, 1946, expressed his personal desire for the renunciation of war in the spirit of the Kellog–Briand Pact of 1928 and that the General concurred with the idea. In fact, MacArthur spoke with emphatic approval of Article 9 in his "New Year Message to the People of Japan" in 1951, saying that "your constitution renounces war as an instrument of national policy. This concept represents one of the highest, if not the highest ideal the modern world has ever known and which all men must in due course embrace if civilization is to be preserved."

The original initiative for the basic idea may have come from Shidehara, but the concrete wording of the Article, as well as the decision to formulate it as one of the articles rather than to incorporate the idea in a Preamble, was in all likelihood the work of MacArthur's office. Some revisions of the earlier text did take place in the course of deliberations in the Diet; but it is significant that whereas the "MacArthur Note" (February 3, 1946) had contained a phrase "renouncing war as a means of self-defence also," this particular point was deleted in the final text. Still, in a Diet discussion in 1947 Prime Minister Yoshida made it quite clear that Article 9 meant what it said and that it "forbade the maintenance of war potential of any kind whether for aggression or for self-defence." Thus it was inevitable that controversies ensued in subsequent years regarding the need for constitutional revision in order to make explicit the "self-defence capability" of the country.

At present, however, it is well known that Japan maintains "land, sea, and air forces as well as other war potential" of a size estimated to be the third biggest in the world *without* any revision of the constitutional constraint.

The economic significance of Article 9, in the minds of Japanese political leaders like Yoshida at the time, was, undoubtedly, the possibility of mobilizing to the fullest the meager domestic resources for the purpose of urgent economic reconstruction while relying on the US warrant of military security. This cunning strategy actually worked in the early postwar years, paving the way for the later economic resurgence.

b. The reform of the civil service system

Unlike other important occupation reforms, the original suggestion for the need for change in this area came from the Japanese side. However, when the idea was taken up by SCAP and a special advisory mission was brought over from the US, the reform proposal turned out to be one of the most unfortunate cases of an alien transplant with only a fleeting appearance of adequacy. Certainly, what was then called the "defeudalizing" of the Japanese civil service was badly needed; but the choice of Blaine Hoover by the US Army Department as head of the mission was not a very happy one. His grasp of the problem was pertinent enough, as can be gleaned from his statement that his reform program "will break up one of the ruling cliques of pre-surrender Japan – the tightly-knit, exclusive and self-perpetuating bureaucracy which exercised the powers of government over the people in the feudal concept of divine right – and will substitute therefore a body of democratically selected officials who will administer the law in the concept of service to the people."[22] But Hoover, then president of the prestigious Civil Service Assembly of the United States and Canada, an umbrella organization of civil service professional societies, was intent on transplanting those principles which had evolved on American soil and would not pay much attention to the characteristic aspects of the Japanese civil service system, in spite of the fact that SCAP Labor Division officials tried very hard to brief him. Ted Cohen, one of these officials, wrote later that: "Hoover's analysis was almost totally irrelevant ... An American arrangement designed historically to eliminate the spoils system was to be applied to a country that had none. I sometimes thought that if the Mission had been sent to the Arctic Circle instead, it would have come up with the same prescription for the Eskimos, seals, and seagulls."[23]

In particular, Hoover ignored perhaps the most striking feature of the tightly knit Japanese bureaucracy, the "old school tie" of Imperial University graduates. He also lent a deaf ear to the problems necessarily arising as a result of wide variety of public service activities in Japan, such as those in public enterprises (the national railroad, tobacco and camphor monopolies, telephone services, etc.) and in publicly supported schools and universities. Thus, Hoover's prescription for reform was essentially a compound of merit examinations, "scientific" job descriptions, wage classifications, efficiency ratings, plus an independent civil service authority. A National Public Service Bill was drafted, implementing all of Hoover's ideas on a central civil service structure, service-wide standards, etc.; and, under strong pressure from the Occupation authorities, it was railroaded through the Diet on October 15, 1947 in a mere fifteen minutes. The Bill had been taken up in a joint Diet committee in advance, where affirmative opinions expressed by four out of ten "experts" who testified were nothing more than the obeisant echo of the Hoover doctrine. It was as if to say "we shall change it anyway after the Occupation is over." And, in fact, the Hoover reform was short-lived. For example, one of the purposes of "defeudalizing" of the civil service was the breaking up of educational elitism in the government bureaucracy; but, as Herbert Passin wrote: "Ten years after the Hoover civil service reform, in 1958, 98 percent of the highest grade government officials, 82 percent of the second grade, and 57 percent of the third grade were still graduates of the seven national, formerly Imperial, universities."[24]

Blaine Hoover was not fully satisfied with this "accomplishment" and went on to do something about what he considered to be the "deadly sin" among government workers of "poor discipline." Whereas in the US federal civil service discipline applied to *individual* behavior, such as arriving on time, staying sober in the office, carrying out assigned duties, etc., Hoover expanded the meaning to include behavior of *groups*, becoming convinced, by the general strike campaign led by government unions in January 1947, that the crux of his problem was discipline of government labour unions. The natural conclusion for him was to prohibit by law collective bargaining and strikes for all government workers irrespective of the type of activities in which they were engaged. Such drastic legislation would infringe upon the very content of the Labor Relations Adjustment Law of September 1946 which the Occupation had approved. Inevitably there arose a head-on collision within SCAP between the Government Section (which supported Hoover) and the Labor Division (headed by James Killen). MacArthur's verdict, on July 22, 1948, was in favor of the position taken by the Government Section, and he sent an instruction to Prime Minister Ashida on the same day, advising (1) to split off the government railways and monopoly enterprises as separate public corporations and let their employees bargain collectively, although not strike. Instead, mediation and arbitration procedures were to be set up. That, at least, recognized a reality that Hoover had defied. (2) On the other hand, the remaining three-quarters of government employees, including 700,000 communications workers and teachers, could now no longer bargain collectively, depriving them of a right they had had *de facto* for three years and *de jure* for two. Immediately after this, James Killen resigned in protest, as mentioned earlier, and the net result of the stiff-backed reform proposal of the Hoover Mission was, as US Assistant Secretary of State Saltzman said, the "polarization of politics in Japan."[25]

c. The educational reform

"There has probably occurred no educational experiment in modern times – with the possible exception of that of the Soviet Union – which is so vast, so important, and so fraught with danger to our civilization as that of the effort to re-educate the Japanese people following the Second World War."[26] Thus wrote Robert King Hall, who served as Chief of the Education Subsection of Civil Information and Education Section (CI&E) of General Headquarters in occupied Japan until the latter part of 1946. Was the educational reform in the postwar Japan such a momentous one, and "fraught with danger," besides? That is the question.

There are a number of aspects to this problem: (a) the basic philosophy of education in a modern society; (b) the administrative setup; (c) the institutional structure of educational organs; and (d) the medium of instruction. Of these, the first was most important inasmuch as it was essential, as the initial lines of educational policy for Japan in the pre-surrender plan of the US government stated, that "dissemination of Japanese militaristic, national Shintoistic and ultra-nationalistic ideology will be prohibited."

There was no doubt that the basic instrumental document, committed to memory by millions of school children up till the end of the war, was the Imperial Rescript on Education issued by Emperor Meiji in 1890.[27] Though designed as a rescript on education, it contained sentences like "should emergency arise, offer yourselves courageously to the State; and thus guard and maintain the prosperity of Our Imperial Throne coeval with heaven and earth" – the sentence which was usually quoted to evoke a sense of loyalty to the Emperor among the conscript soldiers. In fact, the document "contains the distillate of every nationalistic philosophy objectionable to the Allied Powers"[28]; and it was expected at the time that not only would the Occupation authorities order its scrapping but also the Japanese themselves would exorcise it as a remnant of their ultra-nationalistic past. It is, therefore, remarkable that the said Rescript had a tenacious life in the post-surrender period. The fact that the Occupation authorities scrupulously avoided any official notice of its content, authority, or public presentation might have been motivated by MacArthur's determination to keep the emperor system intact for the purpose of facilitating the occupation role itself. According to Robert Hall, there was active opposition to repealing the Rescript on the part of staff officers in the Occupation. And "their objections were three-fold: there is nothing intrinsically wrong with the Rescript; any attack on it would be an attack on the Confucian ethics, Buddhist philosophy, and Shinto mythology which would be interpreted as an attack on religion; and it is convenient for those who are in authority in a military occupation, essentially a dictatorship, to have some centrally dictated statement of goal or aim."[29]

But the maneuvering steps on the Japanese side were more enigmatic. There were three "schools of thought," so to speak, among prominent Japanese who had some influence over public opinion on such questions as the Imperial Rescript. One was the group, represented by Tetsutaro Ariga, professor of divinity at Dōshisha University, which worked for the adoption of "Shōwa Rescript on Education", revising the Meiji Rescript in some important points. The second was the group, most prominently represented by Kōtaro Tanaka, Minister of Education from May 22, 1946 to January 31, 1947, which sided with the idea of continued ritualistic observance of the Meiji Rescript in schools. And the third was a progressive group of scholars and publicists who advocated the scrapping of the Rescript.

The Occupation authorities themselves could not make up their minds definitely as to which one of these groups to support until the US Education Mission arrived in March 1946 and certain members of the Mission violently opposed any proposal that the Emperor should be given the prestige of issuing an "Educational Code" even if virtually dictated by the Occupation authorities. Thus the Mission's Report to the SCAP, dated March 30, 1946, did recommend "the discontinuing of the ceremonial use of the Emperor's Rescript on the occasion of national holidays in schools." But this recommendation was interpreted not to mean "the repeal" of the Rescript itself nor the replacing of it by a new one; and Kōtaro Tanaka, Minister of Education, continued to express the opinion, on the floor of the Diet, for example, on July 15, 1946, that we were not thinking of the repeal of the Rescript at all inasmuch as its contents were basically correct as expressing "the glory of the fundamental character of Our Empire" which should be the basis of our education. Such maneuvering on the Japanese side actually went on for another two years; and it was not until June 1948 that both Houses of the Diet voted to annul the Imperial Rescript on Education.

The logical corollary to the abolition of the Rescript was the formulation anew of the standard of educational philosophy befitting the transformation of the prewar basic concept of national polity. The initiative for this move was actually taken by Kōtaro Tanaka himself, although he felt that the formulation of a new standard of educational philosophy was perfectly compatible with the retention of the Imperial Rescript. But, meanwhile, the new constitution (promulgated on November 3, 1946) was in the drafting stage, abolishing the sovereignty of the imperial institution and making the Emperor "the symbol of the state and the unity of the people" on the one hand, and containing, on the other, a number of Articles guaranteeing such matters as academic freedom, the right to receive an equal education among all people, etc. It should also be noted that the Report of the US Education Mission (March 30, 1946) had the following statement in its section on "The Aims of Education":

Before the reconstruction of education in Japan can be undertaken, it is imperative that the basis of a philosophy of education in a democracy be clarified. To repeat constantly the word "democracy" is meaningless unless it is clothed with content.

A system of education for life in a democracy will rest upon the recognition of the worth and dignity of the individual. It will be so organized as to provide educational opportunity in accordance with the abilities and aptitudes of each person. Through content and methods of instruction it will foster freedom of inquiry, and training in the ability to analyze critically . . .

Education should prepare the individual to become a responsible and cooperating member of society. It must be understood, too, that the term 'individual' applies equally to boys and girls and to men and women. In building for a new Japan, individuals will need the knowledge which will develop them as workers, citizens, and human beings. They will need to apply that knowledge in a spirit of free inquiry as society members participating in the manifold aspects of its organization . . .

Even without such "guidance" from the US Education Mission, there was a movement among non-governmental Japanese themselves in the immediate post-surrender period for the drafting of a "fundamental set of principles for education" completely to replace the Imperial Rescript of 1890, notably a group which called itself "Study Group on Democratic Education." The Ministry of Education, too, could not stand aloof in the face of mounting public desire for a basic reform and established its advisory body called the Japanese Education Reform Council with

Yoshishige Abe, ex-Minister of Education, as chairman. It was this Council that worked energetically during the winter months of 1946–47 to produce a draft for the Fundamental Law of Education in cooperation with the Civil Information and Education Section of the SCAP.

The Fundamental Law of Education was passed in the Diet on March 31, 1947, more than one year prior to the official annulment of the Imperial Rescript on Education, and has remained since then as the basic charter embodying the educational philosophy of democratic Japan to this day. The Law stated the goals of education as "the development of people healthy in spirit and body, who are filled with an independent spirit, respect the value of individuals, and love truth and justice" and provided a turning point in the governmental policies in the educational field. How faithful the Japanese government has been in respecting the philosophy enunciated in the Law during the subsequent decades is a debatable point; but this does not concern us here.

There were other important educational reforms proposed by the Occupation authorities in which the US Education Mission to Japan played a significant role. Apparently this Mission was considered by the United States to be of extreme importance; and the original list of candidate members included such luminaries as James B. Conant, President of Harvard University, Robert Hutchins, President of the University of Chicago, John Dewey, and Howard Mumford Jones, all of whom, however, declined to come in the end. The Mission, which arrived in Japan on March 5, 1946 and stayed until April 1, was composed of 18 members and was headed by Alexander J. Stoddard, Superintendent of Schools in Philadelphia. In response to the request of General MacArthur the Mission was charged with an extremely broad range of tasks for educational reform in Japan and was divided into five committees:

Aims and Content
Administration
Teaching and Education of Teachers
Language Reform
Higher Education

In view of the fact that very few of the Mission members had any first-hand contact with the Japanese prewar educational system or a solid grasp of the peculiarities of the Japanese society, it is truly remarkable that the Mission completed its Report in the short span of four weeks, with concrete recommendations of far-reaching consequences. It is less of a mystery, however, when we go through the entire Report and observe that many of the concrete suggestions were in the nature of transplanting of American practices. To say this, of course, does not necessarily imply irrelevance. The general statement on "aims of democratic education," for example, which has been partially quoted earlier, was quite appropriate for a new Japan and was applauded widely among the Japanese themselves, as was the following statement which appeared in the preface to the Report:

We . . . believe that there is an unmeasured potential for freedom and for individual and social growth in every human being. Our greatest hope, however, is in the children. Sustaining, as they do, the weight of the future, they must not be pressed down by the heritage of a heavy past.

Specifically, many Japanese also applauded the Mission's recommendation for divesting the Ministry of Education of its central control powers and confining it to the provision of technical aid and professional counsel to the education boards elected by popular vote at local levels.

On the other hand, the Mission's specific recommendations for reform of the organizational structure of the school system, replacing it with a "6–3–3–4" system modeled on the American plan (elementary school, lower secondary or junior high school, higher secondary or senior high school, and college or university), met some strong resistance.[30] In the field of higher education, too, the Mission's recommendation for the establishment of locally based universities in each and every prefecture modeled on US state universities was a mechanical transplanting of the American system. The Mission's critical judgment on the so-called "dual-track" system in the institutions of higher learning, i.e. the elite group represented by seven imperial universities and the popular group with lower social standing, was well taken. But suddenly to elevate former professional schools and higher schools to the multi-faculty university status was an adventurous experiment without any assurance of provision of qualified personnel.

One other recommendation by the Mission, which turned out to be abortive, may be mentioned. That was a proposal to simplify the Japanese language drastically. The Mission's Report stated: "The Japanese language in its written form constitutes a formidable obstacle to learning . . . Clearly the question of language reform is basic and urgent. It casts its shadow over practically every branch of the educational reform program, from the primary school to the university. If no satisfactory answer can be found to this problem, the achievement of many agreed upon educational goals will be rendered most difficult."[31] The Mission, consequently, took the rather radical position of "wholly abandoning in time" the use of Chinese characters and adopting a phonetic system, preferably the Roman alphabet. One recalls a proposal, made by Arinori Mori, an influential Meiji educational leader after the 1868 Restoration, to make English the official language of Japan. Mori's suggestion actually went unheeded, essentially because the gradual simplification of the Japanese language in the course of Japan's modernization was found to be effective enough in the raising of functional literacy among the masses, contributing no doubt to the early take-off in economic development from the slumbering feudal past.

It was probably a case of realism prevailing over idealism that led the US Department of State to submit to the Far Eastern Commission a revised policy based on the Education Mission's recommendations one year after the Mission's Report incorporating every important point *except* one on the language reform. The Department commented still later (April 1948) to the effect that "SCAP's attitude is that the reform of the Japanese writing system and the methods by which such a reform is to be achieved are problems to be decided by the Japanese Government, and it favors the adoption of any suitable language form that will contribute to the intellectual development of the Japanese people and the healthy growth of democratic tendencies."[32] In retrospect, many Japanese feel that this was a wise commentary which could have been applied to some other recommendations by the US Education Mission.

2   The road to recovery

It can hardly be doubted that Japan's road to recovery was paved by the coincidental developments on the international scene. With the heightening of the cold-war psychology from about the time of the announcement of the Truman Doctrine (March 1947), reinforced by the demonstrably successful march of communists in China in 1948 onwards, the US government apparently became determined to make Japan "a bulwark against communism." The consequence was a major shift in the US policy in Japan towards expediting the latter's economic recovery. The initiatives of occupation policies came to be taken by Washington itself, firstly backsliding on reparation and *zaibatsu* dissolution programs, then advising strong-armed measures for the arresting of the inflationary trend and setting a single exchange rate, and lastly, hastening the steps for a single separate peace with Japan. What put the finishing touch on the US determination was the eruption of the Korean War in June 1950. This, incidentally, constituted a most significant watershed in the recovery of Japan's postwar economy, with impetus given by special procurements in Japan by the "United Nations Army" for the prosecution of the war. In this chapter again, I tried to be as objective as I could in describing the march of events, although the choice of topics dealt with may be judged as reflecting my selective inclination.

1. The shift in US policy on Japan

The American occupation of Japan lasted for six years and eight months, from September 2, 1945 to April 28, 1952. The period was clearly divided into two sub-periods, reflecting the radical change in the basic policy towards Japan by the US government. The first part was epitomized by a typical statement by the Joint Chiefs of Staff (with presidential approval) to the effect that "the plight of Japan is the direct outcome of its own behavior and the Allies will not undertake the burden of repairing the damage," and was more concretely spelled out by Pauley's statement quoted in the last chapter. The second sub-period was characterized, on the other hand, by the US determination to restore Japan's prewar position as the "workshop of Asia" and to preserve her economy as far as possible from socialist encroachments.[1]

A major policy watershed, undoubtedly, was the decline and fall of the Kuomintang on the mainland China in 1948–49. But it was the landmark speech by Kenneth Royall, Secretary of the Army, on January 6, 1948 at the Commonwealth Club of San Francisco, that made it unmistakably clear to the Japanese, too, that US basic policy had changed. He developed the theme that America's attitude toward Japan had to be re-examined, since the new conditions in world politics had produced "an inevitable area of conflict between the original concept of broad demilitarization and the new purpose of building a self-supporting nation." He went on to say that: "At some stage extreme deconcentration of industry, while further impairing the ability to make war, may, at the same time, destroy manufacturing efficiency of Japanese industry – may, therefore, postpone the day when Japan can become self-supporting"; and further that "if Japan were to achieve political stability and retain its free government, it had to have a healthy independent economy." The Royall speech, a significant point of departure, was rapidly followed by General Frank McCoy's statement before the Far Eastern Commission on January 21, 1948,[2] evincing to the world that the military arm of the US government had shifted its policy on Japan.

On reparations

However, in the background of such a move was the gradual maturing of a thought in the American business world since as early as the beginning of 1947, i.e., a few months after the Pauley Mission's Final Report on reparations was made public – the thought that a rehabilitated Japanese capitalism would, on balance, redound to the benefit of American business, providing a good, growing, customer. It was most likely that it was for this reason that Clifford Strike, head of a large New York engineering firm, was sent to Japan in January 1947 in preparation for the second reparations mission due to arrive in August of that year. Strike, in a controversial piece in *The American Magazine* (September 1947), entitled "Revenge is Expensive," called for revision of the reparations plan even if opposed by members of the Far Eastern Commission and for the creation of a strong industrial Japan for the peace and prosperity of the Far East. One of the most influential actors in the scenario of reversing the US economic strategy was apparently William H. Draper, jr., then Under Secretary of the

Table 2.1. *Successive reparation proposals*

(Unit: millions of yen in 1939 prices)

		Removals of:		
	Date of Report	Industrial Equipment	Military Equipment	Total
Pauley proposal	November 1946	990	1,476	2,466
Strike proposal	March 1948	172	1,476	1,648
Draper–Johnston proposal	May 1948	102	560	662
Actual removal	(before removals were stopped in the spring of 1949)			160

Army. He led a blue-ribbon mission of American business executives to Japan in March 1948 with the determined purpose of bringing General MacArthur into line with the "shift in emphasis" in American policy from reform to economic recovery. The chronicle of reparations proposals over the period of less than two years since the Pauley Mission's Final Report reflects the extent of amelioration, as shown in Table 2.1.

In time, the reparation question became a side issue; and the removal of plant and equipment for that purpose was entirely stopped in the spring of 1949. The issue was reopened in the negotiations for the Treaty of Peace, which was signed on September 8, 1951 and contained Article 14 which specified:

1 The Allies in general will be satisfied with the taking of those assets which were held in their countries by the Japanese state and Japanese nationals.
2 Those Allies which had been occupied by Japan will obtain, in addition to (1) above, service reparations in the form of producing activities and of salvaging sunken vessels.
3 Other Allies are to forfeit any claims for reparations.

The countries in the second category were to negotiate separately with Japan to decide on the details. But India and Chiang-kai Shek's China announced that they would forfeit. Negotiations with other countries, such as Burma, the Philippines, Indonesia, Vietnam (under Bao-Dai's rule), Laos and Cambodia, went on until as late as 1958, the aggregate obligations for Japan coming to 1,012 million US dollars, which sum meant, in terms of annual instalments, a mere 0.4 percent of Japan's national income in the relevant years and was actually about one half of the US aid to Japan for relief and rehabilitation ($2,118 million) over the period from September 1945 to December 1951.

On zaibatsu *dissolution*

As was mentioned in the last chapter, the occupation reform for deconcentration of giant combines (*zaibatsu*) also met with the fate of gradual backsliding in the course of those policy reorientation years of 1947 and 1948. In a summary review of the occupation reforms, Robert A. Fearey, a member of the office of Far Eastern Affairs in the US Department of State during the occupation years, wrote: "Always one of the more controversial aspects of the occupation, the deconcentration program . . . occasioned considerable criticism in Congressional and business circles during the latter half of 1947 and in 1948 because of its alleged 'extreme' character."[3] Most prominent among the American critics of the program in public was James Lee Kauffman, an attorney for most of the major US companies in Japan before the war, who visited Japan in the summer of 1947 and managed to obtain a copy of the still-classified FEC-230 document. Upon his return, he prepared a lengthy report in which he made it the focus of his vitriolic attack.[4] He charged that FEC-230 was socialistic and eliminated Japanese businessmen who were needed for economic recovery. In particular, he concluded, FEC-230 endangered the goal of a self-supporting Japan as a bastion against communism in the Far East.

The Kauffman Report was widely circulated in the American business community and amongst top officials in the American government, catching the attention, in particular, of George Kennan, recently appointed head of Secretary of State Marshall's Planning Staff. Apparently, Kennan repeated some of Kauffman's accusations over lunch on October 16, 1947 to Forrestal, Secretary of Navy, who recorded the conversation in his diary, saying that Kennan feared that "the socialization of Japan had proceeded to such a point that if a treaty of peace were written and the country turned back to the Japanese it would not be possible for the Japanese to support themselves . . . resulting possibly in near anarchy, which would be precisely what the communists would want."[5] Kennan himself wrote in his *Memoirs* much later that: "The ideological concepts on which these anti-*zaibatsu* measures rested bore so close a resemblance to Soviet views about the evils of 'capitalist monopolies' that the measures could only have been eminently agreeable to anyone interested in the future communization of Japan."[6]

Both Kauffman and Kennan were clearly off course; for the intent of the *zaibatsu* dissolution program, as conceived by the Edwards Mission and administered by the occupation officials in charge, was the promotion of a free enterprise competitive system of the economy. This was unequivocally stated by General MacArthur in January 1948: "the Japanese are rapidly freeing themselves of these [oligarchic] structures to clear the road for the establishment here of a more healthy economy patterned after our own concepts of free private competitive enterprise."[7] Nonetheless, the impact of the Kauffman tirade, further stirred up by Senator William Knowland's denunciation of FEC-230 on the floor of the US Senate as "the work of irresponsible New Deal radicals" in early December 1947, created an atmosphere in the business world that a counter-measure had to be taken expeditiously. Here, again, as was the case in connection with the reparations issue, William Draper entered the scene, first by sending radiograms to General MacArthur in early January 1948 complaining about specific measures of the projected deconcentration, and then heading a blue-ribbon mission to Japan in March 1948 to conduct an overall review of the occupation's economic policies. By then, the deconcentration law had already been passed through the Diet and the Holding Company Liquidation Commission (HCLC) had designated 325 companies as chargeable under the law. Draper's strategy was to circumscribe the implementing action by proposing to set up a board of independent American businessmen to review HCLC orders and the corporate reorganization plan under the new law. MacArthur agreed to this and the Deconcentration Review Board (DRB) was duly set up under the chairmanship of Roy Campbell, president of the New York Shipbuilding Corporation. Then, on April 7, 1948, Draper announced in Washington that the US government was abandoning most of FEC-230. From then on deconcentration wound down; and, as was briefly mentioned in the last chapter, by July 1, 1948 the HCLC reduced the list of companies to be dissolved to 100 from the initial list of 325, and announced, significantly enough, that all the banks were being dropped as well. By December 1948, when FEC-230 was formally withdrawn, the DRB had eliminated all but nine companies from the original list subject to deconcentration.

Interpretation of the shift in policy

How does a social scientist explain this somewhat bewildering shift in the US occupation policies concerning reparations and the *zaibatsu* issue? Howard Schonberger, professor at the University of Maine at Orono, attempted an explanation in the following terms:

The rapid deterioration of the Nationalists in China, the worsening inflationary crisis in Japan, the threat that the international economy would not absorb sufficient exports to sustain American prosperity, and increasing tensions between the US and USSR created a new context by1947 in which the capitalist class and state managers thought about US relations with Japan. All state managers agreed that the US had to assist in the economic recovery of Japan . . .

The changes in *zaibatsu* dissolution policy in 1947 and 1948 are a particularly powerful example of the influence of a fraction of the capitalist class on state policy.

But influence and control over policy are quite different matters. What made the influence of Kauffman and the business community he represented so effectively was the lack of any political and social basis for support of the deconcentration program in Japan. Put negatively and conditionally, it would appear that *even without the intervention of* [American] *business interests in the* zaibatsu *dispute the opposition of the Japanese capitalist class to deconcentration would have influenced American state managers to scuttle the* zaibatsu *program* . . .

[In other words,] A changing international environment, especially the opposition of the Japanese capitalist class to the design of American economic reform policies, contributed to the ascendancy of a centrist policy current amongst American state managers that assured the emasculation of the reparations and *zaibatsu* dissolution programs and the perpetuation of a relatively unfettered capitalist class rule in Japan up to the present. (Italics added.)[8]

This analysis, especially the part italicized, was first given credence by Robert Fearey, an experienced Far East specialist in the US Department of State, in a form which went more deeply into the characteristic national traits of the Japanese. He wrote:

Contrary to a rather widespread assumption abroad, the Japanese, with no real experience of the advantages of the competitive alternative, felt little or no resentment or animosity toward the *zaibatsu* before the war, and feel little or no gratification now at their destruction . . . [They] do not have the intellectual or philosophical background of the competitive approach, and regard the matter as a new concept whose advantages must be demonstrated along with its methods.[9]

He explained this national trait partly as rooted in the absence of a sizable middle class in Japan – the class, according to him, which is "normally the mainstay of a competitive economy."[10] And he went on to warn that "if the idea of a competitive economy is abandoned in Japan, the Allies should recognize in that abandonment a major defeat for the cause of Japanese democracy . . . In Japan, where democracy is not firmly rooted, the adoption of socialism or a reversion to the prewar monopoly system with the submergence of individual initiative and freedom which these systems entail would seriously handicap the growth of incipient democratic tendencies."[11]

It may be conceded that Fearey's warning was basically well taken; but we must say that the type of judgment on the problems he dealt with requires more of a historical perspective than he appeared to demonstrate. For one thing, Japanese capitalism was a late comer, like Germany's; besides, Japan did not enjoy a full tariff autonomy until 1899 – the legacy of the unequal treaties of commerce with the then front-rank capitalist nations. This circumstance was a basic factor in inducing the formation of cartels and trust organizations and in strengthening the *zaibatsu* structure in order to be competitive on the world scene.

Secondly, although Fearey speaks of "incipient democratic tendencies" as if they were nursed along through America's tutoring in the occupation period, Japan did have a period of the so-called "Taishō democracy," that is during the era of Taishō Emperor from 1912 to 1926. It was during this period that the so-called "party government," whose cabinets would be based on the strength of political parties in the House of Representatives, came to be accepted and universal manhood suffrage was instituted for the first time (1925). It is also symptomatic of the period that Tatsukichi Minobe, professor of law at Tokyo Imperial University, advanced the thesis (in July 1911) that the emperor was one of the organs of the state, possessing no authority over and above it, and also that under the Kato cabinet (June 1924–July 1925) substantial economies were effected especially in the army and navy budgets despite bitter protests from the military. There was also, during this period, some emphasis on the broader ideals of social democracy including the recognition of labor and tenant–farmer unions and of greater equality for women. In fact, whereas the Public Order and Police Law of 1900 had specified the exclusion of women from politics by forbidding them even to attend political rallies or to join political associations, the New Woman's Association (Shin Fujin Kyōkai), organized in 1920, succeeded in obtaining public support to force an amendment to the said law (in 1922) permitting women to attend political rallies.

There are other indications of progress in the democratic development of Japanese society during the period of "Taishō democracy," such as the advocacy of a free press and the expansion of popular involvement in national affairs. But, as is well known, the reversal of this trend began to take place from around 1928 as the military started to take the initiative in the affairs of the state. It cannot be denied that the seeds of democracy of the Taishō period were still fragile and unstable; but the question remains why they could not germinate and flower into something resembling a mature democracy. This is a big question, going beyond the scope of the current study; but readers may be referred to a painstaking research by Robert Scalapino,[12] whose explanation in terms of the historical timing of Japan's "modernization" is persuasive enough. It should also be remembered that the Potsdam Declaration of July 26, 1945, demanding Japan's unconditional surrender, did speak of the need for removing all obstacles to the *revival* and strengthening of the democratic tendencies among the Japanese people, with the implication that "democratic tendencies" had, in fact, been in existence in an earlier period.

2. Arresting of inflationary trends

The postwar inflation

Once US policy on Japan made a radical shift in favor of the country's economic recovery with the purpose of restoring Japan's prewar position as the "workshop of Asia" and of preserving her economy as far as possible from socialist encroachments, stabilization in the sense of arresting the inflationary trend, which had continued in the early Occupation years, became an imperative necessity.

Losses and damages as consequences of the defeat in the war have been dealt with in the previous chapter; and we can easily see that the dire deficiencies in the basic consumption goods and the means of production would inevitably cause both open and suppressed inflations.

A brief statistical account may be presented here on the progress of inflation during the early occupation years. For this purpose, the monthly index of "effective" consumer prices in Tokyo is chosen, which combines official and black-market prices with the weights relevant to each month under investigation.[13] According to this index, the most inflationary period since the beginning of the Occupation was the first seven months from August 1945 to March 1946, during which time the said index advanced by a monthly rate of about 42 percent. Then there took place the currency conversion in March 1946, coupled with a capital levy tax and other auxiliary measures which siphoned off a substantial amount of excess purchasing power, resulting in a period of six months of relative stability in the price level. But prices turned upwards again from the closing month of 1946, and especially in the months of May, June and July 1947. Food shortages had become most acute, and prices increased at a rate approximating 24 percent per month. It was then that the socialist-led Katayama cabinet was installed with a greatly expanded power in the Economic Stabilization Board; and again relative stability was achieved for about ten months from August 1947 to May 1948, with an average monthly rate of increase of about 4 percent. Katayama resigned in February 1948 over the issue of finding a revenue source for paying inflation-offsetting "living-cost subsidy" to government officials.[14] He was replaced by Hitoshi Ashida, head of the Democratic Party and originally a career diplomat; and a number of senior officials in the Economic Stabilization Board, including myself, resigned *en masse*. A new stage of inflationary trends set in after this, and coincidentally with the shift in the US basic policy over Japan, MacArthur's office became very much concerned with the stabilization issue to the extent of accepting an experts' mission from Washington to put pressure on the Japanese government.

Table 2.2. *Inflationary trend during the Occupation*

		(Annual rate of increase) %
1945	3.5	
1946	16.3	365.7
1947	48.2	195.7
1948	127.9	165.3
1949	208.8	63.2
1950	246.8	18.2
1951	342.5	38.8
1952	349.2	1.9

Note:
The 1934–36 wholesale price index is taken as unity.
Source: Martin Bronfenbrenner, "Inflation theories of the SCAP period," *HOPE*, vol. 7, No. 2, 1975, p.137.

With a longer historical perspective, we may give here a summary picture of Japan's inflationary trend during the Occupation period. For this purpose, we set the 1934–36 Japanese wholesale price index as unity (not the conventional 100) and obtain the multiples in Table 2.2. It can be seen that the postwar inflation in Japan registered about 350 times the level in wholesale prices compared with the prewar (1934–36) level by the end of the Occupation in 1952, by which time stabilization was finally achieved.

It may be noted that this inflation was the product not only of the collapse of the economy subsequent to the defeat in the war, but also partially of the cost of the Occupation incurred by Japan. In fact, Martin Bronfenbrenner, who was on the scene of the Occupation most of the time, counts, as one of three "Occupation failures in the economic sphere," "the Japanese inflation over the four-year interval 1945–49."[15] He points to the fact that "no serious attempt was made, by either the Occupation or the Japanese, to control either the volume of currency printed or the volume of bank deposits created to support not only the Government deficit but also similar deficits of private firms"; and also that "Occupation policy saddled the Japanese with 'termination of war' expenditures, including the support of the Occupation and its dependants in better-than-American style."[16] As a matter of fact, the magnitude of such "termination of war" expenditures, which in 1947 amounted to 64.1 billion yen, was equal to more than 30 percent of the total general-account expenditures of the central government in that year. It further increased to 106.2 billion yen in 1948 and declined only slightly to 99.7 billion yen in 1949.[17]

US government concern

In mapping out a program for economic recovery of Japan, above all for arresting the inflation which again appeared to threaten in the spring of 1948, quiet leadership was taken in Washington by Draper, then Army Under Secretary, who at the time was concerned with the appropriation of funds for Japan's rehabilitation in the new American fiscal year beginning July 1, 1948 and needed the co-operation of Treasury and the Federal Reserve Board.[18] This circumstance prompted him to suggest a new experts mission to be sent to Japan, headed by Ralph Young, Associate Director of the Research Division of the Federal Reserve Board, so that they could make their own survey and recommendations. Thus the Young Mission came to Japan in June 1948; and, after staying only eighteen days, the Mission submitted a report to General MacArthur, recommending that a single exchange rate of 300 yen to the dollar (plus or minus 10 percent) to be established promptly and proposing, in order to dampen the continuing price rises, a number of technical measures dealing with, among other things, bank reserves, credit controls, and income and property taxes. But, as Ted Cohen wrote, "when the impacts of all the recommendations were added up, they amounted to a sharp cut in the nation's current consumption, and specifically to a reduction in workers' real wages."[19] Since SCAP, up to that time, had been trying to *raise* real wages *pari passu* with the stabilization efforts, the recommendations of the Young Mission meant a complete reversal of policy. General MacArthur, supported by the Occupation officials in charge, could not stomach this; and he rejected the Young report *in toto* and ordered it classified as "top secret," ostensibly because of the proposed exchange-rate figure. That was the only time during the Occupation that General MacArthur turned down a report of an outside advisory mission in its entirety.

MacArthur may have won a battle; but it soon became clear that he was to lose his grip on the conduct of the Occupation administration in the economic sphere. For, when Washington received the SCAP radio rejecting the Young report, they, the Federal Reserve and Treasury in particular, banded together and flatly refused approval of Draper's new 1949–50 appropriations request. Draper was forced to come up with a compromise plan. This was to produce a Joint Chiefs of Staff directive, which would compel MacArthur, and to arrange to send a high-level adviser to supervise the implementation of this directive. Thus was born the National Security Council directive of the so-called "Nine-Point Program" of December 1948 and the dispatch in February 1949 of Joseph Dodge, a Detroit banker, with the rank of minister and as personal representative of President Truman. These steps implied an unquestionable vote of distrust in SCAP economic stewardship, confirmed by the President; and, from this time on, General MacArthur was to be only a transmission belt, so to speak, with his authority drastically limited.

This becomes plain when we examine the content of the "Nine-Point Program," which is here reproduced in full:

1 To achieve a true balance in the consolidated budget at the earliest possible date by stringent curtailment of expenditures and maximum expansion in total government revenues, including such new revenues as may be necessary and appropriate.
2 To accelerate and strengthen the program of tax collection and insure prompt, widespread and vigorous criminal prosecution of tax evaders.
3 To assure that credit extension is vigorously limited to those projects contributing to economic recovery of Japan.
4 To establish an effective program to achieve wage stability.
5 To strengthen and, if necessary, expand the coverage of existing price control programs.
6 To improve the operation of foreign trade control and tighten existing foreign exchange controls, to the extent that such measures can appropriately be delegated to Japanese agencies.
7 To improve the effectiveness of the present allocation and rationing system, particularly to the end of maximizing exports.
8 To increase production of all essential indigenous raw materials and manufactured products.
9 To improve the efficiency of the food collection program.

To these nine points was added a supplementary directive, saying that a single exchange rate should be set up within three months of the initiation of the stabilization program.

What was significant was that the "Nine-Point Program" repeated almost exactly the policies that the Occupation authorities had been already following under the much earlier "Economic Stabilization Program" of May 1947 which the Economic and Scientific Section of SCAP had drafted. The only apparent difference was that the NSC directive called for "a true balance in the consolidated budget at the earliest possible date" as against merely "significant progress toward a balanced budget." The very fact that the two programs were so similar had to be interpreted as an indication that the target of the directive was *not policy itself but actual performance.*

The NSC directive was made public both in Tokyo and Washington, in an explanatory press release, only five days later; and it did have a considerable impact on the Japanese public in general since neither the Young report nor the three-year-old directive (preventing MacArthur from assuming responsibility for the operation of the Japanese economy) had been public knowledge at the time. The impact was mainly in the nature of somewhat sudden realization of portents to come from Washington, mixed, however, with a sense of perplexity inasmuch as both stabilization and production recovery were showing definite marks of improvement by the end of 1948.[20] In retrospect, I think it was only natural that when Joseph Dodge came to implement the "Nine-Point Program" his main concern was confined to point (1), cited above, and the question of setting a single exchange rate.

3. Setting of a single exchange rate

Mr Dodge arrives

During the two months between the public issuance of the "Nine-Point Program" on December 19, 1948 and the arrival in Japan of Joseph Dodge on February 1, 1949 there occurred two events in the domestic political scene of Japan which fortuitously worked in favor of making Dodge's mission easier. One was the replacement in February 1949 of Finance Minister Sanroku Izumiyama with Hayato Ikeda;[21] the other was the decided victory of the Liberal Party headed by Shigeru Yoshida in the general election of January 24, 1949. Dodge found a most co-operative team of Japanese bureaucrats for his purpose; and Ted Cohen, who had to contend often with less docile, independent minds on the Japanese side in the earlier period of the Occupation, wrote later that "neither Dodge nor the Washington economists ever fully appreciated the difference those [two] events made, but I always thought that if he had been a gambler instead of a sober banker, he would have been called 'Lucky Joe' Dodge."[22]

Whether Dodge was "lucky" or not, he was at least adamant in insisting on carrying through the tasks charged to him and achieved his objectives apparently for his own satisfaction. On the question of "a true balance in the consolidated budget at the earliest possible date," Dodge used the simile of Japan's economy being dependent on the support of a pair of stilts, government subsidies and American aid; and he proposed, in particular, exposing all the hidden subsidies both in the general and special accounts of the central government budget, so that explicit steps could be taken to abolish or reduce them in order to attain "a true balance in the consolidated budget." Even the well-disposed Finance Minister, Ikeda, balked at a number of specific points; but the "Dodge budget" for fiscal 1949 was in the end thrust down the throat of the Japanese government, and the Diet had no choice but to approve it on April 20, 1949. Understandably, the Japanese press bestowed the title of "Economic Czar" on Joseph Dodge on that occasion.

This nicknaming of Dodge turned out to be soundly appropriate as he surprised both the Japanese government and the Occupation officials with the announcement on April 23, 1949 that he had decided on the single exchange rate of 360 yen to the dollar for the Japanese currency. The exchange rate question, having been recognized as quite complex and extremely important, had been under intensive discussion in relevant offices of both the occupier and the occupied ever since the summer of 1947, and a number of explorative reports had been confidentially exchanged by the parties concerned. But, apparently, Dodge paid little attention to them and chose to make his own decision in consultation, according to his own words, only "with three confidants."[23] He left Japan triumphantly a week later.

The exchange rate problem

The complexity and importance of the exchange rate problem in Japan at the time requires a brief explanation here. As the US policy on Japan shifted around the end of 1947 towards expediting economic recovery, the normalization of Japan's foreign trade came to be placed on the immediate agenda of the Occupation policies, for which purpose it was essential that a unitary exchange rate be decided. Trade conditions in 1947, for example, were extremely abnormal. In that year Japan's exports amounted to 170 million US dollars and imports to 510 million dollars, with a trade deficit of 340 million. However, in order to be able to sell abroad, prices for export goods had to be at whatever level in terms of dollars such goods could be sold in foreign markets, which meant that the actual dollar price for each good had a controlling effect on the specific yen–dollar ratio for each good. For example, a sewing machine, exported from Japan, could be sold, in the initial postwar period, at $40.00 abroad and it cost ¥24,000 to produce it in Japan, the implied specific exchange ratio being 600 yen to a dollar. Such specific exchange ratios ranged, in 1948, from 180 yen to 800 yen a dollar. Rayon yarns were traded at 180 yen and bicycles at 540 yen. On the other hand, imported goods were sold in Japan either at internal official prices or controlled prices; thus very often a product costing one dollar abroad was sold at 100 yen. Such being the case, yen proceeds from the sale of imported goods reflected generally *yen-dear* exchange ratios while yen payment to Japanese exporters reflected generally *yen-cheap* ratios, resulting in a deficit of the Foreign Trade Special Account even in a year like 1947 when the dollar value of imports amounted to three times that of exports.[24]

Subsidies implied in such a "hot-house" character of trade had to be corrected by opening windows to let outside air come in, so that the discipline of the market could effectively be applied in the interest of economic efficiency. The setting of a single exchange rate could be the solution. But the difficulty was that imports at the time consisted mainly of basic foodstuffs and raw materials, i.e. a category of commodities requiring the maintenance of low prices, and exports of significant quantity were raw silk and ships both of which would have been priced out abroad at exchange ratios dearer than 400 yen. Nevertheless, the "hot-house windows" had to be opened sooner or later; and the question was whether to do so step by step or by one stroke; and, if the latter, at what time and, more important, which particular exchange rate should be chosen.

On the Japanese government side, it happened that I was responsible for drafting a recommendation, submitted to the Economic and Scientific Section of SCAP on December 15, 1947, in which the following steps were proposed:

1 A generally applicable single exchange rate is to be calculated as soon as possible by use of the index of official prices (for Japan) with certain practical modifications.

2 But when to make the calculated rate public for actual enforcement is to be decided separately, taking into consideration various related economic problems and trends.

3 The rate once established is to be maintained as long as possible. If, however, subsequent revisions are called for, they are to be made in accordance with a definite formula that was to be beyond political control.

4 For the purpose of successively approaching an "equilibrium" rate, a "balancing formula" is proposed which would reveal a degree of divergence of actual conditions from the non-subsidy equilibrium of trade balance.

Sub rosa discussions continued somewhat intermittently during 1948 among officials on both sides, firstly to grope for a tentative general rate figure and secondly to debate on the advisability of setting a separate "financial rate" on which American business interests clamored for earliest decision. Good enough progress was being made on the Japanese scene by the end of 1948 toward working out a definite plan on exchange problems; but Joseph Dodge, when he entered the scene in the spring of 1949, apparently showed little interest in getting entangled in the ramifying complexities of the exchange rate problem and proclaimed his irrevocable decision out of a clear sky, as stated before.

There was a basic question of some importance if a single exchange rate was to be established in the circumstance of Japan in the postwar period; that is, whether or not it is better to err on the side of a rate which may involve an overvaluation of the currency in question. There had been discussions on this subject among economists even before VJ Day (August 15, 1945), and their recommendations were far from unanimous. Frank Tamagna,[25] in particular, dealing specifically with the problem of exchange rates for currencies of liberated and occupied countries, made a point that "the selection of a high exchange rate is the most practical and effective method of curbing the inflationary pressure resulting from expenses by members of the Allied armies, and particularly by members of the American forces";[26] and he sided with the view that it is better to err on the side of a rate overvaluing the currency in question. Gottfried Haberler,[27] on the other hand, took the reverse position to that of Tamagna on the ground that a lower rate (i.e. undervaluation) would make it easier to abolish or mitigate the then existing economic controls and would entail less need of revision in the immediate future.

In any case, the core of the problem was, as Tamagna suggested, how to determine the equilibrium rate of a currency; that is, "the rate which, under prevailing conditions of national income and flow of foreign investments, achieves and maintains a state of equilibrium in a country's balance of payments."[28] We, on the Japanese side, agreed with this idea; and therefore, with the extremely disrupted conditions of the economy in 1947 and 1948,[29] we had proposed, as stated earlier, a method of approximation by stages through the application of a "balancing formula."

But at the same time we were aware, somewhat optimistically then, that the Japanese economy at the beginning of 1949 was definitely in the convalescent stage, not yet able to manifest its full potential capability. Thus we felt that to decide on a single exchange rate for Japan in such circumstances – the rate which would not shut out a major part of her exports in foreign markets – was quite similar to the case of deciding on the concessional handicap for a convalescent golfer who had been absent from the course for a number of years due to sickness. If his handicap was, let us say, 18 before he fell ill, his friends might, after discussion, permit him to play with the handicap of 24 at the resumption of play. But, even with this special allowance, he may have difficulty competing with his friends. Japan at the beginning of 1949 was in a condition similar to this convalescent golfer. But just as the convalescent golfer who, after finding the concessional handicap of 24 still too strenuous, soon might recover his pre-illness skill with the earlier handicap of 18 and thus be at an advantage as his recovery progresses, we were confident that the dynamic process of recuperation and the catching up in technical progress would enable the Japanese economy before long to take advantage of a concessional exchange rate determined early in the process of recovery. Whether Joseph Dodge paid any attention to this type of problem in deciding on the rate of 360 yen to the dollar is not known; but his decision turned out, just as some of us commented on it at the time, to be erring on the side of undervaluation of yen. We shall have an occasion to discuss the dynamically favorable effect on exports of the static exchange rate of the "convalescent" period.

The Shoup Mission for tax reform

Most likely as a necessary follow-up to Dodge's unilateral surgery on Japan's budget structure creating a super-surplus,[30] the American government decided to send to Japan an experts mission for tax reforms headed by Carl Shoup, professor of Columbia University, with six other well-chosen specialists in different aspects of central and local taxation systems. The Mission arrived in Tokyo on May 10, 1949, stayed for a little over three months, and submitted its report to General MacArthur, which was made public on September 15, 1949. I believe that of all the missions sent by the United States to Japan during the Occupation period the Shoup Mission was the most conscientious in the sense that all of the Mission members took great pains in trying to learn complexities, traditional and contemporaneous, of the local conditions before applying modern principles of taxation of which they were at the frontier. Aided by three Japanese economists[31] as advisers, the Mission labored most energetically through the hottest season in Japan to come up with a lengthy report (some 60,000 words) which, in addition to proposing pertinent recommendations for tax reform for the Japanese economy at the time, presented a most readable summary of the tax systems in Japan, far superior to, and more enlightening than, the bureaucratic or text-book summaries that had been available in Japanese. It is a testimony to the far-sighted wisdom of the Mission that even after forty years the Shoup Report of 1949 is still studied as a reference and guide for tax reforms in Japan.[32]

The main features of the Shoup Mission's recommendations may be summarized under the following three headings:

1 Retaining of the progressive and broad-based personal income tax as the mainstay of the national tax structure, with special emphasis on "horizontal" fairness.
2 Emphasis on the fiscal autonomy of local governments, through the introduction of a value-added tax scheme.
3 Provisions for revaluing land and fixed capital in the light of the war-time and postwar inflation, designed to allow accumulation of adequate depreciation reserves and to prevent the draining away of these reserves by income taxes.

As regards the first point: if we were to place major reliance on the direct taxes for the national government, it was evident that we should achieve both the desiderata of "horizontal" fairness and of "vertical" redistribution. A major flaw in the income tax administration in the period preceding the Mission's arrival was an obvious inequity in the actual tax incidence on the same income level between the self-assessed taxpayers and the collected-at-source group, the latter being wage and salary earners.[33] The Mission's approach was, on the one hand, to be more realistic about the degree of compliance by the self-assessed group through reduction of top bracket rates (from 85 percent to 55 percent) with an apparent sacrifice of progression, while proposing special "blue form" returns for record keeping by them with favorable treatment in re-assessment. Shoup had remarked in Japan that any recommendation which could not endure the test of fairness in tax burden was unlikely to be accepted in the end. This intent, as well as the methodology commanded by the Mission, was laudable enough. But a tax system is like a woven cloth requiring both warp and woof. If the methodology is the warp, actual relevant statistical data constitute the woof; and the latter had to be provided by the Japanese bureaucracy. In retrospect we must say it is unfortunate that the Mission's recommendation on income tax reforms was handicapped greatly by the inadequacy of the woof.[34]

One innovation which the Shoup Mission proposed in connection with the first point above may be mentioned here. That was the institution of a net worth tax, which was to be a national government levy on property in all forms and whose purpose was to make up for revenue lost by lowering the top bracket rates of personal income tax. Probably more important, its proposed function was to use it as checks on income tax enforcement, and vice versa. The proposal was duly implemented immediately afterwards, but the relevant legislation was repealed in 1953 after Japan regained her independence.

As for the second point of the Mission's recommendations, the general philosophy implied, pointing to the need for strengthening of local autonomy, was of much more historical importance for Japan. The principle of local autonomy had been slow to develop in Japan, partly because the national unification through the Meiji Restoration (1868) brought with it a popular psychology of relying on central leadership and guidance for the ascendant nation-building. The immediate postwar reforms did turn over a new leaf in this regard, through, for example, adoption in 1946 of the system of popular elections for prefectural governors replacing the old practice of appointment by the central government. At the same time, the Ministry of Interior was abolished and a new ministry in charge of autonomous bodies (Jichi-shō) was created. However, as regards the fiscal relations between national and local governments, the legacy of old times remained more or less intact in the form of centralized control through (a) "national government disbursement for specific purposes," (b) "agency-delegated functions" and (c) the limitation on bond issues. What the Shoup Mission did was to propose a system of equalization grants with no strings attached in place of (a) above and the abolition of (b) entirely, giving autonomy to local governments supported by newly increased sources of revenue. "Agency-delegated functions," in particular, used to be the most important instrument for the centralized control of local administration, having the mandatory character with a possibility of legal prosecution against non-observant heads of local autonomous bodies. The Mission's recommendation to abolish them was truly revolutionary from the standpoint of the Japanese bureaucracy; but it did receive immediate support from the Kambé Research Committee on Local Administration which was established by the government in December 1949 for the purpose of reviewing the problem of functional redistribution between national and local governments in the wake of the Shoup Mission Report.

Strengthening of local autonomy, of course, needed a substantial reform on the revenue side; and the Mission's answer was the institution of the value-added tax which was considered by the Mission to be preferable to retail sales taxation or to turnover taxation in the specific conditions of Japan. In both respects, that is, as regards the administrative functional redistribution and the proposal of the value-added tax, the Mission's reform ideas were far-sightedly pertinent, in fact too far-sighted in that they were not implemented by the Japanese government at the time but were to be recalled forty years later with the serious intent of possible implementation.

4. The Korean War and the aftermath

The "Dodge deflation"

The so-called "Dodge Line," its imperative of consolidated budget balancing having been carried out with no compromise, actually achieved its objective faster than even its authors had anticipated. The Bank of Japan notes in circulation declined from 355.2 billion yen at the end of 1948 to 300.6 billion by the end of June 1949 and then stood at 355.3 billion at the year end of 1949. The money flow balance between the government and private sectors, which had shown a net outflow from the former to the amount of 59 billion yen in fiscal 1947 and 21 billion in fiscal 1948, turned completely in the reverse direction in fiscal 1949, showing a net inflow from the latter to the amount of 37.3 billion yen. The consumer price index, with the average of 1948 as 100, and which registered 138 in June 1949, started declining from then on to the level of 123 by June 1950. Unemployment, on the other hand, rose steadily from 260,000 at the end of 1948, to 340,000 a year later and then to 430,000 by June 1950. A string of small business bankruptcies captured the headlines, with occasional suicide cases reported. In theory, the "Dodge Line" was intended to create a stable base from which the economy could gradually expand on a sound, sustainable course. In fact, however, for fifteen months afterward, the economy showed little sign of recovery. Industrial activity rose only sluggishly, and durable goods production, the key indicator of the new capital investment awaited by concerned observers to replace the alleged consumer binge, actually fell. It was, in a sense, inevitable that this was the case, due partly to the peremptory decision by Dodge to terminate the use of the Reconstruction Finance Bank (RFB) for industrial recovery.

The RFB was set up earlier in the Occupation to finance the rebuilding of war-ravaged industry because the commercial "city banks" lacked resources; the RFB had played a principal role in resuscitating coal production and in sustaining other important industries.[35] But the bank's only resources were government-appropriated funds in the form of RFB bond purchases; and that was enough to make it, in Dodge's eyes, an additional engine of inflation. Thus, Dodge decided to abolish the RFB and in its stead set up a US Aid Counterpart Fund, into which the yen proceeds of American aid imports were to be gathered for the prime purpose of making long-term industrial loans, like hydroelectric power projects, to aid the whole economy. Imported US food was an "aid"; but, of course, it was not distributed free. Therefore, consumers, when they bought the US aid food, were now to pay, in effect, for capital investment, while the government lowered its expenditures. Food prices actually rose; and the government found it could not possibly invest the yen counterpart of aid food as fast as it could extract the money from the pockets of the consumer at the higher prices. Of the 129 billion yen the Counterpart Fund collected from the sale of US aid goods in fiscal 1949–50, the Japanese government was able to invest only 50 billion in capital projects; the rest, 79 billion, was simply withdrawn from circulation. The government was directed by the Occupation to use some of it to redeem RFB bonds and to keep some immobilized in cash.

Not only did the fiscal retrenchment have sudden deflationary effect, but the demonetizing of a sizable portion of the note issue created a critical condition in the still debilitated business world. A struggle for survival began; and it was only natural that in the capitalistic milieu with the legacies of prewar power relations remaining a shake-out of the weak and a strengthening of the strong would result. For one thing, in the general deconcentration program of 1947–48, the category of banking was made an exception, and the big *zaibatsu* banks could maintain their position essentially intact. And they were able to provide funds for the companies that had been associated with them. Even for them, the Dodge deflation had the effect of drying up their resources for loans. But the Bank of Japan came to the rescue with a securities-purchase operation to the extent of depressing the percentage of securities in the total assets held by commercial banks from the prewar average of 25 percent to as low as 9.9 percent by March 1950. Still, the tight money situation could not be eased, with a consequence that commercial banks in general had to resort to what was then called "overloans," that is, lending in excess of their assets. Thus, between the end of 1948 and the early months of 1950, while deposits in all the banks increased roughly by 100 percent, loans and investments by them rose by 160 percent (from 381.3 billion yen to 994.7 billion), the ratio between the two going up from 0.85 to 1.10, and their borrowing from the Bank of Japan swelled from 48.7 billion yen to 135.4 billion, or a rise of 178 percent.

Such was the monetary background, which, in the generally depressed condition of the economy, had the effect of favoring those Japanese business firms with former *zaibatsu* connections and penalizing small and medium-sized independents. It may be said that while the general public was being subjected to the consequential forced saving, gradual redistribution of wealth ensued through capital accumulation favoring big business and a solid link came to be institutionalized between the erstwhile *zaibatsu* banks and industrial enterprises. Dodge came back to Japan later in 1949 to check up on the progress of his program and commented, with satisfaction, that "it's a textbook example of how a budget can stop an inflation cold."[36] In effect, he constituted, as Ted Cohen rightly observed, "the first postwar channel between the conservative Japanese big business elements and their bureaucratic and political allies in Japan and the top level of officials in the US Government."[37]

Impact of the Korean War

All the economic indicators tell us that the Japanese economy, in mid-1950, was at a stalemate. The "polarization of politics," referred to earlier, partly as a consequence of SCAP's reversal on the rights of labor, found its expression, on the one hand, in the landslide victory of the conservative Liberal Party in the general election of January 1949 and the massive shift in labor alliance away from the Socialists to the Communist Party,[38] and, on the other, in the widespread unrest on labor fronts induced by the government's decision to dismiss a large number of union activists on the pretext of violating the retrogressively revised labor laws.

Three ugly incidents mar the year of 1949, which opened with

MacArthur's congratulatory statement, saying that the results of the January election were a "clear and decisive mandate for the conservative philosophy of government."[39] The first of the three incidents was the death of Sadanori Shimoyama, president of the National Railway Corporation, whose body was found, run over by a train, on July 6, a few days after he had been forced by the government to announce the dismissal of 120,413 men. The second was the so-called "Mitaka Incident" of July 15, when six people were killed by an unmanned electric train derailed at the Tokyo suburban station of Mitaka. And the third was the "Matsukawa Incident" of August 7, in which a train was derailed, allegedly through sabotage, at the town of Matsukawa, about 170 miles north of Tokyo, killing three crew members and injuring a large number of passengers. These incidents, all of them shrouded in mystery, created a social atmosphere of turbulence and fear and aggravated further the gloom born of worsening economic distress as the decade turned to the 1950s.

What prospect awaited occupied Japan in the succeeding months and years, no one could tell at the time. But many of the uncertainties were all of a sudden swept away by the outbreak of the Korean War on June 25, 1950. Literally in a matter of days the US Army turned Japan into a multi-purpose base for its military operations in Korea. First of all, what MacArthur apparently considered to be a security vacuum, created by the transferring of occupying forces from Japan to the scene of combat, had to be somehow filled; and he ordered the Japanese government on July 8 to create a 75,000-strong Police Reserve Corps and to add 8,000 men to the then existing Maritime Safety Corps. Budgetary appropriation was needed for these measures through the Diet; and the Ministry of Finance tried to insist on this, reminding the Occupation that even at the height of the prewar militarist era in Japan the demand for armament expansion by the military had to go through the Diet. Indicative, however, of SCAP's feeling of sudden urgency at the time was the finality with which they overruled the Japanese government on the budgetary procedure. It was also indicative of the internal economic conditions at the time that for the total number of 75,000 to be enlisted in the Police Reserve Corps the applications added up to no less than 382,000, more than five times the number needed, illustrating the pressure of unemployment.

More important from an economic point of view were the rush orders for large quantities of all kinds of support supplies by the US military to the Japanese producers, from galvanized iron sheets and cotton duck to prefabricated buildings and chemicals. These were called "special procurements" paid for in dollars; and the list of goods and services demanded soon was expanded to cover a wide field of economic activities as the Korean conflict became more intense. In fact, Japan's automobile manufacturing, later to become of world top-rank, acquired the momentum of its early growth from orders for repairing US Army vehicles of all kinds which were flooding in.

The tragedy of war in a neighboring country turned out to be a windfall boon for the Japanese economy. By the time the ceasefire agreement was signed at P'anmunjōm on July 28, 1953, that is, for the full three years of fighting on the Korean peninsula, the special procurements amounted to a total of 970 million dollars. This category of extraordinary dollar receipts for Japan lingered on until 1955, by which time the aggregate amount was estimated to have reached 3.56 billion dollars. If we take fiscal 1952 as an example, the dollar receipts due to the special procurements amounted to 62 percent of the total dollar intake of Japan's international payments. Meanwhile, Japan's non-military exports also basked in the world's sellers' market which was itself a consequence of the general expansionary trend in armaments. Thus Japan's foreign exchange reserves, which stood barely at the level of 200 million dollars at the end of 1949, increased to 942 million dollars by the end of 1951, a 4.5 times expansion. Naturally, industrial production enjoyed a sudden boom occasioned by a windfall rise in profit rates (as percentage to equity capital) between the latter half of 1949 and two years later: for example, from 26 percent to 156 percent in the cotton spinning industry, from 32 percent to 194 percent in the synthetic fiber industry, from 5.4 percent to 30 percent in the iron and steel industry, and so on. Prices also rose, stimulated especially by the "price is secondary" policy of US Army procurement. The wholesale price index registered a rise of 52 percent and the consumer price index 24 percent within a year after the outbreak of the Korean War.[40]

As Ted Cohen commented, "no one can say what would have happened to the Japanese economy without the war, but in the actual event it took the Korean War to relieve Dodge's deflation."[41] Although it certainly cannot be denied that the Korean War impinging upon US-occupied Japan constituted a most significant watershed in the recovery of Japan's postwar economy, it should be remembered, as was referred to earlier, that the combination of policies pursued under the command of Joseph Dodge had initiated, even before the outbreak of the Korean conflict, a selective process of "survival of the fittest" in the capitalistic milieu of "the strong preying upon the weak." Development typical of the Korea boom period was the decision, reflecting the radically changed psychology of the Japanese business world, of the iron and steel industry to launch a massive plan of expansion in the name of rationalization. Already in October 1950 both Yawata Steel and Nippon Kōkan made public a three-year program of modernization; and in November Kawasaki Steel announced the projected construction of an integrated steel plant, the first of its kind in

Japan. The so-called "First Rationalization Program for the Steel Industry," with paternalistic backing by the Ministry of International Trade and Industry, covered the period from 1951 to 1955, contemplating a ten-fold expansion in annual new investment in capacity, especially in rolling mills. As for the funds needed for the purpose, major reliance was placed on loans from private banks, to be supplemented by the government source to the extent of 15 percent of the total. The plan of Kawasaki Steel in Chiba appeared to be so ambitious at the time that it caused a quip from the Governor of the Bank of Japan: "We shall make certain that the Chiba site will be covered only by shepherd's purse." The Governor had to eat his words in the end. But such was the unexpected turn of events in the Korea boom period.

5. The peace treaty

The effect of the cold war psychology

In the evolving international situation of the postwar years, the problem of coming to agreement among the Allies on a peace treaty for Japan turned out to be extremely complex. This was natural inasmuch as the Allies which fought against Japan included, besides the United States, the Commonwealth countries, the Soviet Union and China, among whom conflicting interests grew as the years progressed. A series of shattering events, from the fall of Czechoslovakia (1948) and the Berlin blockade (1948–49) to the victory of Mao Tse-tung in China (1949) and the Soviet possession of atomic weapons (1949), heightened the cold war psychology, which seemed to justify, in the minds of US foreign policy planners, the strategy of "containment" and the so-called "domino doctrine." Such circumstances strengthened the resolve of the US government, earlier broached by Army Secretary Royall, of making Japan the "workshop of Asia" ostensibly to serve as a bulwark against communistic encroachments. A corollary to this was the US government's decision to promote the idea of an early, lenient peace with Japan, a separate one if necessary, with an important proviso, however, that the security safeguard be assured.

General MacArthur, the Supreme Commander for the Allied Powers, was actually in favor of a quick treaty, "partly because prolonging the Occupation might cause the United States to seem imperialistic to the Japanese, but also because a treaty would have stimulating economic effects."[42] He was not particularly concerned with the question of security, claiming that Japan above all wished neutrality and should become "the Switzerland of the Pacific." The opinions of the War and Navy Departments, however, were diametrically opposed to those of MacArthur, not only opposing a quick treaty, but also even suggesting the rebuilding of Japan's army if it would be useful as a defense against a possible Soviet invasion. The State Department, too, guided by George Kennan who headed the Policy Planning Staff, was doubtful about attempts to hasten a treaty with Japan, being apprehensive, in the context of still unstable social, political and economic conditions in Japan, that after a treaty there could be strong polarized political forces, nationalist on the one hand and communist on the other, thus disrupting society. Moreover, agreement with the Commonwealth countries was not easy to come by even though they were on the same side as America in the cold-war confrontation. I recall vividly a remark made by the Australian Prime Minister, Sir Robert Menzies, although a little later, to the effect that "it would come as a shock to most Australians to be told that, as a punishment for the Japanese, Australian troops were in future to defend Japan while the Japanese themselves went smiling and bowing about their affairs of production and commerce."[43]

Various documents now available reveal intense wrangling and negotiations within the US government offices and among the Allies before there finally emerged on October 13, 1949 a mature draft for a treaty with Japan, written with full awareness of the cold war, the containment policy, and an earlier significant decision of November 1948 by the National Security Council. Whether this draft was secretly communicated to the Japanese government or not, we do not know; but in November 1949, Prime Minister Yoshida indicated to the Diet for the first time that Japan would accept a peace treaty; and, on January 24, 1950, he made a speech in the Diet to the effect that the anti-war clause of the Constitution did not imply that Japan had forfeited the right to self-defense. By May 1950, Yoshida was indicating that he was willing to accept a separate peace with the West and forgo Soviet participation.

Mr. Dulles' role for a separate peace

Thus the track was laid for the determined policy of the US government for a separate peace with Japan to be pursued before John Foster Dulles, appointed on April 6, 1950 as Foreign Policy Adviser to the Secretary of State, started work on the treaty question.[44] Dulles proceeded to write his first memorandum on Japan, issued on June 6, 1950, in which he emphasized the following points:[45]

1 Japan should be part of the free world and friendly to the United States and should set an example to the rest of Asia by thriving in the free world, thus contributing to a general will to resist communism.
2 Japan's geographical situation makes her susceptible to falling into the

communist orbit, and the West must take the initiative to prevent this from happening.

3 There is a danger of indirect aggression – i.e., subversion – in Japan, and a strong police force must be created to deal with such a contingency.

4 As for the content of the treaty itself, provision is to be made for a progressive reduction of the military occupation; the reforms of the Occupation period are to be noted and preserved; and there are to be no reparations or economic restrictions.

5 Independently of the treaty, but concurrently, a security agreement should be concluded.

Dulles' idea at the time was to hold a preliminary conference of the Allies in the late summer or fall of 1950 in Hawaii, to which were to be invited delegates from all countries represented on the Far Eastern Commission plus those from Indonesia, Ceylon, South Korea and Indochina. As for China, both the Nationalist and the Communist regimes would be invited. The suggestion that all the participants in the preliminary conference should be involved in security arrangements with Japan (under (5) above) was *prima facie* inconsistent with the objective (under (1) above) that Japan was to be aligned with the United States. But in any case, unanimity was not to be required on treaty terms in the conference; and Dulles appeared to have been confident that the US. policy would prevail.

The ground was thus prepared for an early peace, and Dulles began his task of establishing the requisite lines of communication by travelling first to Japan and Korea on June 14, 1950. In Tokyo, he discussed the treaty with General MacArthur, held conversations with a number of prominent Japanese, and also made a hasty visit of inspection to the 38th parallel which divided the two Koreas. Coincidentally, immediately after this, the Korean War broke out and Dulles stayed on in Japan until June 29. Although John Gunther, in his biography of General MacArthur,[46] wrote that "the South Koreans and Americans in Korea, to say nothing of SCAP in Tokyo, were taken utterly by surprise," we in Japan were not as certain that the conflict had not been foreseen by proper agencies of the US government. In fact, on the very following day of the North Korean attack, we read in *The New York Times* a statement by Rear Admiral Roscoe H. Hillenkoetter, director of the Central Intelligence Agency, saying that American intelligence was aware that "conditions existed in Korea that could have meant an invasion this week or next."[47] It was easy enough for us to believe him, inasmuch as an attack on the scale of four divisions, assisted by three constabulary brigades and some 70 tanks, going into action simultaneously at four different points could hardly have escaped the United States intelligence network widely stretched around in that region.

It happened that at the time of Dulles' visit to Japan there came also a mission headed by Secretary of Defense Louis Johnson and Chairman of the Joint Chiefs of Staff Omar Bradley with the purpose of studying the military aspects of a peace settlement with Japan; and they, together with General MacArthur, must have threshed out as far as they could various important aspects of the treaty problem in the light of the new turn of events in the East Asian region. For Dulles, the problem became simpler because he could now pursue his separate peace idea for Japan alone, and exclude communist countries. It was his conviction that in the postwar era the greatest threat to peace was the communist movement, which – regardless of shifts of timing and temporary compromises – was believed to be dedicated to world revolution.[48] Thus, on his return to the United States, Dulles stepped up his timetable for the negotiation of the treaty. The Pentagon, however, thought otherwise on the grounds that the US military position in Japan under the continued Occupation was far superior to what it would be under any conceivable peace settlement and that such superiority was required in the prevailing circumstances. Here was a dilemma that had to be resolved within the US government, inasmuch as the proposed recognition of the full sovereignty of the Japanese people over Japan and its territorial waters would be inconsistent with a provision in the same treaty handing the military power of Japan into the hands of the United States. The only way to resolve this dilemma was to let Japan take the initiative, as a sovereign state, in requesting American military aid, a request to which the United States was to accede. With this basic line of approach the disagreement within the US government could be reconciled; and Dulles went ahead to carry through his separate peace plan by negotiating the treaty terms on a bilateral basis through diplomatic channels, avoiding the use of a general conference method which was most likely to involve direct confrontation with the Soviet Union. Although there were some modifications proposed by non-communist allied countries, a draft plan of peace with Japan was solidly worked out by the time the San Francisco Conference was opened on September 4, 1951. There, the Soviet delegation, headed by Andrej Gromyko, met a stone wall of procedural vetoes which prevented any of their amendment proposals even being discussed. Thus, the American plan for a separate peace with Japan, with the exclusion of the Soviet Union and communist China, became a reality on September 8, 1951. Linked with the peace treaty was the US–Japan security treaty which was signed immediately afterwards.

This security treaty, coupled with the separate peace, may have satisfied the designs of the US government in the context of the cold war at the time. It was then that the Korean crisis aggravated to the point of MacArthur's advocacy of bombing the mainland of China and his subsequent dismissal (April 11, 1951) by President Truman.

Acceptance of the security treaty (between the US and Japan) was made a condition for the signing of the Peace Treaty and turned out to be a source of considerable opposition among the Japanese themselves. For one thing, the security treaty was in the nature of an imposition on the still-occupied nation without sovereignty. Article I of the treaty, in particular, granted the US in effect the right to dispose its Japan-based troops or supplies to meet trouble anywhere in the Far East while making no specific commitment to defend Japan, although it promised assistance to the Japanese government in putting down large-scale internal riots and disturbances. Furthermore, in the preamble there was a statement that the United States expected Japan to "increasingly assume responsibility for its own defense against direct and indirect aggression." This, of course, would be in contradiction to the arms-renouncing clause (Article IX) of the Japanese Constitution. Besides, the term of the treaty was indefinite; it would expire when both governments thought that the United Nations or alternative security arrangements assured international peace and security in the Japan area. In addition, the administrative agreement was negotiated to lay down the detailed conditions for the presence of US troops in Japan. Since this was an executive agreement, it did not come before either the Diet or the Senate, and it automatically went into effect with the security treaty on April 28, 1952.

Japanese reactions

It was evident in the eyes of most Japanese that the security treaty with the accompanying administrative agreement implied an infringement upon Japanese sovereignty in numerous concrete respects; and such misgivings were heightened as the years progressed in the 1950s, finally to culminate in the stormy crisis of 1960 when the revision of the treaty was contemplated.[49] That was the occasion when the projected visit of President Eisenhower to Japan, as part of an exchange in which the then Crown Prince Akihito would visit the United States to celebrate 100 years of relations between the two countries, had suddenly to be cancelled. And George Packard III made a comment that "the blocking of the Eisenhower visit struck a blow at the fifteen-year-old policy of Japanese ruling circles to subordinate Japan to America and at their policy of strengthening the alliance."[50]

The security treaty could be, and was in fact, revised in 1960, removing some features that had been objectionable to Japan in the old one and also specifying that either the US or Japan could terminate the treaty after ten years by giving one year's advance notice to the other. The Treaty of Peace, on the other hand, could not be revised and its *separate* character has essentially remained for forty years now.[51] In the context of Japan's international relations this was considered to be an extremely important point at the time, for the separate peace then meant Japan becoming embraced into the arms of one side of the cold war with the necessary implication of becoming at least estranged from, if not antagonistic toward, the other side. The basic national interest for Japan was, of course, the maintenance of peace; and Japan being too small or too weak to take leadership in this matter even as a moral power with her arms-renouncing Constitution, the least she could do was *not* to contribute even an iota to the intensification or the prolongation of the cold war. Thus arose voices of opposition among a large section of the general public in Japan to a separate peace, asking for an overall one instead. In fact, we knew that opinions were expressed outside Japan, too, deploring the idea of a separate treaty excluding the participation of either the Soviet Union or the People's Republic of China.[52] But Dulles harped on the theme, whenever he had a chance to make a public statement in Japan, that "those who advocate a so-called 'overall' peace are, in effect, advocating no peace at all."[53] It was clear enough, therefore, that the person fittingly called "the architect of peace for Japan" was precluding any efforts toward consummating overall peace settlements with Japan; and the prospect of "no peace at all" naturally had a power of persuasion on the nation which was becoming tired of a long period of occupation.

Discussions which took place in Japan in this connection constitute a major topic in itself and go beyond the scope of this study. But I may refer to one particular point of controversy which was of social scientific significance. That is the point, emphasized by the advocates of an overall peace in the context of the cold war, that *the difference in socio-economic systems as such should not be any cause for aggression of one system against another.* This issue was raised in particular by the Peace Study Group (Heiwa Mondai Danwakai), which acted prominently in supplying the intellectual leadership for the cause of peaceful coexistence from the standpoint of Japan. The group, composed of some sixty eminent representatives from universities and public life,[54] had been organized by the initiative of Genzaburō Yoshino, philosopher-editor of the monthly journal *Sekai*, in 1948 for the purpose of discussing a UNESCO statement (issued on July 13, 1948) on the causes of war and the foundations of peace.[55] The group continued to meet as the peace treaty issue became publicly discussed and issued joint statements concerning the treaty problem twice, first in January 1950 and for the second time in September 1950 after the Korean conflict started. The consistent position they took was the advocacy of an overall peace settlement, opposition to foreign military bases on the Japanese soil, and inviolable neutrality with membership for Japan in the United Nations.[56] Dunn made a critical comment on such advocacy, saying that this was "a remarkable program which largely ignored the realities of world politics of the time."[57] But the detailed explanation of the group's advocacy, given in their September 1950 statement, can be read even now as revealing perspicacious insight into the intricacies of world politics especially in the era when power politics is additionally complicated by the emergence of a new socio-economic system, which after all is a historical process. It is worth recalling in this connection a letter written by Franklin Roosevelt in November 1942 to one of his closest friends in the business world, Thomas W. Lamont.[58] He wrote in part as follows:

In the Autumn of 1933, when I initiated with Stalin the question of renewing diplomatic relations, Litvinoff was sent over and we had a four or five day drag-down and knock-out fight in regard to a number of things, including the right to have American priests, ministers and rabbis look after the spiritual needs of Americans in Russia.

Finally, after further objections on Litvinoff's part, I threw up my hands and said to him, "What is the use of all this anyway? Your people and my people are as far apart as the poles."

Litvinoff's answer is worthy of an eventual place in history. He said, "I hope you will not feel that way, Mr. President, because I do not. In 1920 we were as far apart as you say. At that time you were one hundred percent capitalistic and we were at the other extreme – zero. In these thirteen years we have risen in the scale to, let us say, a position of twenty. You Americans, especially since last March, have gone to a position of eighty. It is my real belief that in the next twenty years we will go to forty and you will come down to sixty. I do not believe the rapprochement will get closer than that. And while it is difficult for nations to confer with and understand each other with a difference between twenty and eighty, it is wholly possible for them to do so if the difference is only between forty and sixty." Perhaps Litvinoff's thoughts of nine years ago are coming true.

Members of the Peace Study group might have been too idealistic in thinking at the time that the cold war confrontation was essentially a short-run conjuncture and that the convergence of capitalism and socialism would be historically inevitable. But forty years since that time, we may say, have proved that they, as well as Litvinoff, were grasping the direction of history in the correct long-run perspective.

At any rate, the Treaty of Peace for Japan, albeit a separate one, came into effect on April 28, 1952; and Japan regained her independence. By then, the postwar inflationary trends had been essentially contained, although the Korean War boom was accompanied by a temporary price rise of 38.8 percent in the index of wholesale prices between 1950 and 1951. Industrial production also registered the index level of 131 (with 1934–36 = 100) in the fiscal 1951 (March 1951 to April 1952), overfulfilling the government target set one year earlier by 40 percent.

3   The period of high growth rate

With this chapter my interpretive analysis begins. First, however, I provide statistical evidence to confirm an unusually rapid growth rate achieved by Japan roughly for two decades after 1954. Extraordinary, in particular, was the growth rate in manufacturing labor productivity compared with other advanced capitalist countries. It was quite natural that in this circumstance the ruling circles of Japanese capitalism regained their confidence; and, as the Peace Treaty became effective in April 1952 and the erstwhile occupation-inspired restrictions came to be largely removed, the former *zaibatsu* groups were reassembled with certain modifications in their conduct, such as the adoption of what is known as "the one-set" principle. Still, a question remains as to whence the effective demand arose to sustain the rapid growth rate of real GNP. The most important item, no doubt, was the export expansion, illustrated below by the sewing-machine episode. Private investment, too, was a portent stimulus, leading logically to the transformation of industrial structure. There was no question but that Japanese capitalism was rejuvenated in the process.

1. The "miracle" of rapid growth

> Past experience shows that a greater cumulative increment than 1 percent per annum in the standard of life has seldom proved practicable. Even if the fertility of invention would permit more, we cannot easily adjust ourselves to a greater rate of change than this involves. There may have been one or two decades in this country during the past hundred years when improvement has proceeded at the rate of 1 percent per annum. But generally speaking the rate of improvement seems to have been somewhat less than 1 percent per annum cumulative.
>
> J.M. Keynes[1]

Keynes was speaking in the middle of the gloomy decade of 1930s, and he might have been psychologically influenced then by the pessimism of the day. But it can also be shown historically that Great Britain, during her radiant half century from 1860 to 1913, managed to raise her per capita real income only at the annual average rate of 0.9 percent. Few economists at the time doubted the truth of the Keynes' observation, which subsequently became a part of common sense among the practitioners of economic science.

Consequently, when the record of West German growth in real GNP was reported as 9.3 percent per annum in the first half of the 1950s, publicists in general did not hesitate to characterize that attainment as "a miracle." The West German economy kept on growing, albeit at a decelerating pace, at the quinquennial average of 6.6 percent for 1955–60, 5.0 percent for 1960–65, 4.7 percent for 1965–70, and 3.0 percent for 1970–74 – still far surpassing the "common sense" rate of improvement suggested by Keynes. All the more was it a source of surprise for the economics profession when Japan came to show, shortly after West Germany, first the quinquennial average growth rate in real GNP of 7.0 percent for 1954–58, followed by 10.8 percent for 1959–63, 10.9 percent for 1964–68, and 9.6 percent for 1969–73, only to have her sustained expansion stalled by the first oil shock of 1973. Japan's case was more of a miracle than that of West Germany; and an explanation is called for, since of all the human and social phenomena economic ones are probably the least accountable in terms of miracles.

Kenneth Boulding has advanced a hypothesis of "creative defeat," saying that "very often there is the creative reaction to defeat; Japan is an example of a fantastically creative response to defeat."[2] One recalls that Schumpeter used to puzzle the students of his "business cycle" course by ascribing the Japanese boom of 1924–25 to the Great *Kanto* Earthquake of 1923. The defeat in the last war brought about, of course, a far greater scale of devastation in the economy of Japan, necessitating a fresh renovating start in almost every aspect. So long as the morale of the population could be maintained, however, the work of reconstruction would not only invite strong incentive but also by necessity involve innovative installations in productive activities. If Schumpeter were alive, he might have predicted a sustained high growth rate for the Japanese economy after the defeat. But was there an element of "creativeness" as Boulding suggests? This may be more of a figurative judgment.

For one thing, there could be a transcendental explanation for Japan's growth performance, which, on the assumption of a country's innate capability of maintaining a certain long-run trend line, would state that Japan was simply coming back to her innate trend line after a lapse caused by the dissipation and isolation incidental to the war. Such an explanation appeared to be plausible up until around 1970 if we could assume that Japan's long-run growth rate of real GNP was more or less what she demonstrated to have been capable of in the course of her development from the early Meiji Era, or from the 1870s, i.e., between 3.5 and 4 percent per annum. If the trend line were drawn with a 4 percent growth rate starting from the 1934–36 average as 100, the hypothetical index would stand at 267 in 1960 and 324 in 1965, against which actual figures stood at 162 in 1960 and 248 in 1965. But by 1970, whereas the former comes up to 395, the latter goes slightly above it to 407, with the implication that the growth up to 1970 was more or less within the range of the assumed long-run trend line. If we go, however, a few more years to 1973, the gap widens to 444 on the trend line against 499 as actual attainment. It is plain that we require a more substantive explanation than this trend line hypothesis. In any case, of course, the 4 percent annual growth, which is assumed here, with the implication of about 3 percent growth in per capita income, may be already too high in the light of the Keynes' dictum quoted earlier.

A statistical analysis

A first step towards explanation could be a statistical analysis of the GNP growth components. We may formulate tautological relations among relevant items in the mechanism of economic growth and try to ascertain which item or items were especially responsible for Japan's high growth rate in the postwar period.

The rate of growth of real GNP (G) can be expressed, by definition, as the sum of the rate of change of labor force (or of aggregate working hours) (x) and the rate of change of labor productivity (or of per man-hour productivity) (y), or alternatively, as the ratio of the gross saving ratio (a) and the incremental capital coefficient (β), thus:[3]

$$G = x + y = a/\beta$$

Focusing upon the relation $G = x + y$, we can first of all point out that Japan was favored in the immediate postwar period by an unusually flexible condition of labor supply, as was pointed out in Chapter 1. At the time when the total labor force gainfully engaged was slightly more than 30 million in the years immediately following the defeat in the war, Japan's labor force supply for *non-war* purposes was suddenly expanded by more than ten million consisting of:

  7,100,000   through demobilization
  2,600,000   through repatriation mainly from Asian countries
  1,600,000   through release of drafted workers in armament-related
              industries
the majority of whom were able-bodied men with one skill or another. As they returned to civilian life in Japan, they could not be employed

immediately and many of them went back to their ancestral rural regions and constituted a large body of disguised unemployment. This was a reservoir which appeared to be unfathomable for some years to come, and the excess of supply over demand thus created weakened the bargaining position of labor, depressing the wage rate to a level lower in the early postwar years than the productivity rise warranted. This circumstance made the supply curve of labor perversely elastic and had the effect of raising the labor participation ratio especially among women and the aged. The rate of growth of the labor force in the first half of the decade of the 1950s, for example, was maintained at the level of 3.5 percent per annum – an unusually high figure. We may say that the x-component in the growth equation was high without requiring a bonus rise in the wage rate to entice people into the labor market.

As for the y-component, i.e. the rate of change in labor productivity, an overriding factor in the situation was the so-called "catch-up" process. While Japan was isolated in the pursuit of the war, there developed, especially under the leadership of the United States, what is known as "the scientific industrial revolution,"[4] which, in close association with the war efforts, combined the innovations in electronics, aeronautics, automation, the use of atomic power and the burgeoning of new synthetic materials. Thus, although at the time the war ended Japan was left far behind a country like the United States in the application of the latest technologies to industries, she was able to catch up very quickly with other advanced countries by importing the innovations and know-hows which had already been developed. By the end of the 1940s Japan was sufficiently advanced in the general skill of her labor force as well as in entrepreneurial capabilities so that she could absorb the fruit of technological progress without much difficulty and even improve upon them as in the case of electronics and cameras. In manufacturing industries, in particular, the rate of growth in labor productivity was maintained exceptionally high as evidenced by the quinquennial averages, shown in Table 3.1, where comparison is made with other advanced countries. Comparison of the cumulative effect is even more striking. With the 1950 level as 100, the index for 1973 was 1,412 for Japan, contrasted to 210 for the US, 210 for the UK, and 411 for West Germany, namely about seven times more rapid in Japan compared with the USA or the UK.

Concerning the alternative formulation of the growth rate, namely, $G = \alpha/\beta$ (the growth rate being the ratio between the saving ratio and the capital coefficient), we may say that since the capital coefficient is known not to differ as widely among advanced countries, an exceptionally high growth rate cannot be sustained unless the saving ratio is high. Again an international comparison does show that the ratio of gross domestic saving

Table 3.1. *The rate of growth in labor productivity in manufacturing – an international comparison*

(Units: %)

	Japan	USA	UK	West Germany
1950–55	17.5	2.8	2.5	9.3
1955–60	6.2	2.7	2.4	6.6
1960–65	8.9	4.6	3.1	5.0
1965–70	17.8	1.3	3.5	4.7
1970–73	10.4	4.7	6.1	3.0*

Note:
* The average figure for 1970–74.
Source: The Bank of Japan, *Nihon Keizai wo Chūshin tosuru Kokusai Hikaku Tōkei* (Comparative Economic and Financial Statistics: Japan and Other Major Countries).

to GNP was markedly higher in Japan than in other industrialized countries in the relevant years under our discussion, as can be seen in Table 3.2. The problem, of course, is how such a high saving ratio was recorded in Japan, and this, in itself, is an extremely interesting and complex problem requiring a much fuller analysis than the space here allows. But one thing is certain: the propensity to save of the household sector in Japan has traditionally been higher than in other countries and such savings have been syphoned off into the corporate enterprise sector via banking institutions of all kinds including post offices. This fact calls for an explanation, answering the question at the same time as to whether this characteristic is likely to persist or not. A number of explanations has been offered in the past, such as: (1) the general practice, especially in the postwar, of "bonus" payments in June and December amounting to the equivalent of three months' salary or more each time induces necessarily a lag in spending and thus a high propensity to save; (2) the inadequacy of the social security system, especially for the elderly, necessitates a higher rate of individual saving with precautionary motives than in most other advanced countries; (3) a rather rigid system of seniority, that still persists in Japan, works toward a higher propensity to save among more elderly employees whose spending needs are actually smaller than those who still have their children in schools and/or expecting marriage; and (4) the household sector includes within it a much larger number of individual proprietors than in some other countries who save not only *qua* households but also *qua* business enterprises.

Table 3.2. *The ratio of gross domestic saving to GNP – an international comparison*

	1964–68 average %	1969–73 average %
Japan	36.2	39.5
USA	15.7	14.8
UK	18.8	19.2
West Germany	26.7	27.4
France	25.7	27.0

Source: White Paper on the Japanese Economy, 1975 (Japanese edition), p.119. Figures for Japan are for fiscal years, i.e. years starting from 1 April.

Problems to be answered

Explanatory tools for economic growth are, of course, hardly exhausted by the statistical components of the growth equation discussed above. Probably far more important would be questions like: (1) what were the major sources of effective demand which warranted the high rate of growth? (2) What was the role played by the government by way of stimulating growth? (3) Was there a significant shift in industrial structure? If so, how was it brought about? (4) What was the fate of the erstwhile *zaibatsu* structure and the subsequent evolution of business organizations? (5) What was the impact of the single exchange rate, set in April 1949, on the country's external economic relations?, and so on. We must now turn to these problems in an attempt to provide a much fuller explanation of the "miracle" of rapid growth in the postwar Japan.

2. Capitalism rejuvenated

It is generally agreed, I believe, that the regaining of independence through the separate Peace Treaty in 1952 against the background of the Korean War marked a most significant turning point for postwar Japan not only in her political position in the world but also as regards her economic development. In particular, the ruling circles of Japanese capitalism regained their confidence. As was described in some detail in the last chapter (Section 4), the sudden burst of demand for all kinds of products occasioned by the Korean special procurements was a godsend for the Japanese economy then stagnating under the Dodge-deflation; and many a business leader commented publicly later that the Korean War was "the divine wind" which turned their despondency to sanguine optimism.

Far more important, however, was the radically changed atmosphere in Japan subsequent to the reversal of many of the former Occupation reforms. The opening sentence of the statement by the Pauley Reparation Mission, issued on December 7, 1945, to wit: "Four years ago today Japan attacked Pearl Harbor. America will never forget the attack. Japan will never forget the consequences," was conveniently forgotten by the Japanese ruling circles as the Occupation ended. Not only they, but also most Japanese people, apparently felt that by the completion of the War Criminals Trial by the Allied Court in 1948 the question of war responsibility was more or less whitewashed as far as the Japanese people in general were concerned. Symptomatic was the retracting by the Occupation of the war-criminal status of Shinsuke Kishi (who later became Prime Minister) and the rehabilitating by the Japanese government of more than ten thousand of those who had been disqualified from official positions on account of their war-time activities. Both of these things happened before the Peace Treaty came into effect on April 28, 1952. On the other hand, the Japanese government, soon after regaining independence, proposed to legislate the Prevention of Subversive Activities Law, ostensibly aimed at mass disturbances; and the Diet, under a conservative majority, passed it in July 1952, as if to echo the McCarthy inquisition in the United States.

Zaibatsu *groups reassembled*

From the standpoint of business leaders in Japan, the two biggest headaches since the beginning of the Occupation were the reparation question and the deconcentration directive. While the first of the two was more or less cleared away by the terms of the Peace Treaty, as has been discussed in the last chapter, the second lingered on. But here again, a new wind began blowing even before Japan regained independence, as "the companies formerly associated with the former *zaibatsu* gradually succeeded in regaining leading positions in the principal industrial branches despite various restrictions. After April 1952 when the Peace Treaty became effective, these restrictions were removed or moderated, and following the lifting of the ban on the use of former company names, trade marks, etc., the former names were revived again."[5] For example, the antimonopoly law was soon revised[6] to permit a manufacturing corporation to hold shares of competitive firms, to raise the upper limit of share-holding by financial institutions from 5 to 10 percent, again to legalize the system of interlocking directorates, and to widen the scope of cartels that could be formed. The revision was taken advantage of immediately, and cartels of all forms came into vogue. But the most important move that gathered momentum after the Peace Treaty was the consolidation and realignment of firms along the former *zaibatsu* lines. Typical was the reassembling into one of all the trading firms which had once been splintered from the old Mitsui Trading Company (Mitsui Bussan). Fig. 3.1 "The Reconsolidation of Mitsui Bussan" depicts this process which, as can be seen, started as early as February 1949 and was consummated in April 1956.

Another wing of major *zaibatsu* groups in Japan before the war was Mitsubishi; and their giant trading firm took a smoother course in reconsolidation and re-established the old Mitsubishi Shōji Company on July 1, 1954. It is noteworthy that in so doing it increased its capitalization fourfold and allocated twenty million of the new shares purposefully to the associated Mitsubishi firms. This resulted in the concentration of share ownership in the hands of Mitsubishi-related firms to the extent of 31.1 percent, compared with the pre-reorganization concentration of 10.4 percent.[7] At the same time, the new Mitsubishi Shōji Company came to hold significant parts of shares in Mitsubishi-related firms, such as Mitsubishi Bank, Mitsubishi Marine Transportation Company, New Mitsubishi Heavy Industry Company, Mitsubishi Chemical Company, Mitsubishi Electric Equipment Manufacturing Company, etc. In this manner, the interlocking in ownership among the former Mitsubishi *zaibatsu* firms became rapidly as close as it used to be before the war.

These examples show quite typically the manner in which the erstwhile *zaibatsu* firms came to be reassembled quickly after Japan's regaining of independence. We might recall here a passage in General MacArthur's New Year Message of 1948, quoted earlier, in which he said, referring to the *zaibatsu* system: "The world has probably never seen a counterpart to so abnormal an economic system. It permitted exploitation of the many for the sole benefit of the few. The integration of these few with government was complete and their influence upon government policies inordinate, and set the course which ultimately led to war and destruction." "The reverse course" (gyaku kōsu) was the term used in Japan with reference to the retrogressive trend in 1950 to 1953; but the expression was too colorless, to say the least, on this *zaibatsu* revival. For, in addition, the banks, each resurrecting the name of historically established *zaibatsu*, came to occupy, to a greater degree than before the war, the central position by responding to the need for an unusually high degree of dependence of manufacturing firms on outside financial capital. A striking example of such dependence is provided by the relatively far higher weights which financial expenses (largely interest payments) occupy in the components of costs among some major manufacturing enterprises in Japan. With labor cost as 100, financial expenses were as high as 90.2 for Nissan Automobile Manufacturing

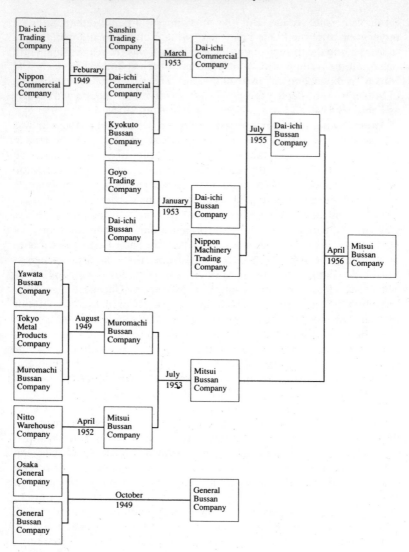

Figure 3.1 The reconsolidation of Mitsui Bussan

Corporation and 50.5 for Matsushita Electric Appliances Manufacturing Corporation in 1965 while the similar relative figures stood at 0.3 for General Motors, 1.4 for Volkswagen, and 0.4 for General Electric.[8]

The fact of big banks, especially those with former *zaibatsu* connections, coming to acquire key positions in the early financing process in the reconstruction period when outside financing was the essential condition for investment activities is eloquently shown by the contrasting picture between prewar and postwar as regards the sources of supply of industrial funds. Whereas in the prewar period (average of 1934–36) the "own capital" (retained profits plus subscription to new shares, not including depreciation allowances) predominated, occupying 86 percent of the total supply, and the "outside capital" (loans from banks, debentures and government funds) contributed the remaining 14 percent, their roles were reversed in the typical early postwar year (1951 fiscal) to the extent of increasing the dependence on "loans from banks" to 62.8 percent while the "own capital" source shrank to 25.9 percent. The share of "government funds" rose, meanwhile, from 0.9 to 7.8 percent.[9] There developed, thus, a situation where commercial banks became a major provider of medium- and long-term investment funds for manufacturing firms, obtaining their resources not only from household savings, which we discussed earlier, but also, to an increasing degree, from the central bank credit. Banks also become active holders of equity shares of corporations to a degree much more prominent than in other advanced industrialized countries. It may be noted also, in passing, that because of such high independence on outside funds manufacturing corporations could enjoy higher profit rates since their interest payments, though a part of value-added, could be deducted as a cost item for corporate tax.

Since the big banks, in particular, were former *zaibatsu* banks, it was only natural for them to associate themselves each with those firms which used to be members of the "family," so to speak, of respective *zaibatsu* structure especially after April 1952 when the Peace Treaty became effective and the consolidation and realignment of firms along the former *zaibatsu* lines progressed. It cannot be doubted that in this way the closely associated *zaibatsu*-type business groups, with a banking institution at the core for each, have come to play, today no less than in prewar days, leading roles in the economic activities of Japan. Organizationally, there exists no holding company to head each group as in the prewar days; but the presidents of major Mitsui-associated corporations, for example, meet regularly under the name of "Nimoku-kai"[10] for the purpose, presumably, of exchanging information. Similar arrangements exist for other groupings such as Mitsubishi and Sumitomo.[11] Thus it was that the percentages occupied by the three major *zaibatsu*-type groups in the total paid-up capital of

Table 3.3. Zaibatsu *groups' weight in the total paid-up capital of corporations 1937–1970*

(Units: %)

	Mitsui Group	Mitsubishi Group	Sumitomo Group	Total
1937	3.5	3.3	2.2	9.9
1941	4.4	4.3	2.1	10.8
1955	3.1	4.1	2.7	9.9
1960	2.9	4.5	3.6	11.0
1965	4.0	6.0	4.6	14.6
1970	3.3	6.6	4.5	14.4

Note:
Summarized from a detailed table given in Yoshikazu Miyazaki, *Sengo Nihon no Kigyō Shūdan* (Business Groups in the Postwar Japan), Nihon Keizai Shimbun, 1976, pp.260–1.

corporations in Japan have been generally on the increase since before the war, as shown in Table 3.3.

"The one-set" principle

The three groups, the Mitsui, the Mitsubishi and the Sumitomo, are the well-known top three *zaibatsu* from the prewar days. It is, however, important to observe that whereas in the prewar days each of them tended to specialize if it did specialize at all, in certain of the industrial fields and very often to hesitate to launch new industrial ventures,[12] the typical behavior pattern for them in the postwar era has been to vie with each other in getting into a new field as soon as technological feasibility appeared on the horizon. Thus, for example, if the Mitsui established a petrochemical complex (Mitsui Sekiyu Kagaku Kōgyō) in 1955, the Mitsubishi followed immediately with their own (Mitsubishi Yuka) in 1956, and so on. In other words, each of the major *zaibatsu*-type groups has behaved as if it were called upon to possess under its wings "one set" of everything, by absorbing, if necessary, burgeoning independent firms into their group structure.[13] This "one-set" principle was followed not only by the major *zaibatsu*-type groups but also by big individual firms with multiple product lines, as in the case of Hitachi entering the computer industry in competition with Fujitsu and NEC (Nippon Electric Company) at the time when IBM was already a dominant factor in the world market.

Why was it that such "one-set" principle came to prevail especially in postwar Japan? For one thing, in the situation created by forced deconcentration measures during the Occupation period it was easier than otherwise for a new entry to take place in almost any industry. At the same time, an indispensable condition for new entry in those areas where latest industrial innovations were involved was a big enough capaoility of advancing capital for a longer period of gestation than usual – a capability that was possessed only by giant corporations whether associated with zaibatsu-type groups or otherwise independent. Also, from the standpoint of the major zaibatsu-type groups there was an element of positive advantage in broadening the area of activities because of the possibility of internalizing external economies. An almost inevitable consequence of such competitive investment based on the "one-set" principle would be overinvestment relative to likely demand for the products. How such an overinvestment was circumvented and the competitive investments retrospectively came to be warranted are questions which will be enlarged upon in a later chapter. The important thing here is to confirm that Japanese capitalism was rejuvenated thus with its institutional framework solidified in a milieu of dynamic expansion.[14]

3. Whence the effective demand?

Export expansion or domestic resources development?

The characteristic mechanism of "compound interest" growth in prewar Japanese capitalism going back as far as the 1870s was the generation of effective demand in two sectors in particular, that is: (1) the expansion of exports based on the relatively cheap labor especially of young females coming from chronically depressed agricultural areas; and (2) the continuous drive for armament expansion *pari passu* with the "successive, successful wars." In other words, the domestic market for the nation's livelihood purposes was narrow relative to the size of the economy. The defeat in the war presumably changed this mechanism entirely. But the narrowness of the domestic market was again the feature of immediate postwar Japan characterized by the oversupply of the labor force resulting in a depressed wage level and sizable unemployment. Of course, armament expansion was out of the question under the new Constitution which declared that "land, sea, and air forces as well as other war potential will never be maintained." Later, from 1950 on, though paramilitary demand arose on account of the Korean "special procurement," it appeared clear enough, during the early Occupation years, that a major reliance had to be placed on export demand if the economy was to continue on the growth path. This presented a genuine issue, discussed among Japanese economists at the time, namely, whether to give priority to the policies for external trade expansion or to concentrate on the internal development of resources, both human and material.

But while we were in the midst of this controversy on the Japanese side, Joseph Dodge made a decision in 1949 on the setting of a single exchange rate of 360 yen to the dollar, which immediately brought about a significant impact on the fate of Japan's exports. We have referred to the case of sewing-machines, one of the earliest export items in the postwar Japan, which could be sold at $40.00 abroad implying the specific exchange ratio of 600 yen to the dollar since it cost ¥ 24,000 to produce it domestically before the Dodge decision was made in 1949. But there was a dramatic decline in its cost of production, so that by 1960 even at the rate of 360 yen to the dollar its FOB price could be reduced to $12. The simile we used in an earlier chapter of a convalescent golfer regaining his pre-sickness skill was most eloquently demonstrated in this case; and the judgment of some of us on the Japanese side that the Dodge decision erred on the side of undervaluation of the yen proved to be correct. As is well known, it was not until 1971 that the yen was revalued upwards to 308 yen to the dollar. Meanwhile, the dynamically yen-cheap exchange rate must have greatly helped the expansion of Japan's exports.

The sewing-machine episode

In view of this, it may be instructive to relate in some detail the case of the sewing-machine in its export venture, inasmuch as the episode reveals at the same time other relevant aspects of the postwar Japanese economy.

Before the war the domestic sewing-machine market in Japan was dominated by the importation of the Singer machines from America and only in the field of industrial sewing-machines, used mainly to satisfy military demand, were the indigenous manufacturers such as "Mitsubishi" and "Brother" able to survive. The end of the war produced a combination of contingencies which, in the eyes of some, favored the prospect of first developing a domestic sewing-machine industry as import substitution and then almost at the same time fostering it as an export industry. Job-seeking mechanics willing to work at low wages were abundant; small scale family-type work shops were idle especially in the Osaka area; about 600,000 machine tools had to be converted to peaceful uses from war purposes; and, most importantly of all, demand in the US market was so strong in the early postwar years that the US producers, mainly Singer, could not satisfy it fully. These circumstances almost naturally encouraged the creation of a type of industrial organization where parts were produced separately in small workshops and the assembling was done again in an independent unit. Such externalized or social division of labor in the production of a single good had a disadvantage in enforcing strict standardization; but this task was assisted greatly by the paternalistic guidance of both central and local governments. On the other hand, there was a definite advantage, too, in this externalized division of labor. For one thing, the economy of scale could be utilized fully; and also, risk, which was attendant on the somewhat unpredictable conditions in America, could in this way be horizontally dispersed. Thus by the end of 1949, there came into existence in Japan a fairly large number of sewing-machine manufacturing plants producing approximately 30,000 machines per month of which about one-third was exported. The share in production of integrated plants at the time was 25 percent. Within two years, however, i.e. by the end of 1951, this share declined to 5.4 percent as the production increased to 135,000 machines per month of which 80,000 were exported. Costs were declining very rapidly in those years; and one of the factors contributing to the productivity rise was the subsidy scheme introduced in 1951 by the government for the importation of up-to-date machine tools. As much as 50 percent of their import price was paid by the government; and, in addition, domestic manufacturing of such machine tools in imitation was in the initial stage subsidized again to the extent of one half of the cost. The purpose of this subsidy scheme was the promotion of machine-tool industry in general. However, since other industries using machine tools were not sufficiently developed at that time (such as domestic electric appliances) or were only in the burgeoning stage (such as automobiles), the main beneficiary was the sewing-machine industry.

As the Japanese sewing-machine industry made a rapid progress in this way, there ensued naturally competitive struggles on two fronts: one in Japan itself with the Singer which attempted from about 1953 to set up a joint concern and the other in Europe a little later where agitation against Japanese sewing-machine imports became increasingly heightened. On both fronts, the role played by the government in support of the industry was paternalistically accommodating. Singer's tactics were, on the one hand, to file claims against the use by Japanese makers of trade marks confusingly similar to that of the Singer (such as "Seager") and also against the alleged plagiarization of the Singer patent (for example on the "dial tension" part) and, on the other, to attempt to establish a joint concern with the Japanese firm called "Pine Machine" which grew out of a munitions plant, a subsidiary of Nippon Steel Manufacturing Corporation. Criticism was also made against the alleged dumping practice of selling the same sewing-machine at ¥10,000 in the export market against ¥25,000 in the domestic market. Singer's attempt to break into Japan as a manufacturer of sewing-machines was persistent; and when the joint venture scheme with the "Pine" was finally approved by the Japanese government in 1958, the approval was predicated on the condition of limiting the number of units to be processed in Japan. Domestic manufacturers were by then sufficiently strong to withstand any competition that Singer-Pine presented to them.

In fact, by the late 1950s Japanese sewing-machines were successfully invading European markets where along with Singer, which was dominant in France, West German manufacturers such as "Pfaff" and "Anchor-Phoenix" were the leading suppliers. The initial reaction of the European Common Market countries against the intrusion of Japanese sewing-machines was to devise a "mixed-tariff" scheme, combining the specific duty with the *ad valorem* tariff, to be applied to the importation of Japanese sewing-machines. Such a "mixed-tariff" scheme had already been applied to Japanese china and porcelain wares. And it was proposed then that the specific duty part would be a difference between the threshold price of $40 and the price quoted for importation from Japan, which at the time was anywhere between $10 and $12. In retrospect, it was a formidable task for Japanese exporters to make the Common Market countries abandon this idea of a "mixed-tariff" scheme and to succeed in obtaining a foothold in the European market. But in the course of 1961 to 1964 this was accomplished; and the role played in this campaign by the Japanese government agencies and officials, in particular by the JETRO (the Japan External Trade Recovery Organization), was again typically paternalistic in the extreme. The major opposition to be broken was in West Germany; and the tactics employed by Japan ranged from (a) advertising in newspapers like *Frankfurther Allgemeine*, to (b) enlisting the support of consumer unions and dealers who favored cheaper products, (c) appealing to German machine-tool manufacturers for whom Japan was a major buyer and to whom the *quid pro quo* argument could be presented effectively, (d) turning to Japan's advantage in governmental negotiations Erhardt's policy of trade liberalization, and (e) inviting influential political leaders and German sewing-machine makers to Japan. A number of other factors helped Japan's cause at the time. For example, the closing of the Berlin Wall in August 1961 caused the clandestine influx of a large number of people into West Berlin for whom the best available job was subcontracting work of sewing manufacture for which inexpensive Japanese sewing-machines were highly welcome. Also, the Japanese "Brother" sewing-machine firm already had an assembly plant established in Ireland which had very good diplomatic relations with West Germany and whose export of sewing-machines to the latter would suffer fatally if the contemplated "mixed-tariff" scheme were to be applied in accordance with the nondiscriminating principle of GATT.

Coincidentally, too, the visit to Europe of Prime Minister Ikeda in 1962, whom President De Gaulle is said to have characterized as "a transistor salesman," smoothed the way to softening the opposition of the German Sewing-machine Manufacturers' Association whose president then was Dr Schwalb, executive in charge of sewing-machines in "Anchor-Phoenix," the company which was very much interested in handling Japanese transistor radios. The Japanese government policy then was not necessarily that of forcing the completed products into the German market, but rather that of selling parts to German manufacturers. And when some representatives of German industry were invited to Japan under the auspices of JETRO, they were guided round a number of parts-manufacturing plants and, it was reported, were shocked to see with their own eyes parts with the "Singer" mark being made in Japan. This clinched the argument of the Japanese side inasmuch as the "Singer" was already the main competitor for German manufacturers. In this way, the Japanese sewing-machine industry finally succeeded in obtaining a foothold in the strongest of European markets; and, from then on, it was more or less plain sailing. The tenderest care and patient devotion with which Japanese government officials assisted and backed the sewing-machine industry at every step of this process to become virtually the first successful export industry in the postwar era was truly impressive.[15]

Other export items

After sewing-machines came the camera industry and then the watch-making industry, both of which expanded as exports grew and were able to capitalize upon the economy of scale fully to their advantage. Table 3.4 gives in value terms the process of expansion of these two industries, showing at the same time how important the share of exports was as the industries grew. There were practically no exports of Japanese cameras around 1953; but in that year the government set up the Export Inspection Agency for cameras with a view to maintaining the quality of the product so that the image abroad of Japanese cameras would not be tainted from the very beginning. Progress was rapid subsequently in establishing the quality image of Japanese cameras and before too long Japan rose to the top of the world export market, as can be seen in Table 3.5, which compares the units of cameras exported from the three major exporting countries.

Success stories of such export industries as sewing-machines, cameras and watches are noteworthy and no doubt are illustrative of the characteristic dynamism of the postwar expansion period of Japan. But, after all, these three industries together provide less than 2 percent of the total exports in normal years and can hardly be said to have played a major role in the expansion of Japanese exports in the high growth period.

Table 3.4. *Production, exports and imports of watches and cameras (selected years)*

(Units: million yen)

	Watches and clocks			Cameras and parts		
	1955	1965	1975	1955	1965	1975
Production (A)	8,039	58,161	227,179	10,649	66,259	242,127
Exports (B)	453	8,633	106,575	1,680	31,236	155,275
Imports	567	2,416	31,967	28	331	10,768
(B)/(A) (%)	5.6	14.8	46.9	15.8	47.1	64.1

Source: Ekonomisuto, June 15, 1976, p.80.

Table 3.5. *Cameras exported by West Germany, USA and Japan 1965 and 1974*

	West Germany	USA	Japan
1965	2,255,000	907,000	1,611,000
1974	3,059,000	1,978,000	4,846,000

Sources: Ekonomisuto, June 15, 1976, pp.80–1 and *White Paper on Trade and Industry (Kakuron)*, 1975 (in Japanese), p.145.

Therefore, we are called upon to examine the products which in recent years have become staples of exports such as steel products, motor vehicles and vessels in order to see how they have grown both in production and exports and how such growth has been made possible. If we do this, we find that the basic element in the success story of the sewing-machine industry – namely, how paternalistic administrative guidance enabled it to strike a happy balance between competition at home and government support for sales abroad raising its productivity markedly in the course of events through innovation and the scale economy while improving the quality as well – was essentially repeated in the leading industries, too. Tables 3.6, 3.7 and 3.8 summarize the process of expansion of the three staples showing at the same time the increasing importance of the share of exports in the total output of each.

As Japan's exports expanded 27.7 times, in terms of dollar volume, between 1955 and 1975, the share in the total of these categories of staples rose more than proportionately, as shown in Table 3.9.

Table 3.6. *Production, exports and imports of steel products (selected years)*

(Units: 1,000 metric tons)

	Production (A)	Exports (B)	Imports	(B)/(A) (%)
1950	3,754.3	399.0	1.5	10.6
1960	17,855.0	2,044.3	176.4	11.4
1970	77,570.2	16,123.3	32.1	20.8
1974	101,970.7	30,765.1	81.4	30.2

Source: Miyohei Shinohara, *Sangyō Kōzō Ron* (A Treatise on Industrial Structure), Chikuma Shobō, 1976, p.286.

Table 3.7. *Production, exports and imports of passenger cars (selected years)*

(Units: Number of cars)

	Production (A)	Exports (B)	Imports	(B)/(A) (%)
1957	47,121	410	6,179	0.9
1960	165,094	7,013	3,450	4.2
1967	1,375,755	223,491	14,352	16.2
1974	3,931,842	1,727,396	42,218	43.9

Source: Miyohei Shinohara, *Sangyō Kōzō Ron*, p.287.

There is no question but that Japan benefited from the happy contingency of exceptionally rapid growth in world trade as a whole beginning in the early 1950s and was further in the position to take advantage of this thanks to the yen-cheap exchange rate that had been set in her convalescent period in 1949. Thus she was able to enjoy a growth elasticity of almost 2.0, or the annual rate of growth in export of twice the rate of growth in world trade as a whole. Especially remarkable was the upsurge of Japan's industries on the world scene in the latter half of the 1960s when the cluster of earlier innovations became solidly established with the economy of scale, and in a large number of industries Japan came to the forefront in productivity and market share. Of the increase in the volume of trade in the non-communist part of the world between 1965 and 1971, Japanese export expansion accounted for as much as 54 percent in the case of steel products, 46 percent for motor vehicles, 90 percent for civilian-

Table 3.8. *Production and exports of steel vessels (selected years)*
(Units: 1,000 gross tons)

	Production (A)	Exports (B)	(B)/(A) (%)
1955	735	384	52.2
1960	1,759	934	53.1
1970	9,917	7,606	76.7
1974	17,541	15,596	88.9

Source: The Bank of Japan, *Economic Statistics Annual 1975*, 1976, p.208, 236.

Table 3.9. *Shares in the total exports of major items 1950–1975*

	Steel products (%)	Motor vehicles (%)	Vessels (%)	Total (%)
1950	8.7	0.0	3.2	11.9
1955	12.7	0.3	3.9	16.9
1960	9.6	1.9	7.1	18.6
1970	14.7	6.9	7.3	28.9
1975	18.3	11.1	10.8	40.2

Source: Calculated from the figures in the Bank of Japan, *Economic Statistics Annual 1975*, pp.205–8.

use electronic equipment and apparatus, 54 percent for steel vessels and 38 percent for general machinery.[16]

Export-led growth or not

We raised a question in this section, asking whence did the effective demand rise in the high growth period, roughly between 1952 and 1973, and we have taken pains to describe, in some detail, the record of remarkable success in the expansion of exports. Here, one recalls what Nicholas Kaldor wrote in 1971,[17] making a point to the effect that, as a matter of policy desideratum for Great Britain, a country's growth rate could be raised by stimulating exports through subsidizing them and/or undervaluing the exchange rate. The foregoing analysis shows that Japan did "enjoy" a period of undervaluation of the exchange rate; and also it may be added that there was a resort made to the dual price system in a number of export industries, which was tantamount to subsidizing exports, though we have not given details of this matter here.[18] Clearly, Japan's exports were stimulated through such contingency and device. However, the question is whether, and to what extent, Japan's economic growth rate in the years under discussion was raised and sustained *because of* export promotion.

It is agreed that in purely descriptive terms Japanese growth was export-led during the period of her rapid growth rate. This can be shown by pointing to the fact (1) that exports grew consistently faster than GNP; (2) that exports of goods and services as a ratio to GNP, both in real terms, rose steadily from 7.6 percent in 1955 to 14 percent or more in the early 1970s; and (3) that particularly in the manufacturing sector the proportion exported out of domestic production more or less kept on rising during the twenty-year period under review. But export-led growth as an analytical concept is something else. Richard Caves, for example, suggests[19] that for economic growth to be export-led there is required an exogenous disturbance which can be shown to have led to a rise in economic rent and in real income quite distinct from that caused by higher productivity in domestic production resulting from larger investments in human or physical capital. According to Caves, a simple test to distinguish an external from a domestic disturbance is to see whether price and quantity changes are positively or negatively correlated. If positive, the disturbance would be exogenous; and if negative, it would be from shifts in domestic supply.

Lawrence Krause, assisted by Sueo Sekiguchi, applied this Caves' test to the case of Japan and found that "Japanese growth was clearly *not* export-led for most of the 1960s since the price index for exports was 92.0 (with 1970 as 100) and 1961 and remained virtually unchanged through 1968, when it was 92.9 despite the massive increase in export volume of 232 percent."[20] Krause does admit that "even though Japanese growth in the main has not been export led in the analytical sense, it does not mean that exports were unimportant in growth," and goes on to point out that one effect of export growth was "to permit greater expansion of certain industries that could capture larger economies of scale, but domestic sales were much the greater part of total output of these industries, so the stimulus to growth was mainly domestic in origin."[21]

Theoretically, Caves may well be right in saying that if the disturbance arises predominantly from external demand, price and export quantity change should be positively correlated. But the theoretical model there implied is essentially a static one. It is quite possible even abstractly that a particular industry succeeds in becoming an export industry through a resort to the dual price system and then in expanding the scale of production to make full use of the economy of scale so that price and quantity changes become negatively correlated. Any detailed analysis of

Table 3.10. *Ratios of fixed nonresidential business investment to GNE – a comparison among OECD countries*

	Japan	USA	UK	West Germany	France	Italy
1962–64	18.9	5.8	7.7	15.8	14.1	13.6
1965–69	17.6	6.7	8.0	14.7	14.6	11.3
1970–74	18.7	6.4	8.5	15.4	15.6	13.1

Source: Units are percentages. Calculated from the statistics given in OECD, *National Accounts of OECD Countries*. These statistics are also summarized in the Bank of Japan, *Comparative Economic and Financial Statistics: Japan and Other Major Countries*, 1976, pp.23–38.

those industries which played an important role in the export expansion during the two decades of high economic growth in Japan would confirm that the improvement in productivity in domestic production resulting from larger investments in human and physical capital was actually made possible because of the successful drive in export expansion and that, as Takemoto suggested,[22] exports cannot be distinguished from domestic sources of growth such as plant and equipment expenditures.

Private investment as a source of effective demand

In view of the above discussion, the strategic significance of exports in the rapid growth process of the Japanese economy can hardly be gainsaid. But in terms of macroeconomic analysis the role played by private investment expenditures was, beyond doubt, paramount. In a schematic way we have already touched upon this point earlier, making an international comparison of the ratio of gross domestic saving to GNP among advanced industrialized countries. Here, we may focus more specifically upon the expenditure side and compare the ratios of fixed nonresidential business investment to gross national expenditures among several of the OECD countries, as shown in Table 3.10. Although the ratios given for Japan (averaging 18.4 percent for the period covered) are higher than those for West Germany or for France by only a few percentage points, they are still consistently at the top throughout the period. If in addition we take the average ratio of inventory increase to gross national expenditures over the same period, Japan again heads the list with 3.3 percent followed by France (2.2 percent), Italy (1.3 percent), West Germany (1.7 percent), USA (1.0 percent) and UK (0.8 percent).

Looking at these comparative figures one may be satisfied to observe that

different degrees of "animal spirits" could account for such differences in
the weights occupied by private investment activities in gross national
expenditures. But when we examine further concrete details of year to year,
industry to industry march of events, one is struck, in the case of Japan, by a
number of characteristic regularities which may well be unique to that
country. These are:

1 The so-called "one-set" oriented behavior of major business groups.
2 Paternalistic administrative guidance by the Ministry of International
  Trade and Industry (MITI).
3 Anticipatory public investment in creating factory sites by reclamation.
4 Various special tax-relief measures favorable to private industries.
5 The low interest-rate policy.
6 Deliberate temporarization of the trade- and capital-inflow
  liberalization.
7 Specific subsidy measures as regards the use of water and electricity for
  industrial purposes.

We have already dealt with the first of these points in an earlier section. The
remainder is concerned with the general topic of the role of the government
in the expansionary process of the economy and will be the subject matter
we shall take up in the next chapter.

4. Transformation of industrial structure

The foregoing discussion suggests quite logically that the two decades of the
high growth period of Japan, from 1953 to 1973, must have involved a
marked degree of structural shift in the composition of industries in Japan.
For one thing, even if there were no change in the specific productivity of
each industry and also no net increase in the labor force, a mere shift from
the low value-added sector to the high can produce an increase in net
domestic product as simple arithmetic can easily show. Suppose an
economy consists of two sectors, one with the per-man productivity of 10
and the other with 30, the labor force being initially divided equally between
the two, let us say, 50 and 50. The total product then is 2,000. Now suppose
that 10 of the labor engaged in the low-productivity sector is shifted to the
high-productivity sector. Then, the total product now becomes 2,200 or a
rise of 10 percent. Such a shift, of course, is most likely to require an
additional provision of capital, for the high-productivity sector is in all
likelihood more capital-intensive.

Now it can be shown statistically that the history of the Japanese
economic development in the postwar era was that of a striking
transformation of the industrial structure. A summary picture is given in
Table 3.11 to show the changing composition of the gainfully employed

Table 3.11. *The changing composition of the gainfully employed labor force 1947–1974*

	Primary industries		Secondary industries		Tertiary industries	
Year	Labor Force (1,000)	Per-centage	Labor Force (1,000)	Per-centage	Labor Force (1,000)	Per-centage
1947	17,810	53.4	7,430	22.3	8,019	24.3
1955	15,360	37.6	11,900	29.1	13,640	33.4
1960	13,400	30.2	14,810	33.4	16,150	36.4
1965	11,130	23.5	18,010	38.1	18,150	38.4
1970	8,860	17.4	21,440	42.1	20,560	40.4
1974	6,730	12.9	22,510	43.3	24,290	46.7

Source: Prime Minister's Office, Bureau of Statistics.

labor force in terms of three major divisions of the country's economy. This changing composition, where the relative decline of primary industries is especially noteworthy, may be perused in the light of relative earning powers of each unit of labor in three sectors, which were 0.41 for the primary industries, 1.20 for the secondary and 1.23 for the tertiary, the economy-wide average being the unity. Furthermore, within the manufacturing sector itself, the relative weight of heavy and chemical industries, which tend to have higher value-added than light industries, increased markedly in the course of rapid economic development during the two decades under discussion. Expressed as a ratio between the production in heavy and chemical industries *and* the industrial production as a whole, such relative weight rose steadily from 51 percent in 1955 to 64 percent in 1965 and to 75 percent by 1975, probably the highest among advanced industrial countries at the time. Corroborating this trend are the statistics which show how the appearance of new products had the effect of expanding industrial production after 1950, as tabulated in Table 3.12. It can be seen from this table that whereas industrial production expanded 18 times between 1950 and 1969 the proportion occupied by the goods in existence before 1951 shrank to approximately 60 percent of the total and the share of new products, notably electronic and petrochemical products, registered a steady, substantial rise. Such a transformation in the industrial structure naturally had the effect of raising the average productivity of the economy as a whole even without any change in specific productivities of individual industries. We may say that here is given another aspect of Japan's so-called "miracle" of rapid growth.

Table 3.12. *The relative contribution of new products in expanding industrial production in the postwar Japan*

(Volume of industrial production in 1950 = 1.00)
(Figures in brackets are percentages of the total for each year.)

Year	Commodities in existence before 1951[a]	Commodities appearing for the first time during 1951–54[b]	Commodities appearing for the first time during 1955–59[c]	Commodities appearing for the first time during 1960–64[d]	Total
1950	1.00 (100.0)				1.00
1955	2.05 (92.8)	0.15 (6.8)	0.01 (0.5)		2.21
1960	4.14 (81.2)	0.65 (12.7)	0.28 (5.5)	0.03 (0.6)	5.10
1965	6.65 (72.7)	1.19 (13.0)	0.93 (10.2)	0.38 (4.2)	9.15
1969	11.19 (61.9)	2.43 (13.4)	2.56 (14.2)	1.90 (10.5)	18.08

Notes:
[a] Includes, among others, iron and steel products, nonferrous metals, machine tools, steel vessels, sulphuric acid, ammonium sulphate, cotton textiles, cement, sheet glass, etc.
[b] Includes, among others, cash registers, electric refrigerators, fluorescent lamps, television sets (monocolor), caprolactam, jet plane fuels, synthetic fibers and textiles, etc.
[c] Includes, among others, tractors, recopying machinery, air-conditioners, vacuum cleaners, transistors, electronic computers, ethylene oxide, acrylonitrile telephthalic acid, polystyrene, synthetic rubber, etc.
[d] Includes, among others, aluminium sash, electronic calculators, adding machines, color television sets, ethylene dioxides, urethane foam, polypropylene, etc.
Source: Compiled from *White Paper on Japanese Economy*, 1970 (Japanese edition).

4 The role of the government in the high-growth period

Fore-glimpse was given in the last chapter on the role played by the government in the expansionary process of the economy. This chapter focuses on this aspect of the rejuvenation of Japanese capitalism since the war. In the earlier postwar period the social climate reflecting the dire condition of the economy was such that the overall planning by the government was thought to be called for; and serious attempts were made repeatedly to draft such plans up until about 1957. The first part of this chapter gives a brief historical review of these plans to show that they evolved step by step in the direction of relying on "the basic framework of free enterprise and a free market" – an antithesis, in fact, of the philosophy of overall planning. Tons of documents compiled in the process turned out to be a Babel's Tower.

Of all the devices practiced by Japanese government in the aid of industries, it is commonly agreed by foreign observers also, that "administrative guidance" has been a most effective, unique feature. Therefore, this topic is highlighted below; but there are other no less important measures of paternalistic support which, though often passed over lightly in discussion, did contribute substantially toward strengthening the competitive power of Japanese capitalism in the world scene. The remainder of this chapter is devoted to the concrete discussion of these items.

1. Overall planning by the government

"State monopoly capitalism" is the term used by left-wing social scientists to characterize the politico-economic system of prewar Japan, where the state and the monopoly structure of the economy were inextricably wedded with an inherent tendency toward militaristic expansion. It was admittedly an apt term for Japan's prewar political economy. But the defeat in the war also meant bankruptcy of this system; and the early Occupation policies attempted to put in its place a genuinely democratic socio-politico-economic system through eradicating the two major components of Japan's prewar "state monopoly capitalism," i.e. the *zaibatsu* monopolies and the war potential of every kind. The Occupation also took steps to "defeudalize" the erstwhile civil service which used to be the loyal and indispensable servants of the militaristic state. Thus it appeared in the early postwar years that a reborn Japan might find a way to develop into a society radically different from the nation-state that had pursued the imperialistic ambition of "Asian Co-prosperity Sphere." As briefly touched upon in Chapter 1, the Foreign-Office-sponsored "Special Survey Committee," composed of progressive intellectuals, produced a report in which a number of radical reforms were proposed, including the point that the planning principle should be introduced in the important sectors of the economy. And the general election of April 1947 resulted in the plurality victory of the Socialist Party, followed by the formation of a coalition cabinet headed by Tetsu Katayama, a socialist. This cabinet promptly set up the Secretariat for Long-Range Planning in July 1947, which initiated the planning-oriented program of economic rehabilitation of Japan, successively revised but kept in spirit for almost ten years. The fall of the Katayama cabinet and the "reverse course" taken by the Occupation in 1948 changed the political scene within Japan; and under the conservative Yoshida cabinet, in particular, the very idea of overall planning by the government came to be cast aside. It was only natural that this was the case as confidence was regained by the capitalist class in the course of the reversing trend along with the resurrection of *zaibatsu*-type groups. Still, it would be instructive to review the brief history of the painstaking labor of the "Planning School" men associated with the government during the decade of 1947 to 1957.

A series of "overall planning" drafted and cast aside

The fact that the agency charged with the task of drafting government plans for economic rehabilitation produced no less than ten reports, revised successively in the fashion of Penelope's web, over the ten years between 1948 and 1957 bespeaks of the nature of those plans as more of *paper plans for expediency* than bases for serious implementation. The only exception, it may be said, was the first of the exercises called the "Draft Plan for Economic Rehabilitation" which was completed in May 1948. This draft plan set a target of regaining the 1930–34 standard of living by 1952, by which time, it was proposed, Japan's external accounts would roughly balance and the number of unemployed would be reduced to a manageable proportion of about two million. It was suggested that in the process of attaining this target the industrial structure should become slanted more and more toward heavy and chemical industries and that outside aid to the tune of some $1.5 billion would be needed during the period 1948–51. The main body of the draft plan itself was a detailed spelling out, year by year, of practically all aspects of the economy from the projection of population and labor-force changes, supply tables for all the major intermediate products and final consumption goods, productivity changes, foreign-trade prospects, and public finance, to social economic accounting. The plan did indicate, in broad strokes, a few practical matters of implementation, such as: (1) that a strong measure of government control was still needed inasmuch as in the disrupted condition of postwar markets the high profit rate did not necessarily coincide with high social desirability; (2) that government control should choose a limited area in which it could be concentrated in order that such control could be really effective; (3) that a few economic activities, such as new development of hydroelectric power and of coal mines, might be undertaken directly by the government itself, and so on. It appears that the authors of the plan were under no illusions as to the incompleteness of their plan especially as regards the practical steps for implementation; but still, they seemed to be satisfied to have shown as realistically as possible the conditions and requirements for rehabilitation, with a given speed, in terms of both macroeconomic relations and detailed materials requirements. As such the draft plan had its positive historic significance.

The second attempt at overall planning was by the Ashida cabinet which followed Katayama in March 1948. Against a background of the still inflation-plagued uncertainties of the economy at the time, the new cabinet, though much less "planning conscious" than its predecessor, apparently felt the urgent need for planned rehabilitation efforts and set up in May 1948 an extensive organization, the Planning Commission for Economic Rehabilitation, headed by the Prime Minister himself. The earlier draft plan constituted a legacy on which the new Commission was to build its own work. Naturally a greater degree of realism was gained through further experience; and it was realized at the outset that implementation of any plan would have to wrestle with the immediate problem of inflation. Thus the planning period of 1949 to 1953 was divided into two subperiods: the first part, 1949–50, to achieve economic stability, and the second part, 1951–53, to attain economic viability, that is, the ability to carry on a full-employment level of economic activity without continuing foreign economic assistance. However, external factors moved rapidly to discompose the Commission. The Commission as a whole was inclined toward the idea of combating inflation through redoubled efforts in increasing the supply of bottleneck commodities. But the Occupation authorities apparently thought otherwise. It was at around this time, as has been discussed in

Chapter 2, that the US government decided to send the Young Mission to Japan in order to draw up a coordinated policy of anti-inflation, followed by the issuing of the "Nine Point Program" and subsequently by the visit of Joseph Dodge for the strong-armed guidance in arresting the inflation and setting up a single exchange rate. Dodge's philosophy could not easily be harmonized with the basic tenets of planning that had dominated the thinking of the Planning Commission for Economic Rehabilitation. Ruffled though many members were by the development of a new Occupation policy, the Commission went on with its work, somehow adjusting itself to the Dodge program and completed its voluminous report, the "Economic Rehabilitation Plan," toward the end of May 1949. It was history's accident that Dodge's arrival in Japan coincided with the formation of the Yoshida cabinet, the most conservative yet since surrender. Prime Minister Yoshida was highly critical of the plan and suggested "recasting the whole thing with more international awareness." What he meant by "international awareness" was never made clear; but the Commission, slightly reorganized, spent the next few months in the work of dress-up revision. However, the spirit was no longer there and the salvaging operation was a failure. Finally in September 1949 it was decided to bury the plan, and Yoshida explained the reason in the Diet in October, saying that "long-range planning is meaningless."

Nevertheless, the "Economic Rehabilitation Plan" was, in a sense, a monument – a monument built on all the earlier plans and projections, initiating a countless number of new statistical studies and issuing 519 documents in the short span of a single year. Within the framework set by the desiderata of the plan, it was an eminently inductive study, pursuing to the minutest detail almost any matter capable of a quantitative estimate. With keen awareness of the limitations of the Japanese politico-economic structure at the time, the plan proposed to limit the areas of leverage for planning to the following four: (1) maximum effort to expand exports; (2) emphasis on capital accumulation and the rational channeling of investment funds; (3) strong measures to limit population growth; and (4) the retention, after streamlining, of effective governmental control.

Yoshida continued in office until December 1954, when his cabinet was dislodged by a vote of nonconfidence in the Diet. So long as he was at the helm it was not possible to draw up an overall plan or projection of the type which he himself buried in 1949. However, before Japan regained her independence in April 1952, through the coming into effect of the Peace Treaty, there appeared a number of governmental studies which could be classified under the broad category of planning and projection. These studies both reflected the needs of the time and constituted a way of asserting, on the part of planning-oriented officials in the government, the *raison d'être* of their own office. Five of them may be mentioned here:

1 "Conditions for Achieving Economic Self-Support," or "Eos Study" – made public in June 1950.
2 "Economic Self-Support Plan" – made public in January 1951.
3 "Document B" – submitted by the Japanese delegation at the San Francisco conference for the Peace Treaty in September 1951.
4 "Economic Table for 1957" – made public in February 1953.
5 "The Okano Scheme" – prepared especially to impress upon visiting experts from the World Bank in November 1953 Japan's pressing need for external loans to attain economic viability.

It is interesting to note how one of the World Bank experts, Robert Garner, reacted to this "Okano Scheme." Upon his return to the United States, Garner made a critical comment at a meeting of the Foreign Policy Association in New York, saying that:

So far as I can see, the Japanese government appears to have neither an overall plan of any sort nor a specific plan of channeling private capital into the most important sectors of the economy. I suggested, therefore, that inasmuch as there was a danger of funds flowing into unimportant sectors the Japanese government might set up an agency which would decide on the priority of investment needs. They objected to this by saying that they always preferred a "free enterprise economy" to a "planned economy." I, for one, however, do not see why the government's determination to have private funds flow into the most important channels should conflict with the requirements of a "free enterprise economy."[1]

The last of the plans and projections attempted by the Yoshida cabinet was the "Scheme for Overall Development," which was completed in September 1954 and which laid special emphasis on the urgent need for regional development programs which would create new employment opportunities by opening up domestic resources within Japan.

With the departure of Yoshida, for whom the word "planning" was anathema, the mood among official circles changed markedly. Under the new Hatoyama cabinet the Economic Counsel Board was renamed the Economic Planning Agency, and preparation for a study of long-range planning for the Japanese economy was ordered by the Prime Minister. Again the enthusiasm of planning officials, long subdued under the reign of Yoshida, was fired; an extensive, multifaceted study was launched, resulting in the publication in January 1956 of the "Five-Year Plan for Economic Self-Support," encompassing five years from the fiscal 1956 to the fiscal 1960 (April 1, 1956 to March 31, 1961). This plan did not stop at simply giving projected framework figures for the target year. It spelled out needed measures to implement the plan both in terms of basic policies and with reference to specific administrative branches of the government. In fact, most of the proposed measures were in the nature of wholesale endorsement of the pet ideas of several ministries and probably were utilized by the latter as excuses for demanding increased appropriations in the budget. This was unavoidable inasmuch as the government which drafted the Plan took pains to make clear that its basic position was the maximum respect for private initiative and the minimum resort to any kind of centralized planning, and further because the office of the Economic Planning Agency was the weakest link in the power configuration of the Japanese bureaucracy. As a result, not much came out of the Plan in terms of specific measures uniquely associated with its objectives and implications. The need for them was felt less and less as time went on, in any case, since the Japanese economy, apparently on its own steam, manifested a growth capacity far beyond the expectation of the most sanguine optimists. It may be remembered that the first decade of the "miracle" of high growth in Japan happened to coincide with the period which was in the purview of the Plan.

Seeing this Plan of 1956 becoming rapidly obsolete, the government was obliged to set its sights anew; and the birth of the Kishi cabinet in 1957 provided a convenient occasion for such a reappraisal. In accordance with a new instruction issued in early August of that year by the Prime Minister, again the machinery of paper-work planners started to function, and it produced expeditiously the "New Long-Range Economic Plan," which was approved by the cabinet in December 1957. This plan covered the five-year period of fiscal 1958 to fiscal 1962. The basic question which it tried to answer was: what is the optimal rate of growth consistent with the constraints of reasonably full employment and of equilibrium in the international balance of payments? The answer given for the optimal rate was 6.5 percent per annum for real GNP – an ambitious enough figure. Still, consistency of the plan as a painted picture and its realistic character as a projection may be said to have shown improvement over the earlier plans. But as regards implementation of the plan, that peculiar lack of practical realism which characterized all the earlier plans persisted. The official document states in the opening sentence that: "The plan is to serve as guideposts for economic operation within the basic institutional framework of free enterprise and a free market." And it goes on to specify as "instruments for implementing the plan" "such indirect methods as fiscal, monetary, and trade-and-exchange policies," stating clearly that "the government shall refrain, to the utmost, from resorting to direct control measures."

In other words, the basic idea of overall planning by the government was finally discarded and, instead, the idea that the plan was "to serve as *guideposts* for economic operation" within "the basic framework of free enterprise and a free market" was enunciated in unmistakable terms. What was to be the role of the "guideposts" indicated by the government? In practical terms this meant that the government was prepared, though did not promise, to do something when marked deviations from the "guideposts" occurred in the conduct of private business and, in this sense, it may be said that a kind of "indicative planning" was contemplated. An effective tool used by the government for this purpose was "administrative guidance," to which topic we shall return in the next section, where we will also discuss other devices which the Japanese government employed in the expansionary process of the economy.

It may be added in passing that at any rate the New Long-Range Economic Plan of 1957 went the way of most earlier plans and was cast aside as out-of-date within a mere two years in the face of a most remarkable growth performance in 1959 and 1960 – the so-called "Iwato Boom" period.[2] Thus the stage was set, at least psychologically, for yet another plan of greater optimism to emerge and the famed "Plan for Doubling National Income" was brought forth in 1960, calling for an average annual growth rate in real GNP of 7.2 percent. This was more of a political slogan and it was clear that the days of any dependence on overall planning were gone.

2. Administrative guidance

The nature of administrative guidance

In an earlier chapter we gave a detailed account of the success story of the sewing-machine industry to show "how the paternalistic administrative guidance enabled it to strike a happy balance between competition at home and government support for sales abroad raising its productivity markedly in the course of events through innovations and the scale economy while improving the quality as well." Such practice of government offices is known as "administrative guidance," and has often been singled out by foreign observers as a peculiar feature of "Japan, Incorporated." A recent American publication[3] defines it as follows:

The term "administrative guidance" refers to a method, not a policy. It is a method widely used by the Japanese government to support or reinforce many sorts of policies, both microeconomic and macroeconomic.

Essentially, administrative guidance involves the use of influence, advice, and persuasion to cause firms or individuals to behave in particular ways that the government believes are desirable. The persuasion of course is exerted and the advice given by public officials who may have the power to provide – or withhold – loans, grants, subsidies, licenses, tax concessions, government contracts, permission to import, foreign exchange, approval of cartel arrangements, and other desirable (or undesirable) outcomes, both now and over the indefinite future. But it is inaccurate to think of administrative guidance exclusively in terms of manipulation of carrot and stick. Rather, the Japanese tradition of private acceptance of government leadership and the wide-spread recognition that government officials have knowledge, experience, and information superior to that available to the ordinary firm, as well as the sharing of values, beliefs, and political preferences by government officials and business leaders, all contribute to the success of the method.

That a responsible government agency or an official can and does, without having explicit legal authority, direct or induce private firms or persons to take or refrain from taking certain actions is the essence of the practice of administrative guidance in Japan. To some degree, other capitalist countries may also share in this type of practice. But it cannot be doubted that in Japan it has been a more widely accepted and solidly established feature of government administration than in other countries, reinforced all the more by the prevalent bureaucracy–industry link through which retiring officials move to high positions in business, usually to companies with which they have had working relations. "This mobility from government to industry . . . nourishes, of course, the supposition that working bureaucrats normally will so conduct themselves as to enhance their prospects for remunerative private employment, and that once retired to industry they will maintain and reinforce the connections between business and government."⁴

The most important of the areas in which administrative guidance has been effective in postwar Japan is its coordinating role in investment programs of major industries. As was explained earlier in connection with the "one-set" principle of *zaibatsu*-type groups, there was a tendency among several of the industries to overshoot the mark in expanding capacities. Unless there was some restraining in advance of actual construction of new plants, it was most likely that the market force itself had to play the role of rudely disappointing investing firms. Here, administrative guidance intervened in two stages, both of which have been aptly referred to in the descriptive simile. The first stage is likened to "treading on wheat nurseries" (mugi-fumi) which is the practice in the wheat field in Japan of strengthening young wheat plants by treading upon overgrown roots. The second stage is likened to the providing of "mountain shelters" (yamagoya) which, if known in advance that they exist, are likely to have the effect of inducing mountain-climbers to become more adventurous than otherwise.

The "mugi-fumi" stage of investment coordination has taken different forms, such as:

1 *direct* administrative guidance by the Ministry of International Trade

and Industry (MITI) as in the cases of the cement industry and the
ammonium industry;

2 setting up a special subcommittee in the Committee on Industrial Funds
of the MITI Council on Industrial Structure as in the case of the steel
industry;

3 coordination through discussion in *ad hoc* bilateral meetings of
government officials and business leaders as in the cases of the
petrochemical, the paper and pulp and the synthetic fiber industries; and

4 licensing of capacity expansion on the basis of specific laws as in the cases
of electricity generation and oil refining.

All these forms of investment coordination, the first three of which partake
of the nature of administrative guidance, are undeniably restrictive of
competition and have the effect of placing a part of the responsibility on the
government for any excesses or shortfalls that may ensue. Such a
circumstance would naturally lead to the second ("yamagoya") stage of
administrative guidance as regards investment coordination. When actual
expansion of capacities turned out to be excessive, MITI would resort to the
method of advising coordinated cutbacks in the operation throughout the
industry concerned. In more recent years this practice has been supplemented by the legal procedure of invoking "anti-depression cartel" by the
Fair Trade Commission, enabling the firms concerned to agree on the
restriction of competitive practices as regards the quantities produced and/
or to be sold, the prices to be charged, and the rate of operation of plants. In
either case, individual firms could plan what otherwise may appear to be
over-ambitious investment programs with a feeling of security of the
mountain climber who knows that emergency shelters are always there to
protect him if the weather suddenly turns out to be adverse.

The steel industry as an example

No doubt, these paternalistic arrangements tended to encourage a high rate
of investment across the board in the manufacturing sector as a whole; and,
not surprisingly, investment breeds investment, and even an over-
ambitious investment plan often turned out to be retrospectively warranted. The case of the Japanese steel industry is especially instructive in
this connection.

In 1955 – that is approximately the year when Japan's per capita income
is said to have recovered to the prewar (1934–36) level – production of crude
steel in Japan was 9,410,000 tons, compared to 106,170,000 tons in the USA
and 45,270,000 tons in the Soviet Union. But, by 1974, Japan's production
rose 12.34 times to 117,130,000 tons, compared to three-fold rise to
136,000,000 tons in the Soviet Union and 1.25 fold rise to 132,200,000 tons

in the USA. The process through which this remarkable expansion took place in the Japanese steel industry was quite orderly under the MITI administrative guidance, exercised through the Steel Subcommittee of the Committee on Industrial Funds. For each quinquennial period the so-called "Rationalization Investment Plan" was set up and the aggregate target sum for capacity-expanding investment was distributed more or less amicably among competing firms through coordinated discussion among bureaucrats and industry representatives. Such quinquennial target investment sums took the following course of fabulous expansion:

1951–55	128.2	billion yen
1956–60	622.7	"
1961–65	1,146.0	"
1966–70	2,242.8	"

Especially in the decade of 1960s and subsequently, the introduction of innovations in the industry was extremely energetic, prominently by way of enlarging the unit-scale of various basic installations such as blast furnaces and rolling machines. It may be a revelation to many to know that of the twenty biggest blast furnaces in operation in the world as of October 1975, headed by the Krivoy Rog Furnace in the Soviet Union with the net furnace capacity of 5,026 m^3, 13 of them were in Japan.[5] In the use of continuous casting method also the Japanese steel industry topped the world then.

As the unit-scale of basic installations became bigger and bigger with six giant steel companies (Yawata, Fuji, Kawasaki, Kobe, Sumitomo and Nihon Kōkan)[6] more or less competing with each other, anxiety arose among MITI officials and the major financing banks as to the possible danger of competition becoming excessive in view of the extraordinary lumpiness of incremental investments involved. Faced with this situation, administrative guidance now came into play in an unabashed fashion to propose the merger of the two biggest firms, Yawata and Fuji. Clandestine moves for this were afoot as early as the middle of 1966 according to Sohei Nakayama,[7] the then President of the Industrial Bank of Japan which has long been the major financing bank for the leading steel companies. According to Nakayama, who became a driving force for the merger, the recession of 1965 was the igniting occasion for his idea, which became increasingly stronger as time went on, that further competitive installations of giant blast furnaces would inevitably involve national economic waste and that the innovations then on the horizon would be more rationally incorporated into the industry if the number of competing firms was reduced. The MITI officials apparently agreed with this judgment and the biggest merger scheme in postwar Japan was quietly being pushed forward. The news of such a move leaked to a newspaper in April 1968, and a tremendous controversy ensued in public, with most of the economists opposing the idea outright. Patient and clever maneuvering, however, by Sohei Nakayama combined with the forceful administrative guidance by the MITI officials finally brought the merger of Yawata and Fuji into realization in March 1970 and thus was born the biggest steel company in the world, Shin Nihon Seitetsu. This company led the world in 1975 by producing 32,520,000 tons of crude steel, followed by US Steel which lagged far behind with the production of 23,950,000 tons.

Other types of administrative guidance

Administrative guidance, of course, is not confined to investment coordination alone. On the matter of price control, for example, even though a specific legislation (the Emergency Measure Law on Stabilizing People's Living) was drawn up and approved by the Diet in December 1973 for the purpose of providing explicit legal authority for price controls, this law was likened to an "undrawn sword" which, being known that it cut well, would, by its mere existence, make the government's administrative guidance "cut better." In fact, the price freeze that followed, covering prices of petroleum products and those of some 50 to 60 other basic commodities at wholesale and 148 at retail, made use of the specific legislative authority only for the price controls on propane, kerosene and toilet paper. All other prices were controlled simply through administrative guidance.

It may be said that the Bank of Japan's window guidance, in dealing out central bank credit, is also an aspect of the prevalent practice in Japan of administrative guidance.

Actually, episodes abound in the postwar history of Japan's industrial policy where clever use of administrative powers enabled specific industries to tide over difficult conjuncture of events. One such example is a measure of hidden subsidy to the shipbuilding industry in the period subsequent to the recession of 1953–54. The export market was then thought to be the only channel of rescue, but the price-cost situation was not exactly favorable while outright subsidy would have been too blatant. Thus recourse was made to an administrative measure of allocating import permits of sugar to exporting shipbuilders. Since available foreign exchange was scarce at the time, importation of sugar had to be severely restricted, causing unusually high prices of sugar in the domestic market. Variables involved in the equation in the minds of MITI officials at that time were: (a) the needed margin of subsidy for making Japanese ships competitive abroad; (b) the retail price of sugar which its domestic market could bear; and thus (c) the premium which its importers could earn. What was done then was to estimate the aggregate amount of (a) and divide it by

(c) to reach at the figure of "needed" imports of sugar, and to allocate import permits to that amount to exporters of ships. Export price of ships could thus be lowered by 20 to 30 percent; and the "hidden" subsidy by this measure is said to have amounted to 10 billion yen in a little over one year from 1954–55. This sum should be contrasted with the annual budget of 500 million yen of the Japan External Trade Organization at around that time.[8] Although there has been increasing criticism, both at home and abroad, against the extensive use of administrative guidance in Japan for a wide variety of purposes, MITI, at least, has "continued to defend the method as one which avoids red tape, complex legal procedures, and an atmosphere of confrontation between business and government."[9] It may well be that the traditional dislike of open legal procedures in the social climate of Japan has nurtured the practice of resolving an issue through informal, quasi-voluntary jawboning and finger-pointing of the type peculiar to Japan.

3. Reclamation for factory sites

Rationale for reclamation

Compared with the availability of capital and labor, that of land for factory sites is often taken for granted. It is quite true that what might be called "land productivity" in the manufacturing industry is incomparably greater than in agriculture. For example, in 1970, some 5,740,000 hectares of agricultural land produced 4,579 billion yen worth of gross products (about 800,000 yen per hectare) whereas 108,566 hectares of factory-site land produced 57,815 billion yen worth of gross products (about 532 million yen per hectare), the ratio per hectare being 1 to 665. Thus it may appear that a slight transfer, of let us say 2 percent, from agricultural use to manufacturing use could immediately double the land space for factories. As a matter of fact, when the Ministry of Agriculture was confronted with what appeared to be a chronic oversupply of domestic rice production in 1970, it was proposed to lay 337,000 hectares of rice land fallow with suitable compensations to the cultivators concerned. And on that occasion, Mr Kuraishi, Minister of Agriculture, revealed that a long-range plan study convinced him that in future 200,000 hectares of rice land could be permanently transferred to other uses. Arithmetically, this would mean a possibility of tripling the factory-site land without much difficulty.

But the problem is not as simple as this. Factory-site land has to meet a number of requirements if it is to satisfy the efficiency condition, such as availability of adequate industrial water, convenience from the standpoint of transportation, proximity to the source of labor supply, etc. Even if by happy coincidence what used to be rice land, now to be fallowed or given up, satisfies these conditions, a crucial hurdle is the price of transfer which would satisfy both the seller and buyer. Naturally, land-owning farmers tend to demand a price which would cover not only the loss of the stream of future income from the land to him but also the cost of transfer of his profession; and it was soon found that it would be cheaper to create a piece of land by reclamation even if cost is incurred concurrently for the compensation of the loss of fishing rights. There was obviously an added advantage in the reclaimed land in that with the remarkable technological improvements in the facilities related to ocean transportation (such as automated warehouses, roll-on-roll-off facilities for transferring supplies to and from giant purpose-built vessels, etc.) the siting of plants at the seaside with adequate enough ports nearby would mean substantial cost reduction for those industries where bulky cargo is involved, such as steel industry.

In acquiring a piece of land as a factory site, it is customary and usual for private firms to be on their own, exercising their own judgment in canvassing and selecting a particular site and signing a contract to purchase a lot. But in the case of postwar Japan, given the circumstance explained in the preceding paragraph, the government took upon itself the task of making anticipatory public investment in creating factory sites by reclamation along with the providing of such infrastructures as ports and feeder roads, and thus private firms could minimize the cost of land needed as factory sites. As early as in 1953, a law was passed, called the Bay Area Infrastructure Promotion Act, to empower the Ministry of Transportation (which happened to be in charge of bay area development) to plan and issue permits for reclamation projects which in actual execution were to be the responsibility of prefectural governors. Planning itself, however, proceeded on a national scale, including the total target area to be reclaimed for the country as a whole and the allocation to specific bay areas. Reclaimed land, of course, was to be sold eventually to private firms seeking factory-site land, but the original cost of reclamation was to be financed by local governments, which could rely on the Trust Fund Bureau of the Ministry of Finance as well as on issuing bonds for the purpose.

The planning methodology for reclamation

The methodology used in the planning of nationwide reclamation is of special interest from the standpoint of economics of planning, and it may be illustrated by a concrete example of the five-year plan for 1971–75. The plan was drawn up in 1969, by which time 27,184 hectares had been reclaimed throughout the country. The steps taken to reach the final target figure for reclamation were as follows:

a The annual growth rate of real GNP during 1969–75 was estimated at 10.6 percent, reaching 95,860 billion yen by 1975 (1965 prices).

b From past experience one could infer a certain regularity in the quantitative relation between GNP and gross production in manufacturing, and thus one could estimate the latter to be 96,000 billion yen in 1975 (1965 prices).

c Land productivity in manufacturing was 330 million yen per hectare in 1965. It was thought reasonable to expect such productivity to rise to 498 million yen by 1975 (1965 prices).

d Dividing gross manufacturing production (b) by land productivity (c) yielded 192,900 hectares.

e Subtracting the area which was already used as factory sites in 1965 (97,500 hectares) from the 192,900, the government estimated that 95,400 hectares of new factory-site land was needed for 1966–75.

f Not all the factory sites were expected to be obtained from reclaimed land. The proportion was 46.2 percent in 1963 and 45.5 percent in 1966. Thus it was assumed that of the total area needed of 95,400 hectares 45 percent (42,900 hectares) was to be provided through reclamation.

g In addition to the factory sites proper there was a need for supplementary land areas for public purposes, which would add 35 percent more to the total, thus bringing the total reclamation to 57,900 hectares.

h Of this total, 14,700 hectares were expected to be completed during 1966–70, leaving 43,200 hectares as the target figure for 1971–75. Of this, however, about 10 percent was to be done under the private auspices, which meant that it was to be the responsibility of the bay area authorities to carry out the reclamation of approximately 40,000 hectares in five years.

At the time this plan was worked out it was estimated that the cost of reclaiming would be on average 45 million yen per hectare – the sum which was in most places less than one-half the price of farm land in the vicinity.

Anticipatory public investment in creating factory sites by reclamation has proceeded in this fashion since 1954 and has facilitated greatly the problem of siting of plants in the period of rapid expansion after 1955. Quinquennial figures of reclamation completed for industrial purpose were:

1956–60	2,321	hectares
1961–65	11,670	"
1966–70	13,287	"

This was to be stepped up, as mentioned above, to the heightened level of 40,000 hectares for 1971–75. However, environmental concern which became notably acute around 1970 put a brake on the transformation of scenic beaches into factory sites; and the actual reclamation completed during 1971–75 turned out to be 12,512 hectares. In fact, in the decade of the 1970s drastic revision appeared to be called for in the thinking both of government and industry as regards availability of convenient factory sites for further expansion. Rethinking was forced anyway by the fact that the actual growth rate (of real GNP) for the five years of 1971 to 1975 turned out to be 4.4 percent on average, compared with the 10.6 percent rate that had been assumed in the prospective reclamation plan of 1969.

4. Special tax-relief measures for industries

Lighter tax burdens in Japan

It is generally agreed that tax burdens on industrial corporations in Japan have been lighter than in other advanced industrialized countries. In the background for this favorable condition are two features of the Japanese economy which are somewhat distinctive. One is the fact that the Japanese tax system imposes, on the whole, a relatively light load on the tax payer. In terms of percentages to gross national product, tax revenues in Japan, including both national and local taxes, comprised 21.1 percent in 1972, compared with 45.7 percent for Norway, 36.0 percent for West Germany, 35.8 percent for France, 34.7 percent for the United Kingdom and 28.1 percent for the United States.[10] This relatively low figure has been typical in postwar Japan, though having shown a slightly rising trend between 1955 and 1974. Contributory factors for this characteristic feature have been, first, the minimum defense program under the constraint of Article IX of the Constitution and, second, the reluctance on the part of the Japanese government, at least up till then, to permit the social security program to expand to a level comparable to other advanced countries.

The second feature in the background of the relatively light tax burdens borne by industrial corporations in Japan is a heavy reliance on external debt in the capital structure of Japanese corporations. Some information was already given on this matter earlier; and what is important here is the point that interest payments on borrowed capital are treated as expenses to be deducted before arriving at the figure of profits which are the object of corporate taxation. The aggregate figures shown in Table 4.1 for relatively large manufacturing firms, relating to 1974 but more or less typical for Japan, are quite revealing in this respect. It can be seen that to the extent that Japanese firms depend heavily on external sources for finance, direct corporate taxes tend to occupy a smaller percentage of the earnings attributable to the use of capital from the macroeconomic point of view.

Table 4.1. *The impact of corporate taxes in manufacturing firms*

(A) Depreciation	1,770 billion yen
(B) Interest payments	2,310 " "
(C) Before-tax profits	1,693 " "
(D) Corporate taxes	755 " "
(E) After-tax profits	939 " "
(F) Dividends distributed	406 " "
(D) ÷ (C) 44.6%	
(D) ÷ [(B) + (C)] 18.9%	

Source: The Bank of Japan, *Comparative Economic and Financial Statistics: Japan and Other Major Countries* (in Japanese), May 1976, p.113. The figures cited here are the aggregate figures for 337 major manufacturing corporations.

Tax incentive measures for corporations

In addition to these generally favorable circumstances there have been instituted, as a matter of policy, a series of tax-relief measures for private corporations. There has been wide agreement in the bureaucracy and business circles alike that the tax system should be actively used to promote economic growth. Thus, although the Shoup Tax Reform Mission of 1949 did the house-cleaning, so to speak, of sundry special provisions in the Japanese tax system and helped Japan launch a set of rationally structured tax laws in 1950, the Japanese government lost no time, especially after regaining independence in 1952, in adding one after another of Special Tax Measures Law, so-called, designed essentially to promote economic growth. These included, initially, accelerated depreciation for important industrial equipment, a special deduction for income from exports, a tax-free reserve for losses from export transactions, and reduced tax rates on interest and dividends.

During the two decades following this initial period of placing heavy reliance on tax incentive measures, proliferation of special tax measures was truly bewildering.[11] In addition to the tax-free reserve stipulations, listed in note 11, there are, of course, other tax incentive measures such as accelerated depreciation, special allowances for expenditures in prospecting for mineral deposits or overseas mineral deposits, tax deferment by succession of book value of old property, tax deferment of replacement of specific business assets, special taxation of capital gains from expropriated properties, special deductions for capital gains from land, special measures relating to the revaluation of currency in 1971, carryover or carryback of losses, special rules for accounting for certain types of income, and so on.

Some analytical problems on tax relief

From the standpoint of economic analysis there are three problems which are of special interest: namely, (1) how were the effective rates of corporate income tax reduced in fact because of these special measures; (2) what was the differential benefit, if at all, received by large corporations which undoubtedly could take better advantage of these special measures than smaller ones; and (3) what exactly was the impact of these measures on the promotion of business investment and export?

The answer to the first of the above questions we may refer to a study[12] comparing Japan with the United States as regards the extent of reduction of corporate income tax rates from the nominal to the effective. The study made such a comparison for the years from 1965 to 1972 and produced the following figures, for example, for 1972:

	Top nominal rate	Effective rate
Japan	48%	20.1%
US	51%	27.2%

The extent of the reduction shown here was quite stable during the eight years for which the comparison was made, and the authors commented that "Japan actually may have gone much farther in this direction [i.e., the direction of making use of tax-incentives for the purpose of encouraging private investment, etc.] than most other countries."

This study, however, suffers from an avoidable simplification in that the lowering of "the effective rate" compared with "the top nominal rate" is made to arise mainly through the use of "profits before the deduction of depreciation allowances" as the corporate tax base for "the effective rate." A far more detailed study on the extent of tax relief through the special measures was carried out by a special committee of experts for the Tokyo Metropolitan Government in 1974 and estimated the extent of relief, both percentage wise (using the same tax base for "the nominal rate" as well as for "the effective rate") and absolutely.[13] The absolute amount of corporate tax relief for 1974 was estimated at 1,790 billion yen as regards corporate income tax and 793 billion yen as regards corporate taxes to be paid to local governments. The former figure should be compared to the actual corporate income tax paid in 1974 of 5,816 billion yen, constituting an overall relief of 23.6 percent.

The study cited here actually gives an item-by-item estimate of tax relief on account of each special measure and in addition works out a table showing differing degrees of relief by size of corporations, thus throwing light on the second of the three questions raised above. Confining itself to the information given in official publications of the Ministry of Finance[14] only, the study estimates degrees of tax relief (for 1974) to have been only 4.5 percent for the smallest corporations (with capitalization of less than one million yen), but generally rising to 42.1 percent for the biggest corporations (with capitalization of ten billion yen or more).

There is an element of progressivity in the Japanese corporate tax system and one would expect bigger corporations to pay a higher percentage of their net income. But, in fact, the reverse is true, as can be surmised from the differential degrees of tax relief mentioned above. There is a study more directly focused upon this problem. According to Masu Uekusa,[15] who made a detailed analysis of actual tax burdens by size of corporations mainly on the basis of official statistics, the *actual* burden of corporate income tax for 1971 turned out to be highest (30.7 percent) for the middle-sized firms of 10 to 50 million yen capitalization, declining smoothly as the size becomes larger, finally to the rate of 21.8 percent for the biggest firms of ten billion yen capitalization or higher.

The third of the questions raised above, namely, what exactly was the impact of the special tax measures on the promotion of business investment and export, is more difficult to answer. The very fact that these special measures were pressed hard through the Diet usually with strong support from business circles and often against the reasoned opposition of academic economists may be said to be an objective proof that they were considered by the business groups concerned at least to be of some assistance. Moreover, the tax relief to the extent of about one-fourth in the payment of corporate income tax is *ipso facto* a highly promotional measure. There are available also the statistics of specific tax-relief figures classified by the objectives aimed at, such as "promotion of exports," "modernization of equipment," "strengthening of corporate bodies through augmentation of retained earnings," etc.[16] But it is difficult to form qualitative judgments from these figures as to the impact of certain special tax measures upon a particular industry inasmuch as such impact could be crucially important at an appropriate point of time even if the size involved might be small.

Of course, a case study could be made, for example, on the effect of the provision which permitted producers of exported goods to deduct 3 percent of their gross sales abroad, up to 80 percent of their net operating income from exports. This provision was in force from 1953 to 1965 and was eliminated in the latter year because it was in direct violation of the rules of GATT which prohibit export subsidies. Such abrupt elimination of a tax-relief measure could cause temporary hardship to those firms which had been made viable thanks to the relief measure. The problem here is somewhat similar to that of studying the impact of an upward exchange revaluation upon export industries. But here again, we cannot but observe that by 1965 Japan's export industries had been sufficiently strengthened to be able to cast off special scaffoldings of the type mentioned, which by then had fulfilled their task.

Although the Brookings' study, mentioned earlier, concludes that "studies of the impact of the special tax measures on Japanese economic growth are, for most part, inconclusive,"[17] the reasons there cited concern more such matters as the relation between the special tax measures to promote household saving and the rate of private saving, which definitely is inconclusive. So far as the impact on business investment (in certain sectors such as steel and machinery) and export (in the certain period such as late 1950s and early 1960s) is concerned, it can hardly be doubted that the special tax measures have played a very significant role.

5. The low-interest-rate policy

Credit rationing with low interest rate

From the fact, mentioned repeatedly in earlier sections, that Japanese firms depend heavily on external funds for financing of their investments, one can readily understand that the level of interest rate as of particular importance. Here is a situation where the proverbial function of the interest rate as a crucial market variable in automatically rationing investible funds could come into play, rising to discourage excessive investment demand and falling to invite new investment through impersonal interaction of supply and demand.

However, what has transpired in postwar Japan has essentially been not the balancing of supply and demand through the free play of market rate of interest, but the rationing of funds at the discretion of (1) the Bank of Japan; (2) major commercial banks; (3) special banks like the Japan Development Bank, etc. and (4) the Treasury Investments and Loans Authority, while keeping the interest rate structure more or less inflexible at relatively low levels. In addition, a resort has been made systematically to subsidize specific industries to keep the interest burden low.

The major instrument of monetary policy used by the Bank of Japan has been what is known as "window guidance," an equivalent in the monetary policy field of administrative guidance referred to earlier in connection with governmental policies regarding economic matters in general. The instrument is used in imposing specific quantitative ceiling on the aggregate lending of each bank; and this is done in the form of "suggestions only" as banks come to the "discount window" of the Bank of Japan. But the guidance is invariably accepted; and in the circumstance where administrative limitation exists on the volume of loans that each bank can make, each bank, in turn, is forced to impose some form of rationing on its loan customers. The natural inclination of commercial banks, then, would be to favor, especially in times of tight money situation, borrowers with traditional ties of the *zaibatsu* type. Furthermore, not only is the aggregate amount of a bank's lending controlled by "window guidance" of the Bank of Japan, but the latter often gives informal instruction of either a positive or a negative character, as for example an instruction in 1973 which suggested that loans for "speculative purchases of commodities and land" should be discriminated against.

So far as the latter two sources of funds – special banks and the Treasury – are concerned, it is in the nature of these institutions that dispensation of funds would take the form of rationing on the basis of specific policy considerations and the rate of interest is of secondary consideration. Further, it is of particular importance to note that the volume of funds at the disposal of the Treasury Investments and Loans Authority is not at all inconsiderable. Sources of their funds consist mainly of the liabilities of the Trust Funds Bureau, of which postal savings occupy more than one half in usual years. The order of magnitude of these items can be appreciated from the following comparison with the balance of deposits of all the banks in Japan:

	1965	1975
Deposits of all banks	20,653	92,921
Liabilities of Trust Fund Bureau	4,754	40,556
Postal savings	2,573	22,958
(Year-end figures in billions of yen)		

It can be seen that postal savings, which are more in the nature of time deposits than of demand deposits, were by 1975 almost one-fourth of all the bank deposits; and they are channeled entirely into the Trust Fund Bureau of the Ministry of Finance to be utilized according to a budgetary plan of the Treasury Investments and Loans Authority. It is true that a large part of the funds thus distributed is destined to such public purposes as housing (about 20 percent), road construction (8–10 percent), transportation and communication (12–14 percent) and construction of other social infrastructure. But a significant sum is reserved for investment in basic industries (as much as 13.6 percent in 1960, but declining to about 3 percent in the decade of the 1970s) and for export promotion and economic cooperation (10 percent or less). The rate of interest charged then was 6.5 percent for the term of 25 years for the funds channeled from the Trust Fund Bureau, which of course was below the rate charged by commercial banks for loans or the fixed rate of return on debentures.

It is quite clear that what is called "the low interest-rate policy" was in actual fact more of a direct rationing policy based upon a peculiar monetary instrument called "window guidance" and the availability of sizable investable funds through governmental or semi-governmental financial institutions. Relatively low interest rates could thus be maintained more or less in an inflexible manner and have contributed to the buoyancy of investment demand in the high growth decades in Japan.

As Ackley and Ishi wrote: "Low interest rates raise the present value of the yield from real investments in plant, equipment, and inventories relative to the cost of those investments. Yet the volume of such investments is restricted (by credit rationing) from expanding to the point at which investment yields would be bid down – or costs bid up – sufficiently to reduce the profits of entrepreneurship to equal the minimum supply price of entrepreneurship. This actually may be the most fundamental reason for the buoyancy of investment demand in Japan."[18]

Supply of saving from public

Just as the level of interest rates has to be judged high or low in relation to the schedule of expected returns to capital, there is also a problem of how high it has to be in order to succeed in making a large enough amount of funds flow into financial institutions. Elasticity of supply of saving relative to the level of interest rate is reputedly small, and yet when we consider the fact that an unusually large amount of liquid funds is channeled from the household sector to the business sector through all kinds of banking institutions, one cannot but wonder how this is made possible. Table 4.2 gives, for a typical year of the mid-1960s, a comparison between Japan and the United States of the interest yield on loans and the cost-ratios for representative big banks. It can be seen that the major difference between Japan and the United States lies in the yield on deposits, explained mainly by the fact that whereas in the United States demand deposits occupy about two-thirds of total deposits in banks they constitute only 10 percent of banks' liabilities in Japan. Such a situation, of course, makes it possible for Japanese banks to hold assets of longer duration. But at the same time, the

Table 4.2. *Cost and profit of banks – Japan–US comparison*

	Japan	US
Interest yield on loans	7.00%	5.61%
Cost for carrying deposits	6.52	3.98
Yield on deposits	4.12	1.86
Operating expenses	2.40	2.12
Profit margin	0.48	1.63

Source: Research Section on the Financial System, Bureau of Banking, Ministry of Finance. These ratio figures refer to the latter half of 1966.

Table 4.3. *Relative shares of various categories of income in the national income distributed (selected years)*

	1951 (%)	1961 (%)	1974 (%)
Individual proprietors' income in agriculture, forestry & fisheries	22.7	11.3	4.9
Interest income received by individuals	1.4	4.6	7.8
Dividend income received by individuals	1.1	1.8	1.2

Source: Economic Planning Agency, *Annual Report on National Income Statistics 1976*, pp.60–65. Years refer to fiscal years, from 1 April of the year indicated to 31 March of the following year.

profit margin is squeezed, leaving only 0.48 percent against the total operating funds compared with 1.63 percent for the US banks. This, however, does not mean that Japanese banks have fared badly as business enterprises. The truth of the matter is that their scale of operation was expanding enormously in the high-growth period, in fact more, proportionately, than GNP at current prices,[19] enabling them to prosper even with the low profit margin. *Pari passu* with the relative expansion of banking institutions, the interest income accruing to individuals has come to occupy, Keynes' prediction of the euthanasia of rentiers notwithstanding, a greater and greater proportion of national income distributed. Table 4.3 presents the percentages occupied by such income in the national income distributed in comparison with some other categories. It may be noted that while proprietors' income in the primary industries was being drastically reduced in the relative weight over the period from 1951 to 1974 the interest income received by individuals showed a remarkable rise, from 1.4 percent of national income distributed in 1951 to 7.8 percent in 1974, in contrast to the approximate stability at a low level of dividend income accruing to individuals.

In sum, it should be emphasized again that the so-called "low interest-rate policy" is essentially a policy of rationing investment funds to enterprises in the institutional setting of an inflexible interest-rate structure utilizing the public's propensity to save a high proportion of income in the form of bank deposits and postal savings. In the analysis of the investment buoyancy of postwar Japan, one can hardly underestimate the important role played by financial institutions of all kinds. And in this connection, it should be pointed out that the Bank of Japan, as a central bank with authority and competence to control banking institutions, is actually much less independent of the dominant policy of the government on each occasion than, for example, the Federal Reserve Board of the United States.

6. The temporization of the trade- and capital-inflow liberalization

Trade liberalization

Japan accepted Article 11 of GATT in 1963 and Article 8 of the IMF in 1964 and further joined the OECD in April 1964. In other words, it may be said that the year 1964 marked a turning point in Japan's commercial policy as regards non-tariff restrictions such as the application of quantitative controls, either direct or through exchange licensing. But by 1964 the Japanese economy had regained its strength sufficiently to withstand competition from abroad in most lines of manufacturing activities, still enjoying a definite manufacturing advantage in the relatively inexpensive labor force while having caught up to a considerable extent with the technological frontier of other advanced countries.

In retrospect, one cannot but be impressed by the delicate timing with which the Japanese government took steps for liberalization, always mindful of "being not too soon and not too late." Actually, for example, the IMF's pressure on Japan to become an "Article 8" country was openly evident as early as in June 1961 when Mr. Friedman, executive director of the IMF, came to Tokyo for annual consultation. Japan's acceptance of Article 8, however, was postponed until three years later; and meanwhile, Japan went on carefully to choose the items to be liberalized one by one in such a way as to minimize competitive disadvantage to a particular industry. The period from 1960 to autumn 1964 is usually referred to in Japan as "the first stage of trade liberalization"; and the liberalization ratio,

Table 4.4. *Tariff rates on automotive products in percentages, 1968 to 1974*

	Tariff rates on completed cars			Tariff rates on component parts		
	Small size	Large size	Large trucks	Engines	Chassis	Bearings
1 January						
1968	40	35	27	30	30	25
1969	36	28	21.6	30	24	20
1970	34	17.5	18.9	30	21	17.5
1971	20	17.5	18.9	30	18	15
1972	10	10	10	15	15	12.5
1973	6.4	6.4	8	12	12	10
1974	6.4	6.4	8	6	6	6

Source: Compiled from *Handbook on the Automotive Industry, 1976* (in Japanese), Nissan Automobile Manufacturing Corporation, p.371.

which stood at 41 percent in April 1960, gradually but steadily rose to 93 percent by October 1964. And in October 1965 a major step was taken to liberalize the importation of completed passenger cars, though reliance was still generally placed on tariff policies in order to protect domestic producers.

With the acceptance of the international obligations under GATT and the IMF, Japan could no longer resort, in principle, to quantitative restrictions in trade and also had to abolish exchange control measures for current transactions. But a certain number of import items were allowed to be exceptions in this regard and specified as "residual items." Reduction of the number of such "residual items" was to be the second stage of liberalization for Japan; but this stage did not come until the early 1970s. Instead, the latter half of the 1960s was characterized by a general trend of gradual tariff reductions stimulated by the so-called "Kennedy Round" agreement. Japan accepted this agreement in May 1968 and afterwards proceeded to reduce tariff levels by as much as 30 percentage points within about three years. An illustration of this process may be drawn from the *ad valorem* tariff rates on automotive products, as summarized in Table 4.4. When strong pressures began to be felt from abroad on Japan to liberalize her trade, around 1961, the Japanese automotive industry was still in its early stage of development, uncertain of its own future, and appealed regularly to the Ministry of International Trade and Industry for the continuation of various kinds of protective measures.[20] But, as can be seen in Table 3.7 presented in the last chapter, the growth of the industry was truly phenomenal after 1960; and both the liberalization of 1965 and the subsequent reduction of tariff rates could easily be taken in its stride by the industry.

The latter half of the 1960s was a period for Japan when the tariff reduction and a heightened concern on the question of capital-inflow liberalization occupied the minds of the business world and the bureaucracy while the process of trade liberalization witnessed a lull. "The residual restricted items," which numbered 120 on April 1, 1966, were actually increased in the following year and recovered the 1966 level of 120 only in 1969. But since this latter date the list of "the residual items" was shortened steadily, finally to the total of 27 by March 1976. These consisted mainly of agricultural products and only of a few products in the manufacturing sector such as electronic computers and leather goods. Thus the first half of the 1970s is usually referred to as the second stage of trade liberalization.

Liberalization of capital inflow

Liberalization of capital-inflow in the form of direct investment was also timed in such a way that the damage to burgeoning domestic industries would be kept to a minimum.

The occupation of Japan lasted for about seven years during which time the dominance of America was indisputable not only as regards major policy-making but also in giving economic aid and in laying the basis for US economic infiltration. The immediate post-occupation years naturally saw the legacy of this dependence on the USA and pressures were strong to bring in American capital either for setting up a branch firm or for proposing a joint venture. An instance of the latter was related in an earlier chapter where the development of the Japanese sewing-machine industry was discussed. In those years, up until July 1963, regulations in Japan were such that firms based on foreign capital could be set up as long as they agreed not to repatriate profits anywhere outside Japan. Agreeing with such restriction, the Coca-Cola Bottling Company and IBM established their counterparts in Japan quite early in the postwar period. This restriction, however, was in conflict with Article 8 of the IMF Charter; and when Japan decided to become an "IMF Article 8 country" in 1964, she had to rescind the regulation which proscribed the repatriation of dividend payments to foreign countries. From this time on, the only way in which Japan could regulate foreign direct investment was through the screening on the basis of the Foreign Capital Control Act. In addition, as Japan joined the OECD in April 1964, she became obligated to liberalize her capital transactions as expeditiously as possible. In particular, the US government had been waiting for this opportunity to press further their continuing demand for Japan's acceptance of US direct investment in such fields as automotive and computer industries.

All this, of course, could be foreseen; and the Ministry of International Trade and Industry, with its instinctive concern for the protection of domestic firms, had sent a team of experts to Europe in the early 1960s to investigate the impact of the infiltration of American capital in various lines of industrial activities. Fruits of this investigation were written up in a memorandum called *The Infiltration of US Capital in Europe*, which, though never made public, was keenly studied by all people concerned. It may be recalled that US direct investment outstanding in Europe had recorded a remarkable expansion from 4.1 billion dollars at the end of 1957 to more than 12 billion dollars in 1964.

The strategy used by the Japanese government was, on the one hand, to encourage what was then called "industrial reorganization," a neutral-sounding phrase for mergers like that of Yawata and Fuji to become Shin Nihon Seitetsu (Steel) Corporation, and, on the other, to propose the so-called "50–50 formula" which would permit the setting up of a new firm with up to 50 percent of the capitalization subscribed by non-Japanese sources. From July 1967 onwards, the liberalization process was taken in several steps to bring one industry after another, again with faithful adherence to the principle of "being not too soon and not too late," into the category of "50-percent-liberalized" industries. This formula, however, was applicable only to the establishment of *new* firms. Participation by foreign capital in *established* firms was much more strictly controlled on the grounds that the characteristically high financial leverage, or a low ratio of corporate owners' equity to total capital, of Japanese corporations would enable foreigners to acquire the control of large existing firms with an extremely small share in the total capital used. It was only in May 1973 that Japan came to agree in principle with the OECD Convention to liberalize capital-inflow completely, leaving only a few industries in the "negative list" as exceptions. By this time, however, most of the industries, including the once-coveted automobiles and electronic computers, had gained sufficient strength with Japan's own capital to withstand almost any competition that might present itself in the form of foreign direct investment in Japan.

7. Subsidies on water and electricity

Unlike the interest cost, the use of water and electricity for industrial purposes is quite uneven among industries. For some, the cost for these items occupies a much higher percentage of the total cost than the interest charges, and the governmental policy of keeping the rates for industrial uses

Table 4.5. *Shares of water and electricity costs in manufacturing industries*

(Unit: %)

	For water	For electricity
Pig iron	0.74	0.55
Steel bars	0.66	0.62
Steel sheets	0.48	1.13
Cement	0.44	4.72
Ammonium sulphate	7.35	34.42
Urea	2.58	2.78
Viscose staple fiber	1.69	0.36
Pulp (DSP)	4.63	9.26

Source: Takeo Sato, *Economics of Water* (in Japanese), 1965, p.191.

of water and electricity as low as possible has been a non-negligible factor in the growth process of some manufacturing industries. Table 4.5 gives some statistics of the shares of cost incurred for water and electricity in the total manufacturing cost of representative industries. The figures shown in Table 4.5 are admittedly crude, being ratios in the final stage of processing. A more sophisticated estimate, by making use of the input–output table for 1961, was made to show, for example, the share of cost for electricity in the case of crude steel was as high as 18.96 percent, for cement 8.54 percent and for chemical fibers 17.95 percent.[21]

Industrial water

As for industrial water, the quantity used has been increasing more or less in parallel with the rise in the index of industrial production, from 35.9 million tons per day in 1962 to 101.5 million tons in 1972. Supply sources for this total, however, have witnessed a significant shift during these ten years, as can be seen from Table 4.6. In relative terms, the use of recycled water increased markedly while that of well water, in particular, declined. This has been the consequence of a deliberate policy by the government of trying to discourage the use of underground water in order not to worsen any further the condition of ground subsidence in the areas of industrial concentration. For this purpose, the supply price for industrial water service was determined in such a way as to keep it more or less at par with the cost of well water, involving necessarily elements of subsidy both in the stage of waterwork construction and at the point of terminal sale. The

Table 4.6. *Supply sources of industrial water 1962 and 1972*

	Cost per ton in 1962 (yen)	1962		1972	
		Quantity used (1,000 tons)	Share (%)	Quantity used (1,000 tons)	Share (%)
Total	3.34	35,931	100.0	101,457	100.0
Public waterworks					
Industrial water service	3.36	2,201	6.1	11,491	11.3
City water service	16.22	3,029	8.4	3,530	3.5
Surface water	1.58	6,237	17.4	8,257	8.1
Underground flowing water	1.93	2,583	7.2	3,163	3.1
Well water	2.83	11,046	30.7	15,243	15.0
Others	1.96	671	1.9	884	0.9
Recycled water	1.95	10,165	28.3	58,889	58.1

Sources: On Basic Direction of Policies on Underground Water, an Interim Report (in Japanese), submitted by the Subcommittee on Basic Policy concerning Industrial Water of the Council on Industrial Structure, November 1975, p.3. "Cost per ton in 1962" figures were taken from *Statistics of Industrial Water Use, 1962*, compiled by the Ministry of International Trade and Industry; and the average for total is the weighted average. Marine water is not included in this table.

extent of fiscal subsidy in the construction stage is estimated to have been approximately 20 percent of the capital cost, and the subsidy on the supply price, though declining in later years, has ranged from 17 to 7.5 percent.[22]

Electricity

Unlike the case of water, where the processing cost is distinctly different between industrial water and tap water, electricity is a homogeneous product whether it is used for industrial or for domestic purposes. Ancillary cost is no doubt cheaper for large-scale users than for individual households. But if we take a typical year of 1962, the share of household use in quantity was 18.7 percent and its share in total payments was 35.9 percent, which figures *prima facie* suggest that there must have been some degrees of cross-subsidization between the household use and the industrial use.

The cost accounting in the electricity industry is rather complex, and divergence in estimates on the extent of cross-subsidization is unavoidable. However, the estimate, which was generally accepted in the early sixties,

Table 4.7. *Rates for household use and industrial use of electricity compared – Japan and England*

	Japan (yen)	England (pence)
A. Household use	11.95	1.665
B. Industrial use	4.59	1.349
C. (B)/(A) (%)	38.4	81.0

Source: International Comparison of Public Utility Rates and Their Background (in Japanese), Tōkei Kenkyū Kai, March 1965, p.19.

stated that "the rates for household use were determined at the level 6.4 percent higher than the cost indicated and the rates for industrial use were determined at the level 4.9 percent lower than the cost called for."[23] The fact of cross-subsidization can be brought out more clearly through an international comparison. Table 4.7 gives such a comparison between Japan and England for the year 1962 in terms of unit-rates per kWh.

Public opinion was aroused, in the late sixties, by this fact of cross-subsidization; and when the upward revision of rates was carried out in 1974, the gap between the two uses was narrowed substantially by raising the rates for large-scale industrial users by 84.8 percent while applying a moderate rise of 28.6 percent for household users. Even after this revision, however, the unit-rate per kWh for the former stood at only 52.9 percent of the latter. Whether cross-subsidization still remains may be debatable. But it cannot be doubted that it played an important role for electricity-intensive industries during the high-growth period up to 1974.

5　A turning point cometh

It was inevitable that a 10 percent growth-rate period would come to an end sooner or later, although the Japanese capitalist class was reluctant to recognize the trend as the decade of the 1970s opened. Then there came the first oil shock of 1973 which caused a rude awakening not only as regards the essentially temporary character of high growth but also to some negative aspects of the high-growth period. For one thing, a paradoxical situation was noted in that in spite of a very high rate of productivity rise (which must have meant cost reduction) an inflationary trend was observed, which called for an explanation. This is attempted here in terms of "structural creeping inflation." Then it was significant that the year 1970 came to be referred to in Japan as "Kōgai Gannen," or the year initiating the era of environmental challenge as the awareness of aggravating incidence of environmental disruption finally gripped the establishment circles to introduce legislative reforms in this regard. Attention thus directed to external diseconomies and non-marketable amenities naturally began calling into question the welfare content of economic growth as represented by the GNP index. In this way, a turning point came definitely to the high growth period of postwar Japan capitalism in the early 1970s.

1. The first "oil shock" of 1973

Signs of transition

The survey given in the last chapter, which attempted to explain a high-growth performance of the Japanese economy during the two decades starting roughly from the early 1950s, could serve simultaneously as an explanation for the eventual deceleration of the growth rate. In the first place, most of the growth-stimulating effects of postwar temporary factors had been more or less taken advantage of by the end of the 1960s, such as the favorable effect of the exchange rate determined with an allowance similar to "a convalescent golfer" along with the catching-up process in latest technologies, the hothouse effect enjoyed during the period while liberalization measures were temporized, and the once-for-all effect of the subsidized provision of factory sites through reclamation of convenient shore-lines.

Furthermore, the structural shift of industries toward high value-added sectors, which contributed to the high rate of growth, had gone almost as far as it could by the first half of the 1970s; and such factors as special tax-relief measures for industries and the so-called "low interest-rate policy" have increasingly come to be frowned upon by the general public and it is doubtful if they could be relied upon with similar assurance as in earlier years. Such unique features of Japan as the general practice of "administrative guidance" and the high propensity to save of households may still remain; but these factors alone could hardly sustain the inordinately high rate of private investment as was observed in the decades of the 1950s and 1960s. As the saying has it, you can pull with a string, but you cannot push with it. On top of all this, as we shall discuss in a later section, entered the new dimension of environmental concern, which on balance could not but have the dampening effect on market-oriented business activities.

On the other hand, the optimism which characterized the mood of the ruling circles of Japan showed no sign of abatement as the decade of the 1970s opened, most likely because what appeared to be an over-ambitious plan of "income doubling in ten years" was in fact over-accomplished. In terms of the growth rate of real GNP, the first half of the 1960s, starting with the "Iwato Boom," recorded the average annual rate of 10.04 percent and the second half, ending with the "Izanagi Boom," recorded the average annual rate of 11.54 percent, resulting in the index figure of 277.7 for 1970 against 100 of 1960. In terms of per capita real national income also, the doubling in ten years was comfortably achieved. Thus only a small minority of Japanese publicists questioned, for example, the projection in July 1970 by the Overall Energy Research Commission, a governmental consultative body, on Japan's overall energy needs and supply possibilities for 1985 on the assumption that the economy would grow, in terms of real GNP, at the annual rate of 8.5 to 10.6 percent during the period of 1970 to 1985. It may be committed in our memory for future reference that the petroleum imports implied in this projection for 1985 were as high as 650–723 million kiloliters.

Riding on this bandwagon of high-growth posture there appeared in 1972 a successor to "the income-doubling plan" in the form of "The Plan for Remodeling of the Japanese Archipelago" championed by Kakuei Tanaka, who became Prime Minister in July 1972. The general philosophy enunciated in the Plan was in a sense quite timely, emphasizing that it sought "to usher in the new era of 'Restoration of Human Rights' where humans, the sun and greens, instead of big cities and industries, become the master of our society."[1] In order apparently to be consistent with this philosophy, the Plan proposed the dispersing of industrial centers throughout the country, for which purpose vast networks of transportation and communications were to be developed. It was no joke for Tanaka to suggest that as much as one-fifth of the plain area of Japan would be required as highway space by 2000 and that by 1985 27 million trucks would have to be active for the transporting of 600 billion ton-kilometers of freight.[2] The annual rate of growth of real GNP during 1970–85 was projected to be "potentially 10 percent" attaining one trillion dollar GNP level (in 1970 prices) by 1985.

The immediate effect of Tanaka's coming to power in July 1972 with this Plan publicly announced in advance was the boom in land prices especially in those regions which the Plan had named specifically as newly to-be-developed industrial centers. All the more was it a shock for the Tanaka regime and its supporters when in October 1973 the dikes that had been erected around petroleum prices were removed and within four months the crude oil price (Arabian light crude) rose from $3 per barrel to $11.65.[3] The so-called "first oil shock" thus visited Japan with convulsive effect. Rightly the occasion was characterized as a "New Price Revolution."

The first "oil shock"

Japan is peculiarly vulnerable to price rises in raw materials and fuels on the world market, and the effect on her economy of the fourfold increase in the price of oil between October 1973 and January 1974 was almost instantaneous, as can be seen in the marked drop of several components of effective demands in *real* terms from the latter half of 1973 to the first half of 1974, as shown in Table 5.1.

It is especially to be noted that "private consumer expenditures" and "private investment in plant and equipment," between them, accounted for practically all the decline in the sources of effective demand; and thus was ushered in, in Japan also, a period of "stagflation" where a recessionary trend coexisted with inflation. But characteristically in Japan, a new situation was immediately grasped, more vividly than in other countries, as marking a historical transition basically conditioned by a new "price revolution," this time involving an irreversible shift upward of the cost of raw materials and industrial fuels. The only way Japanese industries could cope with this "price revolution" in the first instance was through absorbing the cost increase by the cushion of profits which had been ample in the preceding period and, while buying time in this manner, to attempt to

Table 5.1. *Changes in effective demand components from 1973 to 1974*

	Percentage change from July–December 1973 to January–June 1974 (%)	Relative shares of each component in the total decline (%)
Private consumer expenditures	− 8.5	40.5
Current expenditures of government	3.7	− 2.3
Government capital formation	− 6.6	5.4
Private investment in plant & equipment	− 19.8	58.3
Investment in inventories	− 0.6	0.2
Exports and incomes from abroad	1.6	− 2.2
Gross national demand	− 9.2	100.0

Source: Economic Planning Agency, The Institute of Economic Research.
Calculations are based on the real term figures expressed in 1965 prices.

find a new breakthrough. If we make a calculation of "real profits" in the sense of apparent profits minus depreciation and inventory valuation adjustments for major enterprises, they turn suddenly to a negative figure in the accounting period of October 1973 to March 1974, as shown in Table 5.2. "The good old days," which lasted until the first half of 1973 fiscal year, could no longer be recovered after the oil crisis and an overall deficit was again recorded in the first half of 1975 fiscal year (April 1975 to September 1975). The number of unemployed also increased from an average of 735,000 in 1972 to 850,000 in the last quarter of 1974 and to the peak of 1,130,000 in the last quarter of 1975, with the relative decrease of employment being severest among women and older people in the process.

As was indicated earlier, even without the oil shock of 1973–74 the rapturous years of 10 percent growth rate had more or less gone by 1970, although the Japanese capitalist class was reluctant to recognize the trend. Then there came the oil shock which caused a rude awakening not only as regards the temporary character of high growth but also to some negative aspects of the high-growth period. In particular, the structural creeping inflation which concomitantly arose in the growth process and the aggravating incidence of environmental disruption are the major issues which we have to take up. Also highly relevant will be the question of the welfare content of economic growth. We shall now turn to these questions.

Table 5.2. *"Real profits" of major
enterprises in the "first oil shock" period*

(in billion yen)

Fiscal year	
1965–70 (average of half-year periods)	531
1971: First half	570
Second half	570
1972: First half	490
Second half	400
1973: First half	580
Second half	−410
1974: First half	260
Second half	290
1975: First half	−80
Second half	130

Source: Economic Planning Agency, *White
Paper on Japanese Economy 1976* (in Japanese),
p.278, based on statistics given in the Bank of
Japan, *Analysis of Business Conditions of Major
Enterprises.*

2. The structural creeping inflation

Productivity rise and price changes: a theoretical connection

In principle, a rapid rate of growth of real GNP implies a high degree of
productivity rise and/or an increase in aggregate working hours (or the
total active labor force). Both of these factors were significant in postwar
Japan, but in particular the former, as was shown earlier in Chapter 3. Now,
again in principle, the rise in productivity in a competitive market implies
reduction in unit cost and thus a falling trend in market prices. What
actually transpired in England in the last quarter of the nineteenth century
met exactly this theoretical expectation. Nominal per-capita income
declined from £35.15 in 1873 to £34.71 in 1893, but when adjusted for the
price decline, *real* per capita income (at 1913–14 prices) *rose* by 35.4 percent
from £28.81 in 1873 to £39.00 in 1893.[4] This, however, pertained to
probably the most classical period of *laissez-faire* capitalism; and, since
then, it is difficult to find a comparable performance of competitive market
forces except for a brief span of years in the prosperous 1920s in the United
States.

Nowadays, market imperfections enabling oligopolistic firms to resort to mark-up pricing, combined further with the fairly effective counterveiling power of trade unions, has produced, in a mature capitalist country like Japan, a somewhat different situation. The contrasting picture may be presented, in the first instance, in the form of a hypothetical example, as shown in Figure 5.1.

It is assumed that there are four industries in the economy: (1) automobile manufacturing; (b) paper manufacturing; (c) rice agriculture and (d) haircut service. The rate of productivity increase is intrinsically different, as in the actual world, by the nature of technological conditions unique to each industry, such rates annually being highest for automobile manufacturing at 7.5 percent, followed by paper manufacturing at 3.5 percent, rice agriculture at 1.5 percent and haircut service at the bottom with no improvement. Under the simulated classical competitive conditions it may be assumed that one percentage point of productivity rise could result in a price reduction of two-thirds of 1 percent in every case. Thus, for example, an annual rate of productivity rise of 7.5 percent results in a price reduction of 5 percent per annum, and so on. For the haircut service industry, where there is assumed to be no productivity increase, the price level remains constant. These relations are depicted in Figure 5.1 by a straight solid line with a negative slope of 60 degrees on the lefthand side. This line connects a, b, c and d, with d anchored at the origin. Now suppose that technical conditions change in such a way that annual rates of productivity rise double in all the four industries: 7.5 per cent to 15 percent in automobile manufacturing and so on. Under the classical competitive conditions this would mean that the rates of price reduction also become doubled compared with the previous case: 5 percent to 10 percent in automobile manufacturing and so on. The new relations are depicted in Figure 5.1 by a straight broken line connecting a', b', c' and d'. It is to be noted that this line, with the same slope as before, overlies the original one, with d' again anchored at the origin. The average rate of price reduction for the economy as a whole, giving equal weights to the four industries, rises from 2.1 percent to 4.2 percent, reflecting the generally higher rates of productivity rise in the economy.

Now turn to the contrasting picture of the present days depicted on the righthand side of Figure 5.1. The same four industries with the same differing rates of productivity rise are assumed as in the classical days. But the controlling supposition in the new case is: whatever the rate of productivity increase achieved, that industry which enjoys the highest such rate (the automobile manufacturing in our example) remains always on the vertical line which stands for zero rate of price change. And it is generally assumed that differentials in rates of productivity increase compared with

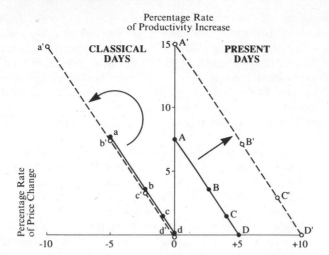

Figure 5.1 Percentage rise and price change – theoretical

		Classical days		Present days	
		% rate of productivity increase	% rate of price changes	% rate of productivity increase	% rate of price changes
Automobile Manu-facturing	a	7.5	− 5.0	A 7.5	0
	a′	15.0	− 10.0	A′ 15.0	0
Paper Manufacturing	b	3.5	− 2.3	B 3.5	+ 2.7
	b′	7.0	− 4.7	B′ 7.0	+ 5.3
Rice Agriculture	c	1.5	− 1.0	C 1.5	+ 4.0
	c′	3.0	− 2.0	C′ 3.0	+ 8.0
Haircut Service	d	0	0	D 0	+ 5.0
	d′	0	0	D′ 0	+ 10.0

the highest productivity-rising industry would result in a price rise to the extent of two-thirds of such differentials, again giving rise to a negatively sloped straight line of 60 degrees. (See the straight solid line connecting *A*, *B*, *C* and *D* on the righthand side of Figure 5.1.) The rationale of such suppositions are: (1) Through mark-up pricing practices in the age of oligopoly the benefit of a productivity increase is shared internally by "capital" and "labor" within the industry concerned instead of being transmitted to consumers via price reduction. (2) The countervailing power of trade unions with their self-centered concern oriented mainly towards their relative position within their own industry or firm helps realization of the practice referred to above. (Management tends not to resist too strongly the demand of unions for wage hike when they can absorb it without raising the sales price of their products.) (3) The labor market being economy-wide, there is a natural tendency for wage rates to become equalized except for such factors as special skills requiring years of training, the intensity of work and the inherent unpleasantness or riskiness accompanying working conditions.

If these suppositions are accepted, not only the relation between rates of productivity increase and rates of price changes will look like the solid AD line in Figure 5.1, but the shift of this line when rates of productivity increase are generally doubled will be in the northeasterly direction by a distance determined by straight upward slide of the point A to A', as shown by the broken line connecting A', B', C' and D'. In this case, the average rate of price rise for the economy as a whole, giving equal weights to the four industries, is doubled from 2.9 percent to 5.8 percent. The contrast between conditions in classical days and at present is strikingly clear. With the same assumptions as regards improvement in productivities, one gives rise to a general price reduction whereas the other to a general price rise; and, furthermore, the higher the rate of productivity increase, the greater the degree of price reduction in the former whereas the greater that of price rise in the latter.

Productivity rise and price changes – current experience

The contrasting picture we have drawn above is admittedly hypothetical. But its relevance to the analysis of recent price rises in Japan is difficult to dispute. For example, when the Subcommittee on Econometric Analysis of the governmental Council on Economic Matters made a detailed econometric analysis of the performance of the Japanese economy from 1954 to 1964 with a view to working out "An Intermediate Report on the New Long-term Economic Plan" (made public in 1966), they arrived at the conclusion empirically that the more rapid the rate of GNP growth the higher also the rate of consumer price rise; and since then it has become a matter of common sense in Japan that to aim at too high a rate of GNP growth would invite so much more of an inflationary trend. That this analysis pertained to the period when the supply flexibility of raw materials and industrial fuel was very favorable for Japan indicates that the covariance implied there was at least not due to the type of "price revolution" which subsequently visited the world through the oil crisis.

The theoretical expectation that can be drawn from our hypothetical

analysis above is in fact corroborated by a statistical analysis of several
industries as regards their rates of productivity rise matched against price
changes of their products, as shown in Figure 5.2. There a comparison is
made between two four-year periods, 1960–63 and 1964–67. For each
period our earlier hypothesis is generally borne out, the lowest productivity-rising industry showing more or less the highest positive rate of price
change. Furthermore, it can be seen clearly that the general rise in the rate
of productivity increase from 1960–63 to 1964–67 shifted the line of least
squares distinctly in the northeasterly direction.

Corroboration of the hypothesis advanced earlier to explain the fact of
creeping inflation co-existing with a high rate of GNP growth will be still
more strengthened if we extend our analysis further to include sectors other
than manufacturing, such as agriculture and service industries. Also it can
be strengthened by detailed examinations of oligopolistic price policies of
several industries and of behavioral patterns of trade unions in their year-
to-year collective bargaining. It is noteworthy that it is exactly in those
industries where the countervailing power of the union is the strongest that
the rate of productivity increase also has been the highest. So long as such
conditions continue to exist, along with market imperfections of various
other kinds, it appears to be difficult for the Japanese economy in the future
to avoid the close association of a high rate of GNP growth and an almost
proportionate degree of creeping inflation unless an effective measure of
incomes policy becomes politically feasible. This type of inflation has been
termed, by some Japanese economists, as "inflation due to productivity
differentials"; but here I choose the expression of "structural creeping
inflation."

In the light of the above analysis, relevant statistics may be cited here in
summary form, in order to confirm, in particular, that the period of
exceptionally rapid rise in manufacturing productivity was actually the
period which witnessed a creeping rise in the wholesale price index and a
considerable upward trend in the consumer price index while the exchange
rate of yen was, if at all, strengthening. In an earlier chapter (Chapter 3
Table 3.1) we cited statistics showing the rising trend of manufacturing
productivity during the high-growth period from 1950 to 1973 in the form
of quinquennial averages of annual rates (except for the period of 1970 to
1973, for which the three-year average was given); we may now juxtapose to
that series the percentage changes in the price level which occurred over
each of the five-year-periods, as shown in Table 5.3. The first and the last of
the sub-periods cited in Table 5.3 reflect extraordinary events of the Korean
War and the oil shock. But even aside from these, it is manifestly clear that
the exceptionally high rate of productivity improvement in manufacturing,
which must have meant substantial decrease in the manufacturing cost, did

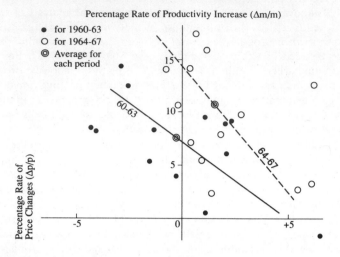

		Δm/m	Δp/p			Δm/m	Δp/p
Manufacturing	60–63	7.4	−0.3	Textiles	60–63	6.3	+2.2
(average)	64–67	10.9	+1.6		64–67	9.4	+2.9
Iron and steel	60–63	8.3	−3.4	Food processing	60–63	0.3	+1.2
	64–67	15.5	+1.1		64–67	2.1	+1.3
Nonferrous	60–63	8.4	−3.7	Rubber products	60–63	5.4	−1.5
metals	64–67	11.6	+6.2		64–67	5.1	+1.0
Engineering	60–63	8.3	−1.4	Leather and	60–63	9.0	+2.2
	64–67	14.1	+0.3	hide products	64–67	2.9	+6.2
Chemicals	60–63	12.1	−2.6	Wood processing	60–63	−2.2	+7.3
	64–67	14.0	−0.9		64–67	2.4	+5.6
Petroleum &	60–63	14.0	−2.9	Ceramics	60–63	9.1	+2.3
coal products	64–67	17.2	+0.4		64–67	7.5	+1.9
Paper & Pulp	60–63	9.4	+1.0	Tobacco manu-	60–63	4.1	−0.2
	64–67	6.7	+0.4	facturing	64–67	10.8	−0.1

Note:
In the table, Δm/m means average annual percentage rate of productivity increase, and Δp/p means average annual percentage rate of wholesale price changes. The former was taken from the productivity studies compiled by the Japan Productivity Center, and the latter was calculated from the sectoral wholesale price index series of the Bank of Japan.

Figure 5.2 Productivity rise and price change – actual

Table 5.3. *Productivity rise and price changes 1950–1973*

	Average annual rate of improvement in manufacturing productivity (%)	Changes in the price level during each sub-period	
		Wholesale prices	Consumer prices
1950–55	17.5	+39.0	+35.1
1955–60	6.2	+2.7	+10.1
1960–65	8.9	+2.1	+35.0
1965–70	17.8	+11.2	+29.2
1970–73	10.4	+15.9	+24.5
(1970–75)		(+56.5)	(+76.8)

Sources: Changes in the wholesale price level were calculated from the statistics given in the Bank of Japan, *Economic Statistics Annual* for 1989, March 1990, p.316, and changes in the consumer price level were calculated from the statistics given in *Nihon Kokusei Zuye 1990*, June 1990, p.589.

not redound to the benefit of consumers in the form of a price decline. It may be added here that the fixed rate of the Japanese yen was raised by 17 percent (to 308 yen for a dollar) in the Smithsonian agreement of December 1971.

3. Environmental concerns heightened

Japan's vulnerable environment

The opening of the decade of the 1970s marked yet another turning point for the Japanese economy, that is, in a heightened awareness of environmental disruption in an industrialized society. The year 1970 has been aptly referred to in Japan as "Kōgai Gannen,"[5] or the year initiating the era of environmental challenge.

In Japan, probably more than in any other country, that familiar abbreviation "GNP" could stand for Gross National Pollution. Extremely rapid growth rate of the two decades we have discussed was, it can hardly be doubted, at the expense of nonmarketable amenities of various kinds and also the cause of non-monetary sacrifices inflicted upon the public at large. In fact, the very measures taken against pollution in the context of a market-oriented economy would help generate additional effective demand to help GNP grow as in the proverbial anecdote of a community that succeeded in solving the unemployment problem by deliberately "importing" mosquitoes to create markets for insecticides and mosquito nets. In addition, it should be noted that in spite of frequent reference in other countries to the environmental problem being "a luxury to be indulged in only after income has reached fairly high levels,"[6] the problem areas in Japan as regards environmental disruption have generally been character-ized by the selectively detrimental effects, if at all, on the poorer section of citizens in the region concerned.

This is not at all surprising when we reflect upon the fact that Japan is unique, probably more than in other respects, in having the densest concentration of industries per habitable land space. In the early 1970s, for example, petroleum consumption per 1,000 km² of habitable land space was 87.7 million barrels in Japan, contrasted with 49.9 million in West Germany and 31.5 million in the United Kingdom. Similarly, electricity used per 1,000 km² of habitable land space was 268 billion kilowatt hours in Japan, contrasted with 133 billion in West Germany and 109 billion in the United Kingdom. Such was the background for the most energetic effort by "Japan Inc." to create land space through reclamation, as was discussed in the last chapter. This effort, however, was highly disruptive of the environment, as is most typically exemplified by the present condition of the Seto Inland Sea. Designated as one of the national parks, the Inland Sea area was described in the Act for Environmental Conservation of the Seto Inland Sea (1973) as "not only a natural endowment of incomparable beauty of Japan and the world but also a treasure-house of valuable marine resources for the nation." But reclamation for industrial purposes had proceeded for a decade or more; and along the coast of this sea, with an expanse of 22,000 km² surrounded by three major islands of Japan and connected with the Pacific Ocean and the East China Sea via three straits, are now concentrated 53 percent of the total steel-making capacity of Japan, 40 percent of oil refining, 35 percent of petrochemical, 63 percent of copper-refining and 76 percent of lead-refining industries of Japan. Altogether, industrial capacities of the region are bigger than the total such capacities of the United Kingdom, and over 500 kilometers of the coast has now become artificially filled in by concrete walls. What was once a pride of Japan's natural beauty has become a problem area of the first order from the environmental viewpoint and, in spite of strenuous counter-measures, the condition keeps on deteriorating. The average measure of transparency at representative points in the region, for example, declined from 9.3 meters in 1953 to 6.3 meters in 1972 and the concentration of ammonia and phosphoric acid increased from 1.5 ppm to 3.6 ppm and from 0.33 ppm to 0.54 ppm, respectively, during the same period. Red tide or the abnormal proliferation of marine flora was reported to have occurred 298 times in 1974, compared with 79 times in 1970 and only four times in 1950.

What has happened to the Seto Inland Sea area is more or less typical of
the manner in which the animal-spirited-stampede for high rate of growth
went on with little regard for environmental amenities. In particular:

1 An extremely rapid *relative* expansion of heavy and chemical industries
  (as discussed in Chapter 3) which are generally more polluting than other
  industries.
2 Progress in the degree of urbanization far in excess of demographic
  changes.[7]
3 The explosive character of boom in mass consumption markets, notably
  private cars.[8]

All of which cause woeful lags in the provision of complementary social
overhead. These are the salient features of the environment-disruptive
process of the high-growth period.

What then are the concrete degrees of environmental degradation in
Japan which one may associate with the high-growth process?

Generally speaking, quantitative measures of such degradation can be
set forth in three dimensions: (1) emissions of pollutants at source; (2)
objectively measurable phenomena of polluted conditions; and (3)
damages inflicted upon humans and other objects of value. It is important
to distinguish between these three. Passing from one dimension to another,
there intervene all kinds of specific characteristics of a region concerned, so
that international comparison, or even an intertemporal comparison
relative to one and the same region, in terms of a single measure of
"pollution" could often be very misleading. Furthermore, there is a highly
important point to be remembered, namely that in the field of environmental disruption quantity often changes into quality especially as we pass from
the first to the third dimension indicated above. In other words, for any
international comparison it is important to assess the absolute physical
figures of pollution always in relation to such matters as the absorptive
capacity of the environment, the geographical configuration, the density of
population, the antipollution measures taken by government bodies in the
region concerned, etc.

Ashio compared with Ducktown

It is instructive, therefore, to compare the histories of two copper-refining
centers in the prewar period, namely, Ducktown in the US and Ashio in
Japan. The story of Ducktown, often related in connection with the
multipurpose development of the Tennessee Valley Authority, tells of the
transformation of a beautiful village perched on the western slope of the
Appalachians and surrounded by stately hardwood trees into a prosperous
copper-refining center just before the First World War and subsequently

into a place of desolation with surrounding forest land denuded, the river water contaminated and no longer serving as a habitat for fish, and the erstwhile green pastures made bare and eroded. Prior to Ducktown, however, there is a story of Ashio[9] which is somewhat similar to the Ducktown story and is usually cited as a classic example of *kōgai* in Japan. A major difference between the two cases was that whereas Ducktown was located in a sparsely populated area in any case, Ashio was close to a river which within fifty kilometers affected directly 200,000 hectares of cultivated and closely inhabited land. The protest movement against the Ashio copper-refining began at first in rather timid fashion and, naturally, did not make a dent in the composure of a rising capitalist firm. The firm took a superior attitude by denying any causal connection between their operation and the woes of the farmers along the river. It is noteworthy that the government at the time, by taking an attitude of noninterference, actually sided with the copper interest. The protest movement, however, went on intermittently and gained momentum after Shōzō Tanaka, a Diet member from the region, made it his cause and took its leadership. Tanaka's energetic activities, now dramatizing the issue in the Diet, now spending days and nights with farmers in the region in order to solidify the protest organization, and now making a direct appeal to the Emperor (in 1901), were instrumental in wresting some concessions from the copper-refining firm and also in causing the government to establish an *ad hoc* committee for investigation. But the concessions by the firm were in the form of (1) the payment of a solatium calculated more to bribe village elders than in proportion to damages suffered; and (2) the announcement that "a filtering device" would be imported from Germany and installed. This turned out to be a device for recovering reusable waste and did not have the ameliorating effect that the protesting farmers were led to expect. The protest movement went on in a more violent form than before, reminiscent of tenants' riots of the past. The most radical at the time were the farmers in the village of Yanaka; and the government struck a fatal blow to the movement by designating the Yanaka area a reserve land for the emergency overflow of Toné River. Farmers were forced to give up cultivating the land there and, with a pittance as compensation, had to disperse. Tanaka fought as hard as ever against the move but could not change the policy of the Ministry of Interior. And, with this episode of defeat, the Ashio protest movement went into a rapid eclipse.[10]

Lessons learned and forgotten

It is characteristic of the story of Ashio that the *kōgai* problem was fought mainly as a political issue and did not even become a legal one. One could have expected that an incident as glaring as the Ashio *kōgai*, with the source of spillover so clearly identifiable, should at least serve as a stimulus for developing a new legal framework to contain the kind of strife that was inevitable. But even to this obvious challenge there was no response from legal specialists of the day. The spirit of the times were such that the engine of economic growth and prosperity should have no muffling impediment to weaken its function. But it is clear enough that the history of environmental disruption in Japan is as old as the history of the industrialization of Japan. Many instances can be reported in this connection, but we shall not dwell upon them. It may be more important to point out that through the experiences of some outstanding instances which created conflict of interests, Japanese capitalism had learned, though gropingly, the basic elements of antipollution measures and put them into practice, namely:

1 suitable choice of industrial sites and, if necessary, the transfer of establishments to new places;
2 control of pollutants at source;
3 diffusion measures;
4 emergency measures such as cut-back of production;
5 compensation to victims.

Such lessons, however, were conveniently shunted aside in the period subsequent to Japan's militaristic adventures beginning in the late 1920s and they were almost completely forgotten in the postwar reconstruction period. Early harbingers in the postwar period of the latter-day concern over environmental disruption were:

1 The reporting of the convulsive deaths of cats and crows in the Minamata area in 1953, followed by the first filing of a report in May 1956 by the Chisso Company to the local health office on "the incident of unexplainable disease" among some residents of Minamata.
2 Citizens' complaints reaching the municipal office of Yokkaichi (a site of one of the earliest petrochemical complexes in Japan) in 1959, citing a sudden increase in bronchial ailments.
3 Reporting in 1955 at the 17th Conference of Surgical Specialists on the existence of a peculiar disease in a certain region along the Jintsū River locally known as the "itai-itai disease."

All these cases erupted subsequently into nationwide disputes of major proportion, each one having been brought into court. But the decade of the 1960s was that of the forward stampede and the importance of such environmental problems was appreciated only by a small minority of concerned scientists at the time.

A new turn in awareness

However, the dangers of the technico-economic juggernaut getting out of hand or splashing mud of external diseconomies became more and more patent as Japan's growthmanship continued, and also citizens' movements against the actual and potential industrial polluters, as in the case of Mishima-Numazu incident of 1964, which successfully prevented the siting of an industrial complex there, became increasingly frequent and effective. Thus finally, the government had to address itself seriously to the *kōgai* problem in a general way and drafted the Basic Law for Environmental Pollution Control, which passed the legislature in July 1967. Momentum gathered as the UN General Assembly, in December 1968, called for a convening of an international conference on the environment and, further, as Japan served as a host country for an international symposium of social scientists in the spring of 1970 to discuss environmental disruption.

This latter symposium, one might say, marked a turning point in many ways. In particular, the Tokyo Resolution which was adopted in the closing session said in part:

Above all, it is important that we urge the adoption in law of the principle that every person is entitled by right to the environment free of elements which infringe human health and well-being and the nature's endowment, including its beauty, which shall be the heritage of the present to the future generations.

And this statement served as a springboard for a basic reorientation in the matters concerning environmental rights of citizens. One of the significant effects was the revision in the wording of the Basic Law referred to above. This law, as it was enacted in 1967, contained a compromise with the interests of private business. The compromise consisted of adding a paragraph in Article I which spelled out the purpose of the law: "In conservation of the living environment provided in the preceding paragraph, harmony with sound economic development should be considered." The implication of this so-called "Harmony Clause" was that the need for environmental pollution control was not absolute but might, in certain cases, yield to the interest of promoting economic activities. But this clause generated a great deal of criticism at the time of the enactment and developed into a focus of heated controversy in the subsequent years. Thus the government finally decided to propose a revision in the law to strike off the paragraph in question. The 1970 Diet Session passed this revision; and the purpose enunciated in paragraph one of Article I – that of "protecting the health of nation and conserving their living environment" – became less relativistic, one might say, than before. This Diet Session came to be called in later years the "*Kōgai* Session," because aside from this revision of the Basic Law, it passed and/or revised fourteen other acts of law, all related to the matter of environmental protection. It also called for the setting up of a new Ministry, the Environment Agency, charged with the task of formulating and promoting basic principles with regards to the conservation of the environment and of coordinating the activities of other administrative agencies in the field. The Environment Agency came into existence in July 1971.

Anti-pollution litigations and standards

Progress made in litigations on environmental issues had also been noteworthy during the early years of 1970s. In the brief span of less than two years, between June 1971 and March 1973, four major *kōgai* trial cases all ended in the victory of plaintiffs representing the victims of environmental disruption. The cases are:
1 The "itai-itai disease" case of cadmium poisoning.
2 The "Niigata Minamata disease" case of mercury poisoning.
3 The "Yokkaichi pollution" case of respiratory ailments.
4 The "Kumamoto Minamata disease" case of mercury poisoning.

Excepting the "itai-itai disease" case where an article in the Mining Act, which provides for absolute liability, was invoked, all the other cases relied mainly upon Article 709 of the Civil Code which reads: "Whoever has infringed on another's rights by intention or negligence shall be held responsible for compensating the damage thus incurred." The article sets out liability for breaches of the law in general and was never intended to cover cases like, for example, the Yokkaichi pollution damage; and, therefore, the court faced, in each one of the above, the difficult task of handling a case without a legal framework pertinent to the purpose and was forced to find an innovative solution.

Nevertheless, it can be said that the court did manage to establish, through the decisions on the above four cases, a number of legal principles which are likely to be cemented further in pollution trials in the future. In the "itai-itai disease" case, *the epidemiological proof was accepted as a sufficient proof of cause–effect relationship.* This principle will make it easier to bring relief to victims expeditiously in those cases where scientific dispute is involved, for the necessary and sufficient proof in science could take years to acquire. In the "Niigata Minamata disease" case, *the burden of proof was placed on the defendant enterprise rather than on the accuser* so that the former had to show that their effluents were not responsible for causing the Minamata disease. This principle, when established, will be an important step towards regularizing and facilitating the procedure for victimized citizens to bring the matter to the court. In the "Yokkaichi pollution" case, *the joint-tort principle was effectively applied.* This case was of the character where both plaintiffs and defendants were plural in number and the specific causal link between the damage suffered by any one of the former and the action of any one of the latter was practically impossible to prove even by

Table 5.4. *Standards for air quality and automobile exhaust –
international comparison*

	Air quality objectives, 1975[a]				Automobile exhaust standards		
	SO$_2$ (ppm)	Particulates (mg/m^3)	NO$_2$ (ppm)	Year Applicable	CO (g/km)	HC (g/km)	NO$_X$ (g/km)
Japan	0.04	0.10	0.02	1976	2.10	0.25	0.60
Japan				1978	2.10	0.25	0.25
USA	0.14	0.26	0.13	1975[b]	9.30	0.93	1.93
Canada[c]	0.06	0.12	0.10	Future	2.13	0.25	1.94
France	0.38	0.35	n.a.		n.a.	n.a.	n.a.
Sweden	0.25	n.a.	n.a.	1975	24.20	2.10	1.90
Italy	0.15	0.30	n.a.		n.a.	n.a.	n.a.

Notes:
[a] All figures are average daily values or their equivalents.
[b] Federal government standards.
[c] For Ontario.
Source: Compiled by the author from various governmental sources.

the lenient criterion of "preponderance of evidence." A way was now
opened for broadening the coverage of Article 719 of the Civil Code to
include cases of pollution damage typified by the Yokkaichi case. In the
"Kumamoto Minamata disease" case, the judicial innovation consisted of
(a) broadening the concept of responsibility of the pollution firm *to date it at
the time the natural environment as such* (even before the health damage
occurred) *was impaired*; (b) *calculating anew the amount of compensation to
be paid to the victims regardless of the solatium that had been paid earlier by
the firm*; and (c) *defining the responsibility of the firm in question in terms of
the internal structure of the enterprise as well as of a unitary corporate person.*
It remained to be seen how these innovations were to be developed further
in face of still-increasing occurrences of litigations in the field of
environment.

No doubt, the Stockholm Conference on the Human Environment of
June 1972 provided a renewed stimulus for anti-*kōgai* policies and
movements in Japan, both public and private, at least in the immediately
following years. For one thing, the social attitudes then prevalent in Japan
reflected themselves in much stricter standards set for air quality and
automobile exhaust than in other advanced industrialized countries. A
study made at the time showed the comparison as given in Table 5.4. It can

be seen that the air quality objective for NO_2 and the automobile exhaust standard for NOx were especially strict in Japan; and, in fact, they were the foci of heated controversy within Japan between auto manufacturers and the concerned public, resulting later (1978) in the ameliorating revisions by the Environment Agency itself.

Another index which bespeaks Japan's marked efforts to provide anti-pollution measures in that decade was the relative weight given to anti-pollution investments by private enterprises within the total business expenditures on plant and equipment. Such a ratio stood at 3.0 percent in 1965 in Japan, a figure more or less prevalent in most other countries. But the ratio picked up steadily in subsequent years in Japan, to 5.0 percent in 1969, 8.6 percent in 1972 and finally to 18.6 percent in 1975.[11] In absolute value terms anti-pollution investments by private enterprises increased 40 times in one decade, from 29.7 billion yen in 1965 to 1,178.3 billion yen in 1975. It must be added, however, that, as was briefly mentioned at the beginning of this section, GNP accounting subsumes not only "goods" and services produced but also "anti-bads" which are marketed with the purpose of offsetting "bads" incidental to the production of "goods," thus no less a component of effective demand.

Citizens' movements heightened but handicapped

In spite of all these efforts, general public sentiment in Japan continued to be critical of all those activities, both by private business and government bodies, that tended to cause environmental deterioration of any kind; and, as the high-growth period proceeded, the environmental concern gradually became a matter, less of cost-benefit calculation than of human rights, expressed concretely in such forms as "the right to environment," "the right to physical integrity," "the right to beach access," "the right to sunshine," and so on. These concepts pertain to basic citizens' rights which could serve as ideological instruments for citizens' movements in the fight over the environment. But, as we study each one of the cases of such movements, we cannot but be impressed with one feature that is common to practically all of them. That is the tremendous amount of energy and time that is voluntarily put into a campaign without any monetary remuneration on the one hand and the quiet stone-wall character of the opposition which has all the paraphernalia of the establishment on its side including "the law's delay and the insolence of office" on the other. Some of the readers may remember seeing that classical Japanese film *Ikiru* which was the story of an ailing ward official who, with the support of local citizens, finally succeeded in overcoming all the hurdles and resistance in creating a small park for citizens, and died smiling alone on the swing in the park. Contrast this with the smooth, matter-of-fact way in which hectares and hectares of new land have been created for industries by filling up the shore-line sea. This latter project, once conceived in the minds of some government officials, goes through steps which are well grooved for eventual fulfilment. The contrast is like the one between a large number of people, women and children included, trying to push a heavy cart over an uncharted wild terrain without a road, and a team of trained staff driving a stream-lined train over a polished rail.

It is clear enough that with public awareness in Japan having become keener over the environmental problem in general in the course of the high-growth period, the climate of public opinion has shifted more and more in favor of acts of conservation of nature and the prevention of pollution. But what is needed is the building of "roads" and the "laying of rails" over which the cart-carrying citizens' demands for a better human environment can be pushed with greater ease than heretofore. In this connection, Japan could learn a valuable lesson from the legislation enacted in 1970 in the State of Michigan, called "Thomas J. Anderson Gordon Rockwell Environment Protection Act."[12] This was the brair-child of Joseph Sax, then professor of the University of Michigan, a participant in the Tokyo symposium mentioned above, to whom we owed more than to anyone else in drafting the Tokyo Resolution quoted earlier. Sax's basic idea in the formulation of the Michigan Law was that ordinary citizens should be able to play the role of attorney general, as it were, in the judicial prosecution of polluting agents as early as at the stage when the specific pollution damage could be presumed.

4. Reflection on the welfare content of GNP index

It is generally accepted that we discuss the problem of economic growth in terms of gross national product (GNP) or national income. And, further, it has been customary in public discussion to equate the growth of GNP at least in an approximate sense, with that of economic welfare. This habit, shared by most economists, used to be firmly enough grounded. There was a time, for one thing, when mass unemployment in capitalist countries was a direct cause of severe suffering for millions of people and any measure that expanded effective demand, even including the nonsensical digging and refilling of holes in the ground, was regarded as a positive step towards increasing welfare so long as it brought about a net increase in employment. In fact, the close association of growth in GNP with that of economic welfare, in the minds of economists, developed in the period immediately following the Great Depression, thanks largely to the Keynesian revolution in economic thinking. It is further agreed among most of us that for those countries in the Third World which have been stagnating on subsistence level an economic growth measured in terms of GNP is most likely to mean an improvement in economic welfare.

Regressive effects of growthmanship

The common sense thus established, equating the growth of GNP with that of economic welfare, however, came to be seriously questioned in Japan in the course of the exceptionally high rate of growth of the two decades after the outbreak of the Korean conflict. Some of the concrete manifestations of this ambivalence have been discussed in the preceding sections of this chapter. Indeed coming to the fore of such reflection on the welfare content of the GNP index constitutes an important aspect of the turning point in the growth process of postwar Japan.

We may begin by giving some concrete examples of the regressive effect that accompanied the dynamic change inherent in the rapid economic growth as measured by the magnitude of GNP. An important point here is that such regressive effect has never been intended in the course of events but has rather been a consequence of the market mechanism responding more or less faithfully to the short-run stimuli of presumably "sovereign" consumers. An example we draw is from a pedestrian aspect of daily urban life. Two generations ago it was customary for Tokyo citizens to go to a public bath house for their daily bath, not having any private bathroom installed at home. Public bath houses used to be a most democratic institution in Japan where everyone except the very rich met unclothed and exchanged greetings and gripes, joy and sorrow, and went home refreshed and satisfied. Especially in the postwar period, however, one home after another began installing a private bath as the income levels rose and members of the family with a bathroom at home ceased going to public bath houses. By the late 1960s the number of customers in these houses started declining rapidly with the natural consequence of an increase of bath rates to make both ends meet. Such hiking of the rates had the double consequence of discouraging customers from patronizing public bath houses and inducing citizens to wait for the earliest opportunity to install a bath at home. Even with the raising of the rates, many of the public bath houses in Tokyo found themselves unable to carry on and were forced to close their business. As of 1970 there were still 2,000 odd bath houses in Tokyo (23 ward areas) catering to about one-third of the population of the areas. But the decline continued with some 20 to 30 bath houses going bankrupt each year. The citizens who still had to rely on public bath houses were generally poorer people who could not afford, or had no space in their home, to install a private bath. What can they do when a neighborhood bath house is closed? Either they will have to go without taking a bath (which is intolerable for Japanese) or to walk double the distance to the nearest bath house which still survives. In any case, poorer people are in effect discriminated against and yet no one can blame the bath-house owners who are only being faithful to the dictates of the market. Affluence has brought comfort for the well-to-do and hardship for the poor.

A somewhat similar process has taken place in connection with the intrusion of private automobiles into the lives of urban and suburban populations. Forty years ago privately owned cars were a rarity in Japan and almost everyone commuted by one sort or another of public transport. But with affluence an age of automobiles has come very quickly in Japan. Think of a bus line which was smoothly running from a suburban center to downtown forty years ago. First, Mr A, let us say, having been successful in raising his income, decides to buy a car and use it for commuting. The addition of only one car has a negligible effect on the congestion of roads and Mr A can smartly pass the buses by which his colleagues are commuting. They all envy Mr A, and soon one of them, Mr B, buys a car and drops out from the ranks of bus customers. Mr C, Mr D and so on will follow as affluence becomes pervasive. Then, the road begins to be congested; and buses will lose their speed and lose their customers, too. The bus line is now forced to raise the rate, accelerating further the process of losing their customers to the ranks of car owners. The more demand there is for automobiles the cheaper they become and thus the easier for the general public to buy them. By the time two-thirds of the commuters forsake the bus, the bus line may find itself forced to discontinue the operation of that particular route. When this happens, the remaining one-third of the commuters are suddenly deprived of the accustomed means of transport and are made painfully aware that to own a private car has become a necessity. By then, too, the road has become intolerably congested and everyone may feel that the original situation of smoothly running buses was much better. But one must remind oneself that at each step of this process the market was responding faithfully to the dictate of consumers and the market mechanism itself cannot reverse this process. It has aptly been said that "it is one of the eternal verities of history that as societies become wealthy they are no longer able to afford pleasures that were well within their reach when they were poor."[13]

Examples can be multiplied to attest to the regressive effect incidental to the rapid growth of GNP magnitude in Japan, notably the instance, discussed in the preceding section, of the social consequences of environmental disruption which have been structured in such a way as to make the weakest link in society suffer most. However, reflection as to the unreliability of GNP as a welfare measure extends still farther into its relevance to various aspects of our society because of the inherent limitation of the GNP concept itself.

"Market failures" specified

To begin with, the concept of GNP (or its allied concept of national income) is predicated on the exchange of goods in the market, and is intended to cover these goods and services that are exchanged in the market. As a corollary to this, it may be added that the unit of measurement of GNP is money value as registered in the market. If one gram of opium, baneful as it may be, has the same market value as one kilogram of rice, these two items are considered equivalent in national income accounting. Welfare content is essentially *concrete*; but when aggregated into GNP or national income, all goods and services acquire a single dimension, namely that of market valuation, and the quantitative expression obtained does not necessarily relate to *concrete* welfare content.

But a question may be raised immediately: who is the judge of the welfare significance of any particular good or service? If one holds to a view that the freedom of individual decision *is* the most important value in this world, one might say, as did Milton Friedman, that it is better that a man act unwisely of his own will – provided his action harms no other persons – than that he be coerced into a wiser course of action. This is the philosophy of *laissez-faire* which elevates the system of competitive market economy to a position superior to any other system. Even the protagonists of this philosophy, however, would admit that there are such things that are subsumed under the category of "market failures." These are at least of two types: (A) there do exist "goods," or desirable things – "goods A" – which escape the market valuation almost entirely, such as natural beauties; and (B) there arise quite often, even in well-functioning market economies, what are known as "external effects," both of a positive and negative character – "goods B" and "bads B." Such instances of market failures may be reflected indirectly in market valuations in one way or another. But, as in the case of an expansion of developmental activities at the sacrifice of natural beauties, the GNP measure takes full account of the developmental side while ignoring the minus effect of the sacrifice; and, in addition, those offsetting activities against "bads B," if marketed in the form of anti-pollution measures for example, are counted on the positive side of GNP.

In other words, aside from the short-run policy orientation of the GNP concept, a longer-range association between the size of GNP and the magnitude of economic welfare could be predicated if certain assumptions could be justified, in particular, if market failures can be considered to be insignificant. More specifically, the assumptions are: (1) that external effects, either positive or negative, are unimportant; (2) that the condition of consumer sovereignty obtains; and (3) that the failure of the reward system, for whatever reason, is of little consequence. True, even in the heyday of competitive capitalism these three assumptions could not be fully justified. Negative external effects were often serious enough, as is evidenced in the pollution damage caused to agriculture and forestry by the Ashio copper-refining plant in the late nineteenth century. The doctrine of consumer sovereignty, too, one may say, was never more than a complacent rationalization by economists. In an address to manufacturers, John Ruskin perorated, more than one hundred years ago:

You must remember always that your business, as manufacturers, is to *form the market* as much as to supply it [. . .] But whatever happens to you, this, at least, is certain, that the whole of your life will have been spent in corrupting public taste and encouraging public extravagance. Every preference you have won by gaudiness must have been based on the purchaser's vanity; every demand you have created by novelty has fostered in the consumer a habit of discontent; and when you retire into inactive life, you may, as a subject of consolation for your declining years, reflect that precisely according to the extent of your past operations, your life has been successful in retarding the arts, tarnishing the virtues, and confusing the manners of your country.[14]

Ruskin was no doubt a sensitive soul; but here is an insight – that "manufacturers form the market" – which could not easily be refuted, even in the days of a *laissez-faire* market economy. As for the third assumption, it may be sufficient to make reference to the discriminating bias, due to inheritance, which gave a head-start to a select group of persons, enabling them to capture a share in the national pie independently of their own efforts.

In spite of these deviations, however, we may say that, in the heyday of competitive capitalism, the presumption of a close association between magnitude of GNP and that of economic welfare was relatively free of seriously misleading connotations. But today matters are different in advanced capitalist societies. Not only is it true that technological progress has heightened the possibility of negative external effects of gigantic proportions,[15] but at the same time the preference scale of consumers is gradually evolving in such a way that amenity rights of all kinds, not susceptible to quantification, are acquiring greater importance than before.

Non-welfare components of GNP

A viable market is a market that can be sustained by the "money votes" of final consumers, who in turn part with such "money votes" in order to satisfy their wants and needs. But here is the rub. People's needs in a society are often relative to institutional and other conditions of that society which may be contrived; and people's wants are often artificially stimulated by suppliers of goods and services who, in extreme cases, are actually capable of embracing the market under their wings. In other words, among the "money votes" which consumers cast, and which thus enter as components into the GNP, there are some whose welfare significance is questionable; and here we may summarize them under four headings, namely:

1 "The cost of life" type
2 "Interference of income" type
3 "The institutionalization of waste" type
4 Depletion of social wealth

A brief explanation for each will follow.

We are all aware that, within our own consumption expenditure, there are certain items which fall into the category of necessary cost, which we wish to remain as small as possible. Heating costs in a cold climate would be the simplest example. High commuting cost without compensating advantages in environmental amenities, as we have increasingly observed in a dense urban sprawl such as Tokyo, is another.[16] But there are more sophisticated examples of cost-type consumption which induce citizens to part with their "money votes" on account of certain institutional and social developments. One example of this kind relates to the widespread use, reported in the United States,[17] of expensive burglar alarms to cope with the mounting incidence of burglary in homes. True, it is often very difficult to draw a hard and fast line between cost-type consumption and end-object type. But there are fairly clear-cut cases of what used to be a luxury or a semi-luxury becoming a necessity in a dynamic situation. Good examples, from postwar Japan, would be the disappearance of public bath-houses and commuting buses, as has been described earlier in this section.

As for the "interference of income," the term was used originally by Schumpeter who, in the playful mood of cocktail conversation, disparaged the profession of American lawyers on whose services he had to depend when he went through the red tape of naturalization. Keynes, no doubt, would have sympathized with him for he, too, apparently felt the ubiquity of lawyers in the United States as essentially redundant. The story he told in his closing speech at the Bretton Woods Conference is quite well known.[18] The "interference of income" phenomenon might be defined as the generation of income by otherwise dispensable services, which are made indispensable through built-in institutional arrangements in the society concerned. There is usually a historical background explaining why a particular service acquires built-in indispensability in a particular society, and there is, of course, no opprobrium implied in singling out a particular profession as "income-interfering." As a matter of fact, an "income-interfering" profession in a particular society draws very often the best of brains in that society and its members distinguish themselves as outstanding citizens of the community. If lawyers serve as an example of "interference of income" in the United States, we may say that bankers and real estate dealers do so in Japan. Another category of business which may be included under this heading in postwar Japan would be the inordinate expansion of tutoring schools for the young generation of all levels, from kindergarten to college, aspiring to pass entrance examinations of the elite course in the educational structure. Household expenditures for such extra-regular training are variously estimated in recent years as surpassing basic food expenditures in a large number of households; and the industry concerned has become one of the most successful, with paraphernalia of all the modern telecommunication and audio-visual devices at their command. What the industry does is to inflate the intermediate service expenditures for attaining a certain objective; and to the extent such inflation takes place, it may be said that the phenomenon of "income interference" becomes a significant factor.

Next, a word about "the institutionalization of waste." Veblen wrote as early as in 1904:[19]

The absorption of goods and services by extra-industrial expenditures, expenditures which, seen from the standpoint of industry, are pure waste, would have to go on in an increasing volume. If the wasteful expenditure slackens, the logical outcome should be a considerable perturbation of business and industry, followed by depression.

This is a prophetic statement; but it is misleading to refer to these wasteful expenditures as "expenditures which, seen from the standpoint of industry, are pure waste." Business enterprises by nature abhor waste in the context of their own calculations. Whether a certain good or service is wasteful or not is not to be judged "from the standpoint of industry" but only from the standpoint of final consumers. What is at issue here, however, is not a moralistic assessment of extravagance or dissipation. Economists *qua* economists have nothing to say to a person who knowingly wastes something for his own enjoyment. But when waste is institutionalized in such a way that a less wasteful alternative, which may well be preferred by consumers, is deliberately withheld from the market, we are called upon to analyze the mechanism which makes this possible, and to draw out the necessary implications for economic welfare. Examples of built-in obsolescence, etc., are legion, as popularized by the writings of Vance Packard, and the mechanism which encourages this type of GNP-inflating expenditure has been fully analyzed by Galbraith. The high growth period of postwar Japan did supply us with many an example of "the institutionalization of waste," most notable of which might be the deliberate obsolescence of consumer durables, such as cameras, refrigerators, television sets, etc., matched by overgrown advertising expenditures by producers and sellers. The last of the points which cause us to question the welfare significance of the GNP measure concerns the depletion of social wealth. Now, just as we can increase our monthly household expenditure by drawing upon our past savings, we can make our GNP larger than otherwise would be the case by depleting our store of resources without replacing them. It is true that there are certain resources used in the process of production that cannot be replaced. The earth's mineral deposits are of this type. So far as these resources are concerned, it would be meaningless to speak of replacing them, and the only alternative open to us is to find ways of economizing their use when the depletion process goes too far. There are, however, various other types of social wealth which, in different degrees and with differing time patterns, can be replaced after having been used. Forestry and marine resources come immediately to mind in this respect; but we may also include here clean water, natural beauties and other environmental endowments, all of which, after all, provide the source of a healthy and enjoyable life. By ignoring the need for conserving such amenities, a country can raise the growth rate of its GNP more rapidly than if it paid heed to them. The high growth period of postwar Japan has provided a good example of this in the manner, as described in the preceding section, of "expanding the kitchen at the sacrifice of the garden."

Fisher's conceptual scheme preferred

The unusually rapid growth of Japan's GNP during the two decades under review can be shown to have entailed all four of the GNP-inflating factors mentioned above. However, those who are committed to "growthmanship," when pressed on this point, do admit that some of the growth components of GNP have been of doubtful character from the welfare point of view and suggest that for welfare-oriented purposes we could compile an index of Net National Welfare as an overall measure or a welfare index based on specific indicators, such as hospital beds, park areas, the literacy rate, sewage facilities, per-family housing space, etc., all of which are quantifiable separately. Of course, one need not dispute the usefulness of such welfare indexes. But for the purpose at hand it may be much more fruitful to resuscitate Irving Fisher's concepts of "capital" and "income."[20] Attention was called to these concepts by Kenneth Boulding forty years ago.[21] Nicholas Kaldor,[22] too, found them useful in making a case for his proposal for "an expenditure tax." For Fisher, "income" consists solely of services as received by ultimate consumers, whether from their material or from their human environment which together might be called "social wealth" or "capital." Social wealth consists not only of producers' real capital such as plant and equipment but also of what are nowadays called "common property resources" as well as geological capital and consumers' real capital. In this scheme, "production" is defined as an addition to this social wealth and "consumption" as a subtraction from it. Since "income" is essentially proportional to the stock of social wealth, "consumption" would have a negative effect on "income" while the effect of "production" would be positive. It is worth recording that Pigou, who took issue with Fisher over this problem, conceded that Fisher's conceptual scheme would be appropriate if one were interested in "comparative amounts of economic welfare which a community obtains over a long series of years."[23] It is precisely for this purpose that we might resuscitate the Fisherian concepts which focus upon "stocks" rather than "flows" when we are interested in the welfare aspect of the economy.

The questionable effects of the exceptionally rapid rate of growth in terms of GNP in Japan made us keenly aware of the significance of such an alternative, broadening farther the scope of social wealth to include not only nonmaterial elements of "common property resources" such as natural beauty but also knowledge and skills accumulated and embodied in the human factor of production. The heightened awareness in this respect marks an aspect of the turning point in Japan's "growthmanship" at the beginning of the decade of the 1970s; and coincidentally, the Club of Rome Report of 1972 and the Stockholm Conference on Human Environment with the slogan of "Only one earth," also in 1972, echoed the similar awareness on an international scale.

It was only logical perhaps that the disaffection with the GNP-focused "growthmanship" prompted many of us in Japan to recall, with concurrence, a long-forgotten dictum of John Stuart Mill, namely: "It is scarcely necessary to remark that a stationary condition of capital and production implies no stationary state of human improvement. There would be as much scope as ever for all kinds of mental culture, and moral and social progress; as much room for improving the Art of Living, and much more likelihood of its being improved, when minds ceased to be engrossed by the art of getting on."[24]

6   The double "price revolution"

The oil-shock "price revolution" was external in origin; but the "price revolution" in urban land was internally caused. And the coincidental impact of the two, the most important factors of production, oil and land, both ubiquitously essential for industrial activities, caused upset and exhilaration to the capitalist class. Upset, because a major readjustment was required in the accustomed use of industrial energy; and exhilaration, because opportunities for speculative gains on urban land could be seized.

Price effects of the oil shock were big enough; but needed policy adjustments in search for alternative energy sources and the attempts to economize the use of petroleum were more far-reaching than what the official experts at first envisaged. Thus the supply and demand schedules of primary energy sources had to be drastically revised during the decade of the 1970s, with a consequential appeal by the government to the public for the acceptance of the "nuclear age."

The "price revolution" in urban land, on the other hand, was concerned with a factor of production for which alternatives are essentially nonexistent and the efficiency improvement in use is generally limited. Thus the out-of-balance rising trend in urban land continued unabated till the end of the 1980s, creating the "myth of land value" with a widespread orgy of speculative actions. Hesitancy on the part of the government in dealing with this was rooted in the century-old precept of the inviolability of private property rights, which is critically examined here.

This chapter closes with a brief discussion of macroeconomic mismanagement in connection with the inflation of 1972–74, the time when the double "price revolutions" were visiting on Japan.

1. The coinciding of two "price revolutions"

It was becoming patently clear as the decade of the 1970s progressed that the special growth-promoting factors which had sustained a 10 percent growth rate in Japan for almost two decades were weakening in their vitality and a turning point was in sight. Then, the first oil shock of 1973–74, constituting a kind of "price revolution," had a dramatic effect upon the Japanese business world, making them suddenly aware that major cost adjustments were needed in many of the industries that had prospered under the condition of abundant availability of oil at a magnanimously low price.

It happened, however, that another "price revolution" was visiting Japan almost at the same time – the "price revolution" of urban and factory land, stimulated by the Kakuei Tanaka's "Plan for Remodeling of the Japanese Archipelago" of 1972. Inordinate rise in land prices had started already at the time of the "Income-Doubling Plan" of 1960; but there was a breathing spell in this upsurge for about a decade until 1972 when the second period of high tide in land prices in postwar Japan began. Then, the expression "maddening rise" was used by government officials themselves. Although the annual rate of increase in urban land prices during 1972 to 1973 was within the range of less than 40 percent, compared with the fourfold rise in oil prices within a mere three months, a degree of out-of-balance inflation of urban land price measured against the rise in wholesale price index was 13 to 1 by March 1975 taking 1956 as the base year for both.[1] The rising trend of land prices, in other words, had been more sustained, though by some fits and starts, with the first high tide during 1960–62 and the second one almost coinciding with the first oil shock of 1973–74.

Thus we speak of a double "price revolution" visiting Japan in the early 1970s, occurring in two of the most important factors of production, oil and land, both ubiquitously essential for industrial activities. It may be appropriate, therefore, to insert a brief digression on the classical case of price revolution.

2. The classical case of price revolution

We usually understand the expression "the price revolution" to be referring to the inordinate rise of prices in European countries during the early sixteenth century and the first half of the seventeenth. According to Earl J. Hamilton, "Early in the sixteenth century the trend of prices turned upward in Spain, first and most rapidly in Andalusia, and rose for a hundred years, with practically all troughs and peaks above the preceding ones. Andalusian prices more than doubled in the first half of the sixteenth century and more than quintupled by its close. Prices increased fourfold in New Castile, the region closest to Andalusia, and three and one-half-fold in Old Castile-Leon and in Valencia."[2] There is no doubt that "the chief cause of the Price Revolution ... was the great increase in the money supply ... [In particular] it was the explosive rise in silver production after the conquests of Mexico and Peru; the discovery of the fabulous mines of Zacatecas, Guanajuato, and Potosi; and the introduction of the mercury amalgamation process of mining in the middle of the sixteenth century that generated the Price Revolution."[3]

It is noteworthy that in the process of this price revolution money wages lagged significantly, to the extent, for example, of only a one-fifth rise in England in the sixteenth century when prices were rising 150 percent. Keynes accepts this fact of wage lag to mean that "the greater part of the fruits of the economic progress and capital accumulation of the Elizabethan and Jacobean ages accrued to the profiteer rather than to the wage-earner,"[4] and he goes on to say that "never in the annals of the modern world has there existed so prolonged and so rich an opportunity for the business man, the speculator and the profiteer."[5]

So it was. It was characteristic of this classical instance of price revolution, caused by an exogenous disturbance of the balance between the metallic monetary stock and the supply of commodities, to have had the effect of bringing about a new *relative price structure*, in favor of profits against wages, that contributed to the development of the modern capitalist system.

To be sure, in the annals of economic vicissitudes of many countries there have occurred numerous instances of inflationary price rises comparable to, or often larger in scale than that of the "price revolution." Consider, for example, French hyperinflation in the 1790s under the assignats and mandats, the US experience of greenbacks during the Civil War of 1861–65, the astronomical inflation of Germany in the wake of the First World War, the hundredfold price rise in Japan between 1944 and 1949, and so forth. These instances, however, were cases of *general* price rise occasioned by abnormal imbalances of aggregate supply and demand and were allowed to occur through the uncontrolled or uncontrollable issue of inconvertible paper currency.

The case of the Spanish price revolution was distinctly different from these in that a more or less sudden and considerable shift in the relative price structure was caused by an exogenous single factor, whereas the major factors in the other cases were the excessive demand due to war and its concomitants and the unrestrained use of inconvertible paper money. Considering this contrast, we may speak of a "new price revolution" in connection both with the oil shock of 1973–74 and the upheaval in urban land prices of 1972–73 in Japan. In both cases, the price item which went out of balance was an almost universally used factor of production, and it could be expected that the general principle of economic efficiency would dictate either a substitution by another factor wherever possible or adoption of an alternative method with a more economic use of the factor in question. We

Table 6.1. *The rise in wholesale price indexes compared with one year earlier (%)*

	October 1973	July 1974
USA	16.5	20.4
UK	13.1	25.1
West Germany	6.8	15.6
France	16.9	25.8
Italy	20.6	41.3
Japan	19.1	34.2

Source: Yoshikazu Miyazaki, *Atarashii Kakaku Kakumei* (A New Price Revolution), 1975, p.117.

shall see how the "double price revolution" affected the Japanese economy as the decade of the 1970s advanced and beyond.

3. The consequences of the oil-shock price revolution

Price effects of the oil shock

The consequences of the oil-price revolution were naturally world-wide. The price of Middle East oil of standard quality rose within three months (from October 1, 1973 to January 1, 1974) from $3.01 per barrel to $11.65, or almost four times. Actually, there had been a gradual rise from the end of 1970, when the price quoted was $1.8 per barrel.[6] Subsequent to such price rises of crude oil, the wholesale price indices of major advanced countries registered more or less sudden upward trends almost without exception, as shown in Table 6.1. True, contributory to this inflationary trend were the consequences of the US decision in August 1971 to abandon gold convertibility. Immediately following Nixon's announcement of this policy, the price of gold in the London market started to rise, registering $115.60 per ounce in July 1973 compared with $37.375 in 1970. And, along with the price of gold, the prices of various internationally traded commodities began surging upward, starting from the spring of 1972. Thus the Reuters Index of agricultural and mining products nearly doubled between June 1972 and June 1973. Still, the quadrupling of the oil price in 1973 was a major factor in the subsequent realignment of the *relative price structure*, in which the cost of energy and raw materials began occupying a permanently greater share. It is also noteworthy that in the case of the oil-price revolution, as contrasted with the case of the classical price

Table 6.2. *Energy consumption and its sources – selected years*

Total energy consumption (1933 = 100)	Sources – relative shares (%)				
	Petroleum	Coal	Hydro	Others	Total
1933	100	8	69	12	11	100
1948	100	5	60	21	14	100
1966	500	60	26	11	3	100
1975	1,000	72	18	6	4	100

Source: The Institute of Energy Economics, Japan.

revolution, which provided a great opportunity for the burgeoning capitalist class, Third World countries – in particular, the OPEC countries – have been in a position to benefit by the development of their economies out of the centuries-long oppression and exploitation by advanced countries. The significance of price revolution in both cases, the classical and the latest, has lain in a historical shift in the power relations of an enduring character.

Policy adjustments in Japan – desiderata and constraints

What then were the consequences of the oil-price revolution on the Japanese economy? As for the more or less immediate *negative* consequences of the first oil-shock, we have already given a summary review in the last chapter.[7] The question remains here to take up the problem of *positive* policy adjustments, i.e. the search for alternative energy sources and the attempt to economize the use of petroleum.

For this purpose it might be appropriate here to review the trend of increase in energy consumption in Japan and also the changing composition of the sources of primary energy, as shown in Table 6.2. In roughly thirty years following the war, energy consumption in Japan increased tenfold and the sources shifted dramatically from coal to petroleum, the latter in 1975 occupying 72 percent of the total – relatively the highest among the OECD countries.

We may also summarize here the characteristics of the energy situation which came to stay with Japan in the period of rapid economic growth of the early 1950s to the decade of 1970s. The following features can be cited:

1 The degree of dependence on imports is extremely high – approximately 88 percent in the more recent years.

2 The share occupied by petroleum in the total supply of primary energy is

very high – 60 to 72 percent as shown in Table 6.2; and almost the whole of it is imported.

3 The share of industrial consumption is higher than in most countries – 57 percent (in 1975) of the total primary energy use as compared with a one-third level in most western countries.[8]

4 The part which goes into generation of electricity out of primary energy sources is higher than most other countries – approximately one-third.

Against such background the Japanese government had to face up to the inevitable impact of the oil-price revolution in various spheres of the economy, forced in particular to revise the demand and supply projection for overall energy. It was immediately foreseen that the search for alternative energy sources other than petroleum and the attempt to economize the use of petroleum were urgent. For one thing, an important consideration constituting a datum for the discussion of energy problems is the time required for dynamic adjustment of any sort. For example, the lead time needed for setting up a new electricity generating plant in Japan is said to be about ten years; and the replacement of an oil-burning plant by a coal-burning one would also require a gestation period of considerable duration. Thus, the starting point for any overall discussion on energy policies of a country has to be a projection of the country's demand and supply of energies at least ten years ahead based on the most complex assessment of desiderata, possibilities and feasibilities of all kinds. One can start such a projection first by placing major emphases on more or less objective constraints and then introduce adjustments that can predictably be counted on as consequences of deliberate policy measures.

What were the desiderata and constraints which the Japanese government had to take into account as they proceeded to respond to the impact of the oil-price revolution? One overriding desideratum was the maintenance of reasonably full employment in the decade that followed, which could be expressed in terms of a certain *minimum* rate of growth in real GNP. Most experts, in and out of the government, felt at the time that the figure of 6 percent per annum for the following decade was the floor below which unemployment would accumulate unless a work-sharing system of a fairly revolutionary character could be instituted. Given the industrial structure, which would necessarily take time to make a radical shift, the full employment desideratum set the boundary for the overall demand for industrial use of energy.

What were the constraints other than the lead time for new construction mentioned above? The major consideration on the supply side constraint for Japan were the problems related to the importation of petroleum. At the time of the oil-price revolution, i.e., in the middle of the 1970s, the major source of supply for Japan was the Middle East area, with Saudi Arabia

(33.8 percent), Iran (17.0 percent), United Arab Emirates (11.4 percent), Kuwait (8.3 percent), Oman (3.7 percent) and Iraq (3.1 percent), together supplying 77.3 percent of the total in 1977, and Indonesia (13.6 percent) and Brunei (3.4 percent) in the Asian region filling up 17 percent. In other words, the Middle East oil was of paramount importance for Japan, with a further implication that the shipping route from that region to Japan had to be secured under all circumstances. The stranding of a mammoth tanker (Shōwa-maru) in the Malacca Straits in January 1975 with the resulting oil spill of 4,500 kl triggered restrictive measures by the countries in the region on the navigation of supertankers through the Straits and brought to the fore dramatically the precariousness of the shipping route of petroleum to which Japan had been accustomed. Thus, inevitably, the energy problem for Japan spilled over into international political and diplomatic complications, even to the extent of Japan being pressurized by America to extend its "defence" sea-lane as far out as 1,000 nautical miles, allegedly to lighten the burden of the US fleet in the area which constituted a life line for oil imports to Japan.

Another constraint, of course, is an environmental one, which has been gaining much more importance in recent years. At the time of the first oil shock, the environmental concern as regards energy problems in Japan centered especially upon the use of nuclear power, on which the authorities were placing major emphasis as an alternative energy source to replace petroleum. For some time until about October 1975 the official target for 1985 was the generating capacity of 60,000,000 kW in the nuclear power field, with an interim target of 31,770,000 kW by the end of 1980. Public consensus, however, was slow to come in Japan in the nuclear field, the country having had the unique experience of atomic bombing towards the end of the last war. Some people refer to such sensitivity as a case of "nuclear allergy"; but, as is now well known, the Japanese are not exceptional in being hesitant to accept what is often called the "Faustian Bargain." Meanwhile, the government attempted to expedite the construction of new plants by increasing further the degree of subsidy to those regions agreeing to site the new nuclear plants. But citizens' opposition flared up in a number of places, forcing a slowdown in the pace of construction. Thus the earlier target of 60,000,000 kW for 1985 (in the 1970 projection) was far from attained, the actual capacity in 1988 being 28,900,000 kW.

Another source of energy with environmental implications is geothermal energy developed by tapping the deep subterranean layer of 3,000 meters or more. Exploratory research had already begun with a prospect of eventually constructing an electricity generating plant of 2 million to 3 million kW capacity at each site. Practically available total resources in this sphere in Japan are estimated to amount to 145 million kW capacity of electricity. A major hurdle here, however, lies in the fact that most of the sites suitable for the purpose are within the boundary of national parks so that environmental considerations stand in the way.

The environmental implications of the energy problems we have discussed above concern the search for alternative sources of supply; but, needless to say, the relation of the energy problem to environment is far broader and more complex, as Dr Charles J. Hitch, president of Resources for the Future, wrote:

Energy is an environmental problem. Energy production and consumption combine to form the world's greatest environmental assault. The list of effects is long and ugly: death for coal miners from cave-ins and black lung; air pollution from electric power generation, industrial processes, and automobiles; an increase in the proportion of carbon dioxide in the atmosphere, perhaps leading to adverse changes in climate having far-reaching implications; ocean oil spills; water pollution from acid mine drainage; scarring of strip-mined landscapes.[9]

We could easily expand the list of specific environmental implications of the energy problem in Japan, notably, for example, the damage to natural beauty and coastal amenities due to the construction of power-generating plants on reclaimed land. But for our purpose here it is not necessary to dwell upon such problems any further, except to emphasize the importance of environmental concern as one of the non-negligible constraints on the development of alternative sources of energy.

Projection of supply and demand of energy

On the basis of desiderata and constraints and also of the practical possibilities of economizing of energy in industries and household, the Overall Energy Research Commission (OERC), a governmental consultative body, proceeded to tackle the question of revising the near-future outlook of supply and demand of energy for Japan as they foresaw the irreversible trend of the oil-price rise following the first oil shock of 1973–74. Such a revision took place almost every other year, the latest (at the time of this writing) being the one in 1990. When we review this process of revision, we cannot but be impressed by the vagaries of the age of uncertainty, such that even the collective wisdom of competent experts had to undergo a series of drastic overhauling of their own product in the manner of Penelope's Web. We may summarize here a few bench-mark figures of major items in the OERC projection along with some actually attained statistics (see Table 6.3). It is remarkable that the actual figures for 1988 for the three items turned out to be one-half or less than one-half of the projected figures for 1985 as estimated in 1970 and that even the most recent

Table 6.3. *The energy supply: projection and actual*

	Total primary energy in petroleum equivalent (10^6 kiloliter)	Petroleum imports (10^6 kiloliter)	Nuclear power capacity (10^6 kW)
Projection for 1985			
July 1970	933–1,029	650–723	60.0
June 1977	660	432	33.0
Projection for 2000			
June 1990	597	308	50.5
Actual			
1975	390	288	6.6
1988	482	276	28.9

Source: Overall Energy Research Commission.

projected figures for 2000 are still substantially below the projected figures for 1985 as estimated in the post-oil-shock year of 1977 except the one for nuclear-power capacity.

Compared with the earlier table (Table 6.2) which showed that petroleum occupied 72 percent of the total energy consumption in 1975, the actual figures for 1988 shown in Table 6.3 reveal that the share of petroleum imports[10] in the total primary energy declined to 57.3 percent and suggest that alternative sources filled the gap. Shares of coal and hydro remained more or less the same between 1975 and 1988, whereas those of nuclear power and natural gas increased significantly. Still, the fact that the total primary energy actually consumed in 1988 was about one-half of the projected figure for 1985 as estimated in 1970 must mean that a sizable economy was achieved in the use of energy as an inevitable consequence of the oil-price revolution.

Possibilities of economizing of energy

How then was the economy achieved? Table 6.4 gives average annual rates of change in the consumption of energy by three sectors (industrial, household and transportation) between bench-mark years. The second oil shock came in 1979; and we gather from Table 6.4 that its impact was greater in every sector than that of the first oil shock and also that the industrial sector was able to economize the use of energy following both. Since the index of industrial production recorded the average annual rates

Table 6.4. *Changes in energy consumption by sectors*
(unit: %)

	Industries	Household	Transportation	Total
Between 1969 and 1973	+ 8.5	+ 11.5	+ 9.2	+ 9.2
Between 1973 and 1979	− 0.8	+ 3.3	+ 4.2	+ 0.9
Between 1979 and 1986	− 2.1	+ 1.9	+ 1.3	− 0.4
Between 1986 and 1988	+ 5.4	+ 5.3	+ 4.8	+ 5.3

Source: Ministry of Trade and Industry.

of increase of 2.0 percent between 1973 and 1979 and of 3.1 percent between 1979 and 1986, it can be inferred that energy efficiency was definitely improved in the industrial sector as a whole.

As for the household sector, the record of the economy drive showed only a modicum of success. But this might be partly explained by the fact that as of around 1975 the average use of primary energy by Japanese households was relatively smaller than in other Western advanced countries and was in the process of catching up. The energy intensity of per capita GNP can be compared among several countries by the ratio of the relatives of both of the two quantities with the figures for the US as 100, as in Table 6.5 which refers to the year 1975. It is instructive to note that the relative energy intensity of per capita GNP in 1975, with the then prevailing exchange rates, was lowest for Japan compared with other Western countries. This relation would turn out to be more strikingly clear if the more recent exchange rate were applied for Japan *vis-à-vis* the US – 150 yen to a dollar instead of 300 yen which prevailed in 1975.

Compared with most other countries in the West, Japan may be said to have less leeway in economizing the use of energy in the household sector, favored as she is with a more moderate climate than others and being able to rely on an efficient and economical mass transport system for urban centers. More important in the order of magnitude would be the energy-saving consequences of the shift in Japan's industrial structure and also of the shift in the media of transportation in general. In particular, the latter harbors non-negligible possibilities depending on the policies adopted by the government. Table 6.6, which presents energy coefficients per unit of transport on the assumption of 100 percent load factor, suggests such possibilities that exist in Japan today.

The use of energy for transport purposes in 1975 amounted to 70×10^{13} kcal, or almost 20 percent of the total primary energies in Japan in that year; and energy economy in this sector could make a significant enough

Table 6.5. *The energy intensity of per capita GNP – an international comparison (1975)*

	Per capita GNP (dollars)	Relatives (A)	Per capita consumption of energy in the household (10^3 kcal)	Relatives (B)	(B) (A)
USA	7,120	100	26,304	100	1.00
West Germany	6,670	94	14,774	56	0.60
France	5,950	84	11,253	43	0.51
Japan	4,450	63	7,173	27	0.43
UK	3,780	53	13,420	51	0.96
Italy	2,810	39	7,408	28	0.72

Source: The per capita GNP figures are taken from *World Bank Atlas*, 1977, and the energy consumption figures from the Institute of Energy Economics Studies, Japan.

Table 6.6. *Energy coefficients per unit of transport*

For freight	Mode	Capacity	kcal per ton-km
	Trucks	8 ton	320
	Electric railway	500 ton	50
	Freight-ships	499 G/T	60
For passengers	Mode	Capacity (persons)	kcal per man-km
	Bus	50	60
	Passenger car	5	190
	Commuting train	144	30
	"Bullet" train	100	70
	B747-SR	498	100

Note:
100 percent load factor assumed.
Source: The Ministry of Transportation, Japanese Government.

contribution to the achieving of energy viability for Japan. But, in actual fact, the choice made by household and business of the media of transport is dependent on so many factors that the market mechanism does not necessarily achieve the state of maximum efficiency in energy use. In recent years the use of energy-efficient railroad media has been steadily declining in relative shares, especially in the field of freight transport, and the per-unit coefficient of energy in the transport sector as a whole has been on the increase. The problem involved here is not only that of changing the patterns of user preference *cum* cost factors but also the institutional peculiarities which pertain to the public-corporate character of the national railroad together with the different degrees of internalization of external effects for various modes of transport. It was to be expected that the imperative of energy efficiency would force the authorities to tackle these seemingly intractable problems more seriously than before.

In spite of the drastic reduction in the overall energy use by 1988 compared with the erstwhile projection before the first oil shock visited Japan, the prospect for the future at the time the OERC presented its so-called "Interim Report" in June 1990 was an exceptionally gloomy one. Although Masashi Yamamoto, who had served as head of the Resources and Energy Agency of the government, did congratulate himself in achieving an energy economy of 36 percent per unit of GNP between 1973 and 1988, or the reduction in the use of energy (in petroleum equivalent) per 100 million yen of GNP from 225 kl in 1973 to 144 kl in 1988, Shūzō Inaba, chairman of the OERC, made it clear that the overall reduction called for between 1988 and 2000 would be such that this per-GNP energy use would have to come down further to 92.3 kl even under the assumption that nuclear power capacity could be increased to 50 million kW, that is, by 40 percent in 12 years. Inaba has appealed in particular to the general public, saying that: "Either accept the nuclear age for our energy supply, or reduce substantially your use of electricity at home and of gasolene for your cars!"

Consequences of the oil-price revolution still linger on.

4. Price revolution in urban land

Skyrocketing of urban land price

Although both energy and land are indispensable basic factors of production and consumption in the present-day life of every society, there is a marked contrast between the two when confronted with a price revolution. In the case of energy, as we have discussed in the last section, alternative sources of supply are available in various forms and the economizing methods are often effective even in the short run. But, in the case of land, alternative sources are essentially non-existent and the efficiency improvement in use is generally limited. Of course, reclamation of shallow beach areas can increase the supply of land and the measures to shift agricultural land to factory sites can respond to the changing demand; but the order of magnitude here is not very large, limited as these steps are by the constraints of complementary requirements. Efficiency improvement in the use of land is also possible, as exemplified by intensive cultivation in agriculture and also by the construction of sky-scrapers in cities. But here, again, in the context of urban congestion in Japan today, environmental constraints of various kinds as well as the woeful lag in the provision of sewerage facilities stand in the way of constructing high-rise buildings. Thus, in a sense it was inevitable that in the process of rapid economic growth demand for urban land tended to outstrip supply, causing a more or less continuous rise in its price.

As a matter of fact, the price of urban land in Japan did not keep its pace of upward trend with the general inflation during the war and immediately after the war. If we take September 1936 as our prewar base, the land price of urban districts (national average) registered only a 2.6 times increase by January 1946 while the wholesale price index showed a 7.6 times rise, and by March 1951 the gap between the two indexes became still wider, the former rising by 76.0 times against 318.7 times in the latter. It was only in 1956 that the two indexes with the prewar base came to be balanced. Thus, there is a good enough ground for us to take 1956 as the base year for the purpose of comparing the price movement of urban land with the movement of wholesale prices. Incidentally, the choice of 1956 as our base may further be justified by the fact that the per capita real income of the nation more or less regained its prewar level in that year.

Since 1956 the wholesale price index kept a fair degree of stability until the time of the first oil shock, rising by 17 percent over those 17 years. On the other hand, the trend of urban land prices tells a different story. As was mentioned at the beginning of this chapter, there was a distinct period of upheaval at the time of the "Income-Doubling Plan" of 1960 and then another one, associated with the "Plan for Remodeling of the Japanese Archipelago" of 1972. This latter upheaval almost coincided with the first oil shock and we chose to refer to it as the "price revolution" of landed property. The high tide of land prices did not quite subside even after this "price revolution" period, and the third upheaval began in 1986. Thus altogether, it may be said that Japan has experienced three high tides of urban land price in the period after 1956; and it will be convenient to deal with them as a single, interrelated topic.

Let us, first of all, summarize statistical records in the form of comparing the price movement of urban land with that implied in the wholesale price index. For this purpose we take the index of urban land prices of the six largest cities and the Bank of Japan wholesale price index, rebase them both to March 1956, and then take ratios between the two by dividing the former by the latter. If the two indexes moved *pari passu*, such a ratio would be unity; and if the ratio is shown to be 2, it means that the urban land price rose twice as fast as the wholesale price index, provided of course that both were on the rise. Now, the following series shows how such ratios turned out for bench-mark years after 1956.

1956 (March)	1.0	
1959 (September)	2.2	"First high tide"
1962 (March)	6.1	
1971 (September)	15.0	"Second high tide"
1973 (March)	20.2	
1986 (March)	25.2	"Third high tide"
1990 (March)	68.2	

We can see that the gap which kept on widening was of horrendous size. Between 1956 and 1990, the wholesale price index rose approximately twice while the average of land prices in big cities rose 145 times, creating the gap of 68.2 to 1.

Capital gains generated

What does this mean? It means that while a commodity costing one dollar wholesale in 1956 was priced at two dollars in 1990, a unit of urban land which cost one dollar in 1956 was priced at 145 dollars in 1990. *Prima facie*, this may sound unbelievable; but this was actually the case. The implication is that there was generated a huge volume of capital gains in the process. How large was such a volume? One official estimate made by the Economic Planning Agency[11] reveals that in *one* year, 1987, it amounted to 416 trillion yen for the country as a whole – an amount which exceeded Japan's GNP of that year (343 trillion yen) by more than 20 percent. A similar calculation made for the US recorded the capital gains in landed property in 1987 as occupying about 5 percent of GNP,[12] and we can see the quite extraordinary uniqueness of the Japanese situation. Needless to say, during the thirty odd years between 1956 and 1990, while the urban land price rose 145 times, the total accumulated amount of capital gains in landed property must have been a multiple of the figure cited for the year of 1987; and a question immediately comes to our minds as regards the forms and destinations of these capital gains.

The first round in the destination of capital gains consists of three forms: (1) direct absorption through taxes; (2) gains realized in the market; and (3) latent gains which remain unrealized.

As for the direct absorption through taxes, we have a fairly accurate estimate inasmuch as the relevant taxes are the real estate tax, the gift tax and the inheritance tax, all of which are based on unambiguous records of land areas. It is true that the *effective* rate of the real estate tax is as low as 0.05 percent of the market value of land, as compared with the rate of 1 percent or more in other developed countries. But while the market price of land has risen 145 times in thirty odd years, it was inevitable that the effective rate had to lag. If the effective rate were 1 percent, for example, in 1990, the real estate tax alone would exceed the annual income of most house-and-land-owning urban dwellers. A more plausible comparison with other countries would be to take the ratio of the total real estate tax paid to the country's GNP; and such a comparison reveals that the burden of the real estate tax in Japan in recent years has been higher than in France or West Germany, i.e., 1.6 percent of GNP in 1988 against 1.2 percent in France and 0.8 percent in West Germany. In fact, such ratio nearly doubled between 1970 and 1988 in Japan.[13] Absorption of capital gains in land via the inheritance tax has been of relatively much bigger magnitude, occupying in recent years around 70 percent of the total inheritance tax liabilities and increasing from 700 billion yen in 1980 to 2.4 trillion yen in 1987, or more than three times. It is, indeed, paradoxical that the very act of attempting to save the tax liability, which has inordinately risen because of the speculative rise in land prices, is creating an increased demand for landed property for the reason that the debt incurred for the purchase is fully deductible from the inheritance tax liability while the assessment of the land value is on the basis of the so-called "route rates" which are far below the market price.[14]

The second destination of the capital gains in land pertains to the part which is *realized*. When the price has risen as much as 145 times in thirty odd years, creating what has come to be called "The Myth of Land Value," it is only natural that even lay people, let alone financial experts, would be tempted to take advantage of the circumstance to make money through the purchase and sale of land. Capital gains tax could be an impediment. However, not only has this tax been quite lenient, but also it has been a common practice to draw up two contracts, one for the actual transaction and another, with a much lower declared price, for tax purposes. Thus, the official revenue statistics on capital gains tax do not convey to us the true picture of the extent and magnitude of the realized part of capital gains. Concrete episodes abound, however, as reported in the mass media, of the so-called "land-rolling," which means repeated purchase and sale of the same piece of land at a successively higher price often within a short span of a few years. There also arose a new profession of "Ji-age-ya," which, distinct from ordinary real estate dealers and speculators, engages in the job of enclosing, as it were, adjacent small pieces of land owned by different persons into a bigger unit and selling it for a big profit. Many a place in the heart of big cities has lost its historical neighborhood atmosphere in this manner. Needless to say, the profession of ordinary real estate dealers, as well as that of lawyers associated with them, has prospered markedly during these decades of land price boom and as a consequence increased its membership, if not its prestige.

Finally, the third form which capital gains in land takes in the initial round is the *unrealized* latent gains remaining in the possession of owners. It is not easy to estimate the part which remains in this form through the duration of each of the "high tide" periods. But there is an official estimate by the Economic Planning Agency showing that capital gains accruing to land-owning households during a single year of 1987 amounted to 267 trillion yen (whether realized or unrealized), which figure should be compared with the aggregate income of the gainfully employed in the same year, amounting to 189 trillion yen. From this fact it is safe enough to infer that a major portion of the capital gains in that year must have remained unrealized in the case of land-owning households – a circumstance that is understandable for the case of most small-size individual shop-owners in cities (classified in the category of households) for whom their land-ownership is nothing less than their living right itself. For the house-owning salaried men also, any temptation to realize capital gains in the small plot of land they own is likely, in most cases, to be overcome by their much stronger desire to continue to live at the same place with accustomed associations with the neighborhood shops, parks, schools, etc. Moreover, the cost in time and money in finding and moving to an alternative place of abode is often prohibitive.

The case for corporate business firms as regards latent capital gains is radically different. For them, also, the magnitude of unrealized capital gains is inordinately large. The National Land Agency submitted an official report to the governmental Tax Deliberation Committee in which the contrasting figures for 1970 and 1988 as regards the land holdings of business firms were given as follows (in billion yen):[15]

	Book Value	Value at "Posted Prices"	Latent Capital Gains
1970	7,600	42,500	34,900
1988	80,600	514,500	433,900
Increase	73,000	472,000	399,000

In other words, capital gains remaining unrealized increased by about 400 trillion yen in 18 years. What is more significant in this report are the answers given by the investigated firms to the question of what the reasons were for keeping their land unutilized: 9 percent of them replied in 1978, saying that they "had no intention of utilizing such land from the very beginning." The percentage of firms replying in this manner in 1989 increased to 50. Furthermore, in this latter year, the report reveals, there were no plans for utilization for no less than 78 percent of the unutilized land area owned by the business firms. From this report, the inference is unavoidable that corporate business firms in general have been engaged in speculative investment in land, taking full advantage of the "ratchet effect" of land prices. The role played by financial institutions of all kinds in this orgy of land speculation can hardly be doubted; and it is a topic in itself when we come to the question of countermeasures against the land price revolution.

One significant implication of the latent capital gains in the possession of corporate firms is their favorable effect on the security price of the firms concerned. An example may be taken from the case of the giant corporation: Shin Nihon Seitetsu (New Japan Steel Manufacturing). It owns 8,300 hectares of land, valued at "at least 8.2 trillion yen."[16] The company reported a deficit in the current account of more than 100 million yen for the term ending in March 1988. However, the market price of its common stock kept on rising in the following fashion (unit in yen):

	Highest	Lowest
1986	276	153
1987	454	168
1988	969	353

When a newspaper man commented critically on the effect of a large holding of unutilized land on the company's stock price, Mr Eishiro Saito, the leader of the company, made an extenuating reply, saying that "our stock price has not yet risen to a four-digit figure."[17] He added in strong words that any idea of taxing unrealized capital gains is tantamount to the negation of the basic tenet of free enterprise, reflecting as he did the dominant opinion of the business world in Japan at present.

We have reviewed the first round in the destination of capital gains, generated through the 145 times rise in urban land price in 34 years while the wholesale price index was only doubling. There are, of course, subsequent rounds, such as how the realized gains were spent and what were the effects on the governmental tax revenue situation as a whole. But we must now turn to a discussion of the major causes of the land price revolution.

5. Major causes of price revolution in land

The meaning of private property right

An event in the socio-economic sphere can be caused by both actions and inactions; and, in the case of the price revolution in land, inactions might have been more important than actions. We suspect this, because three successive "high tides" in land prices beginning in 1960, resulting in the 145-times increase in urban land price over thirty odd years, must have made the Japanese government aware during that time that positive countermeasures were called for, to ward off, if nothing else, a threatened outbreak of mass protest movement in urban areas. In spite of this, the government did little or nothing by way of putting the brakes on and countering the trend. For one thing, many of the politicians in the ruling party[18] have been beneficiaries of the land-price revolution and had a good enough reason not to dry up an important source of their political funds. But the typical excuse given in justification of the "do-nothing" policy on the land-price upheaval was that "we can do nothing in breach of the constitutional clause guaranteeing the right to own property as 'inviolable,'" as was remarked in 1965 by Mr Ichiro Kōno, a leading conservative politician who had served as Minister of Construction as well as Minister of Local Autonomous Bodies.[19]

True enough, Article 29 of the Constitution of Japan, promulgated in November 1946, reads: "The right to own or to hold property is inviolable." And this clause repeats Article 27 of the prewar Constitution of Japan of 1889, the "inviolability" concept going back to the French declaration of the rights of man (1789) and repeated so often in the capitalist world ever since. Jeremy Bentham, in particular among economists, defended the right of property as an aspect of natural rights, "a right which it is the business of law not to infringe but to secure."[20]

But it has been well said that "concepts of property are subject to the endless erosion of time" (Ernest Beaglehole).[21] And it was none other than the occupying authorities, under General Douglas MacArthur (SCAP), who proposed in a draft constitution for Japan in 1946 the concept that "the ultimate fee to the land and to all natural resources reposes in the State as the collective representative of the people." We had an occasion to take up this problem in Chapter 1 in some detail in connection with the postwar Occupational reforms, and there we related the manner in which the Japanese government strongly resisted this SCAP proposal and succeeded finally in replacing it with the wording we now find in the Constitution. Subsequently, however, heated discussion ensued among legal specialists in Japan, a discussion that centered on the question of what was meant by "the guaranteeing of the private property right." On the one hand, an opinion was expressed by Professor Teruhisa Ishii, for example, to the effect that in Japan "the social and public-interest aspect of property rights" has not been sufficiently appreciated and that as a result the government authorities have been unnecessarily timid in restraining aberrant claims allegedly based on property rights. On the other hand, a pertinent point was made when Professor Masamichi Rōyama called attention to the fact that the economic value of properties is bound to change in accordance with the mutations in social structure and conditions, and that it is impossible to guarantee property rights as a "basic human right" independent of their quantitative dimensions. Japan's legal minds wrestled with this problem and finally arrived at the formulation on the content of property rights by Professor Sakae Wagatsuma, which came to be accepted by many of the specialists in the field. His proposal was to define "property rights" in Article 29 of the Constitution as "the right pertaining to that property which individuals have earned and accumulated through their own labor and/or capital in the conditions of free competition."[22]

From the standpoint of economists, this definition is fairly restrictive. For one thing, the conditions of *free competition* prevail in a modern society only in very limited spheres of activities. More important, external factors (e.g. the increasingly social character of production that accompanies technological sophistication) create positive and negative effects for individuals. There are almost no isolated cases of individuals who can claim that they have "earned and accumulated [their property] through their own labor and/or capital" *alone*. This is especially evident in the case of an individual for whom a piece of land he had owned appreciated in value through, for example, the opening of a new railroad line nearby. The windfall gain in such a case could be as high as 300 percent of the initial value of the land within 8 years, as the 1988 government White Paper on Construction has officially admitted. It is a commentary on this feverish situation that a transferable membership deed for the Koganei Golf Course is priced at 400 million yen (approximately twice the lifetime earning of an ordinary salaried man) in the market, because the said golf course, situated fairly close to the urbanized area in Tokyo, is rumored to be undergoing liquidation in the near future for urban development. The windfall involved would be more than one thousand times the price forty years ago. It is clear enough that some kind of tax measure is called for to absorb this kind of windfall. In other words, in speaking of "the inviolable property right" as regards landed property, it is essential that we analyze the components of price formation for land, particularly for urban land, in present-day Japan.

Price formation of urban land

As with any other object for sale, it may be said in the first instance that the price of land is a function of supply and demand. Supply of land, on the one hand, is often said to be fixed, depicted for the textbook purpose as a straight vertical line on the P–Q quadrant. But this would be a drastic simplification inasmuch as the relevant supply, aside from the possibility of creating new land space through reclamation, is usually regional and of a specific quality, whether for agricultural, residential, or commercial purposes. Demand, on the other hand, is generally a derived demand, and the imputed price offered is based on the value of the products and the marginal productivity of the land concerned.

We can discuss the price formation of land in these terms, but we have to warn ourselves immediately that such discussion is premised on the productive use of land; that is to say, here is implied the right of utilization, not necessarily the property right as such. When the property right is the major concern, the holding of land for speculative purpose would be a normal pattern of behavior, and it is most likely, in the period when a sustained price rise is expected, that what is known as "reserved demand" will arise. Given the ratchet effect of land prices, this is a kind of speculative action, constituting demand for capital gains from the land: a piece of land is held in reserve, appearing as if a part of the supply, but with the owner's intention of reaping capital gains sometime in the future. If such "reserved demand" is significantly large, demand as a whole exceeds genuine supply, and the pressure for a price rise becomes much stronger. The textbook version of the "economics of uncertainty" tells us that there could be a positive role accorded to speculators' action, since, through their behavior of buying cheap and selling dear, they may be helping to even out the price differences between regions or over time. This would be true in the case of speculators on commodities like grain or cocoa or financial instruments. Even land speculators might perform the function of improving the allocation of resources through their action if their action were based upon the expectation of a rising trend in income gains from the land concerned. But the speculative demand for urban land in Japan in recent decades, taken against the backdrop of a 145-fold rise in prices over 30 odd years, can hardly be justified as a reflection of a rising trend of genuine income gains.

Thus we come to a consideration of the components of price formation of urban land in recent Japan, in which the speculative element has to be set aside as an extraneous factor of significant size. It has been suggested by some experts, in the course of discussion on the alleged "inviolability" of private property right to land, that the land price is like an onion with many layers around the core part and that it is necessary to peel off one layer after another before coming to the very core, which alone could be considered the object of private property right. The first and the biggest layer to be peeled off should be the speculative component in the price formation of urban land.

What, then, are other component layers, and which are the ones to be peeled off before we come to the core?

Suppose we start with a piece of land utilized for agricultural purpose but situated in the suburb of an expanding urban center. Demand for that piece of land is a derived demand reckoned from the demand for its products; its price reflects the market value of such products and could rise, if it rises at all, only *pari passu* with the rise in that market value. But once that piece of land becomes the object of urban development, various kinds of developmental costs are incurred, such as new roads, waterworks, sewage facilities, and other public utilities. Before long, schools, hospitals, and public parks may also have to be constructed. These developmental costs are usually borne in the first instance by local autonomous bodies (and in some cases by the national government) and are naturally reflected in the land price. If the base price as agricultural land were, for example, 1,000 yen per unit area, the price might go up to 1,500 yen in consequence of the development. Who pays for this difference of 500 yen depends on the regulatory systems and other conditions that are relevant in the region concerned. The difference may be absorbed in the form of a capital gains tax imposed on the seller, or it may be borne partly by an intermediate real estate dealer or again partly by the buyer, as in the case of sewage facilities and public utilities. But, in any case, this additional price component of 500 yen cannot be counted as a portion of the property right of the original owner of the agricultural land in question. In other words, here is one layer of the onion that has to be peeled off before reaching the core.

Another layer that has to be peeled off is the price rise due to the emergence of an external economy. A reference was made earlier to the case of a windfall gain obtained through an opening of a new railroad line. Such an occurrence has been quite common in postwar Japan, and many episodes have been reported of political insiders, privy to the planning of a new line, purchasing the strategic land area cheaply in advance and selling it after the plan is made public. What was priced originally at 1,000 yen per unit area could easily rise to 4,000 yen, as the official White Paper itself admitted. In such cases also, the original landowner is not in a position to claim the property right over the windfall that may come into his pocket. Even when the gain is not realized through sale of the land, a tax measure may be justified in the form of a land appreciation tax.

Thus it may be said that the extra layers to be peeled off in order to reach to the core of the onion for the purpose of ascertaining the quantitative dimension of the private property right on land are (a) the part of the price rise that is due to speculative activities; (b) the part of the price rise that is due to the effect of an external economy; and (c) the part of the price rise that is a consequence of incurring necessary developmental costs.

"Myth of Land Value"

If the foregoing analysis of the price formation of urban land is accepted, it is clear enough that the so-called "inviolability" of private property right is restricted only to the "core of the onion" in our simile. And yet, this "inviolability" tenet was used as a pretext by conservative political leaders in power for not taking positive countermeasures against the inordinate price rise of urban land which continued for more than three decades. The inaction was ostensibly based on that tenet, citing a constitutional clause for support, but the resulting "Myth of Land Value" – the myth that the land price will never go down - was fully taken advantage of by politicians and money-makers, afflicting Japanese society with what Veblen would have called "pecuniary orgies in a respectable form."

There is no question but that in the 145-fold price rise of urban land in three decades the speculative element was by far the biggest continuing cause. The two other "layers of the onion" to be peeled off can hardly provide an explanation for the land-price revolution of the recorded scale. If any evidence is required for this observation, it is sufficient to recall the result of the governmental inquiry into business firms in 1989, cited in the last section, which revealed that for no less than 78 percent of the unutilized land area owned by them they had no plans for utilization. This was clearly a confession that the land was being held for speculative purposes.

On the other hand, we should certainly not ignore the positive stimuli given to the price rise of urban land. We mentioned earlier that the second high tide of 1972–73 was closely associated with the "Plan for Remodeling of the Japanese Archipelago" championed by Prime Minister Tanaka. This political leader of Lockheed scandal fame, in particular, was himself a master of alchemy in land speculation and contributed by his example to the social atmosphere which accepted the legitimacy of "land-rolling" for developmental purposes. As for the third high tide from 1986 onwards, most observers agree that almost a meteoric rise of Tokyo as an international financial center in 1980s created a large volume of demand for office space and residential units for foreigners, for both of which higher than normal rent was of little impediment. The so-called "intelligent building" like Ark-Hills in Roppongi, with the latest informational devices for 24-hour operation, charges monthly rent of ¥ 62,000 per unit (6 feet by

6) of office space; and a typical residential unit nearby with four bedrooms is rented at ¥ 1.5 million, or 10,000 dollars a month. No doubt, construction business catering to such demand is able to absorb the high cost of land for its purpose.[23]

In any case, whatever the stimulus which gave positive impact on the price of urban land, when it once happens, the "Myth of Land Value" assures subsequent speculative rise far beyond the level that could be warranted by the enhanced income-generating possibility of the antecedent stimulus. Such was the mechanism causing 145-fold upheaval of urban land price in thirty odd years while the wholesale prices were only doubling.

6. The socio-economic consequences of the land-price revolution and the countermeasures

Some socio-economic consequences

Socio-economic consequences of the land-price revolution have been so diverse and far-reaching that the best we can do here in a limited space will be to give a few illustrative examples in summarized forms.

First, the ordinary citizens' dreams of owning their own houses, however small, in a city like Tokyo are being crushed. The average aggregate income of a college graduate over a lifetime of employment is estimated at present to be around 166 million yen, which would be barely sufficient to purchase a meager one-room condominium apartment of 500 square feet near the central area of Tokyo. Five times one's annual disposable fund, consisting of one's earnings, savings and borrowed money, is said to be a standard measure for the purchase cost of one's house in the western world. If this measure is applied to a regular salaried person in Japan, the amount comes to about 30 million yen – not enough to buy even one *tsubo* (6 feet by 6) of residential land in the heart of Tokyo. Thus, a prevalent tendency nowadays is for big corporations to vie with each other in providing comfortable enough company houses for their employees in order to attract the cream of job seekers. On the other hand, seeing that the affluence attained does not enable the purchase of a family home, the younger generation of Japan is turning to the type of expenditures that are said to give "the feeling of richness," such as the purchase of expensive imported cars and luxury travel to foreign resort places with their families. This, we might say, is a case of perverted conspicuous consumption.

Second, as might have been expected, the distributional effect of the land-price revolution has been highly iniquitous. This fact is eloquently revealed, for instance, in the list of "high income-tax payers" annually made public by the Internal Revenue Office. It used to be the case that this list was typically topped by business tycoons, but the picture has changed in the last few years in such way that the top fifty on the list would consist almost entirely of the persons who sold their land for profit.[24] Even for those individuals who have not realized capital gains on the land they own, the possibility of obtaining loans secured on their landed property is greatly facilitated by the rise in the latent asset value. General public impression of the widening asset disparity was reflected in a public opinion survey conducted by Yomiuri Shimbun in June 1990, registering 71 percent of the respondents agreeing to the widening disparity in contrast to the 48 percent figure with the same answer recorded in the January 1988 survey.

Third, the effect on public works has been very marked. A proposal, partly in the form of pressures from abroad, has recently been repeatedly advanced in Japan to reorient the country's macroeconomic policies in the direction of stimulating *internal* effective demand in lieu of export drive. Since the time of the Nakasone cabinet (November 1982–November 1987), the government has officially favored such a proposal and has tried to emphasize the expansion of public works – a major area in which the government could take initiative and pay for the cost. It was only to be expected, however, that the sphere of public works was precisely the type of activity for which the acquisition of land was usually essential and that the exorbitant price rise of land therefore stood as a major impediment to the scheduled fulfillment of many of the projects. Just to give one example, the completion of the so-called Metropolitan Loop Road No.2 has been stalled for several years because of the difficulty of financing the purchase of a mere 1,350 meters (0.84 miles) between Toranomon and Shimbashi. The government has found itself unable to meet the cost of procurement of the needed land, which has now risen to the level of 428.7 billion yen or 99.7 percent of the total cost of construction. The National Land Agency announced in March 1987 that the completion of the project would be delayed 108 years if the price of the relevant land should continue to rise 4 percent annually. One recalls the popular Chinese adage: "It's like waiting one hundred years for the waters in the Yellow River to clear."

Especially deficient in the city of Tokyo are provisions for pedestrian roads, parks and children's playgrounds. Here again, the authorities concerned are greatly handicapped in their efforts by the price revolution in land. Somewhat related to the problem confronting construction projects for public purposes is the unprecedented appeal by a group of ambassadors in Tokyo (representing thirty-one countries) to the Japanese Foreign Office to do something about the land situation, which has become so constrictive that a few countries, e.g. Uganda, have already decided to close their embassies in Tokyo, and several others, e.g. Australia and Spain, have chosen to offer for sale a sizable portion of their embassy premises. It is a sad commentary on the nature of affluence in Japan that foreign embassies are being pauperized.

Fourth, a longer-range consequence of the price revolution has been noted by those people who set store by the warm and sociable neighborliness of an urban community that is being increasingly broken up. Referring to the process of divesting community life of its once fertile components through the centrifugal effect of the unconscionable price rise in land, a noted publicist has commented recently: "The familiar noodle shop and then another old friend the laundryman disappeared from the street corner, and the vacant site left behind is now surrounded by barbed-wire entanglements through which the cold blasts sweep down from nowhere . . . Abiding, tried-and-true neighbors are gone almost unnoticed, and in their place nondescript strangers come in, we do not even say 'hello' as we meet . . . How can we ever bring back sanity in the city of Tokyo?"[25] This can hardly be said to be an exaggeration, as the sense of hollowness spreads here and there in the erstwhile sprightly corners of downtown Tokyo. A grave enough consequence of the price revolution in land!

Basic premises for countermeasures

Our discussion of the land-price revolution would be incomplete if we did not touch upon the countermeasures needed to prevail over this intractable malaise. However, so much has been written ever since the time of the first high tide of early 1960s and still more is likely to be written and proposed in the immediate future (as I write this in August 1990) that it will be wiser for me here to confine myself to the statement of basic observations which I consider important in the discussion of countermeasures.

First of all, I should like to emphasize the importance of two basic premises for the entire discussion:

1 The property right, as such, on land is *not inviolable*, and the land policy should be oriented rather toward giving full recognition to *the right of utilization*.

2 The antecedent to the urban land policy should be well-considered *planning* as regards the type of city we would like to have – planning in which constituent *citizens participate* in one way or another.

It follows, then, that legal and regulatory frameworks have to be worked out, for the implementation of these premises, as practical guidelines for which public planning is indispensable.

Since I do emphasize in particular that the recognition of the right of utilization as superseding the private property right is essential, a brief historical review of the problem may be in order at this point.

To begin with, we may ask why the private property right was considered inviolable in the historical context of the development of modern society. That right, along with the right to subsist, was an essential component of civil rights in the evolutionary process of society.

The modern civil society is a society in which a citizen maintains his own economic subsistence as commodity owner through exchanging his commodity. Therefore, his *right to subsist* as man is grounded on the *property right* in his capacity as a commodity owner. For those independent burghers (proprietor farmers, handicraftsmen, independent manufactory owners) for whom ownership and work process are united, it was clear enough that the guaranteeing of the property right was *ipso facto* the guaranteeing of the right to subsist, so the property right came naturally to be regarded as being as inviolable as basic human rights. The evolution of the capitalistic process, however, meant that "labor power" became a commodity embraced, as it were, within the domain of "private capital." As has been pointed out by economic historians, for labor power to become a commodity the sellers of labor power, i.e., laborers, had to become "free" in a double sense of the term: first, "free" in the sense that, not subservient to anyone, they could freely offer their labor power in the market, and second, "free" in the sense that they were separated from the ownership of the means of production and freed from the task of marketing the products of their labor. In other words, here arose the separation of ownership and labor. Not only did this separation mean that the property right of owners of the means of production became separated from the subsistence right of laborers who did not own the means of production, but also it implied further an antagonistic relation between the two major classes: capital and labor.

Basically, this separation of the property right and the subsistence right has continued and further sharpened in the process of capitalistic development. But at the same time it should be pointed out that there do exist, even in highly developed capitalist societies today, a fairly large number of individual proprietors who are conducting small-scale business on the basis of ownership of a small piece of land and some instruments of production and trade. For such people it cannot be denied that the property right and the subsistence right are synonymously conjoined in the concept of human right. Conversely, in a country like Japan, where public ownership of land is meager, a property right independent of the subsistence right (e.g. that of capitalistic enterprises or parasitic land-owners) is being claimed with a strong voice by a significant majority. Such a property right may be termed a "nonsubsistence property right," and, being unrelated to the basic human right, it should be subject to restraints in the interest of public welfare.

Even in the case of landownership for which the nonsubsistence property right is claimed, what is essential is the right to the land's *utilization*. From the standpoint of a capitalist enterprise, for example, a rational interest in the use of a factor of production, such as labor power, is to be able to hire and fire the owner of that labor power, not to establish ownership of him as a slave. The same may be said of land as a factor of production. So long as the use is guaranteed on terms agreeable as to the duration and rent, a capitalist enterprise with its main interest in the production of commodities should find maintaining such an agreement less cumbersome than having to insist on the property right over the land it decides to own.

It can generally be stated that land policy, whether as regards agricultural or urban land, had best be oriented with its central emphasis on *the right of its utilization*, and that those who nowadays favor the principle of "inviolability" of the property right are those whose major interest is in an expected speculative gain from the owned land in their asset portfolios. This latter point is especially pertinent to the recent land-price controversy in Japan.

Countermeasures proposed

Now, we may go on, after this historical review, to a few other basic observations related to the current problem of countermeasures against the land-price revolution.

It is almost axiomatic that land policy planning by public bodies is greatly facilitated when, as was specified in the Land Commission Act (1967) of Great Britain, legislative backing is given to ensure that the right land be available at the right time for the implementation of national, regional, and local plans. For this purpose, a logical solution would be to give to an appropriate government body the power to buy land compulsorily at a price net of increase due to betterment. The compensation provision is a key to land acquisition by public bodies. One recalls in this connection a 1962 Italian attempt to create a self-financing program of municipal land acquisition for low-cost housing, according to which the land was to be acquired at prices prevailing two years prior to the time of the planning decision. This provision was subsequently declared unconstitutional, and a concessional compromise was made to allow for the market price rise during the interval between the date of the planning decision and that of actual compulsory purchase. In the case of Japan it has been customary in recent years that the time interval referred to above lingers on for several years, during which time the official "posted prices" themselves frequently have more than doubled. Expansion of publicly owned land in urban areas is definitely called for in Japan now, but at the same time the compensation provision has to be drastically improved in the direction of minimizing windfall gains to private land owners.

This observation brings us to the next problem which is closely related to the task of paring the speculative element of the price formation of land. Generally speaking, a more direct policy instrument in this connection is a system of taxation, of which there are three major types: (a) real estate tax; (b) capital gains tax for realized income; and (c) asset appreciation tax on latent gains. The controversy in Japan, ever since the first high tide of land price inflation in the 1960s, has centered on the problem of which tax measure should be given a greater emphasis as an effective instrument for combating the rising trend of urban land price. At the time of this writing (August 1990) it appears that a majority of experts, including those in the national business organizations, favor the type (a), or the raising of tax rates on holding the property, thus encouraging presumably more rational factor mobility. It is suggested by them that if such raising of the holding tax is combined with the disburdening of capital gains tax the landowners would be prompted to part with their land for sale, thus increasing the supply of land in the market. This argument is generally combined with a presupposition that the capital gains tax even of moderate burden will have a "locked-in effect," or the effect of "locking in" a particular type of asset in the owner's portfolio on account of a specific tax measure on that asset. The issues involved here are fairly complex, especially in the context of continually rising price trend which creates a sizable volume of "reserved demand" and modifies significantly the applicability of the "locked-in effect" presupposition. So we shall not here dwell upon the details of discussions on tax measures required for the task of paring the speculative element in the rising trend in land prices, except to say that the opinion favoring the strengthening of the type (b) above, or the capital gains tax for realized income, is fairly strong especially among some leading theoretical economists.[26] It is worth a special mention that the National Land Agency supported, in its "Basic Policies for the Tax Reform on Land" made public in April 1990, the idea of applying progressive schedules on capital gains tax and also the instituting of a new type of holding tax on latent gains in the landed property held by business firms, an equivalent of the type (c) cited above.

Lastly, we may briefly touch upon a group of proposals which have come up especially since the third high tide of urban land price, that is, 1986 onwards. They relate to programs of deconcentration of the metropolitan functions of Tokyo, which has experienced the exceptional price rise of land during recent years, presumably as a result of the convergence of international financial activities in Tokyo. The government has proposed that each ministry should take steps to move at least one agency or bureau from Tokyo to a less-congested locality, but resistence to this idea has been, as expected, very strong. However, a number of plans for gigantic construction on reclaimed islands in Tokyo Bay are being offered by private groups of experts, the most ambitious of which is by the Kishō Kurokawa group, which proposes to create a land area of 30 thousand hectares in Tokyo Bay in order to move over all the central ministries and parliament and construct a residential center for five million people. Such a plan dodges realistic problems which are inseparably associated with manifold functions indigenous to Tokyo Bay and cannot be taken seriously. Still, almost everyone agrees that the present concentration trend toward Tokyo has to be countered somehow and, if possible, reversed. Here again, certain tax measures may be in order, such as a special enterprise tax levied against additional acquisition of office space in the central part of Tokyo, a special surtax on employers proportional to the number of employees who commute to the city center by public transport systems, and the revoking of the exemption clause as regards the real estate tax on governmental and otherwise public institutions situated in Tokyo and so on.

"Fundamental Law on Land"

Ever since the first high tide of urban land prices in the early 1960s, the Japanese government, either through its component authorities or with reliance on the advice of governmental consultative bodies, made repeated announcements of their intention of taking appropriate steps to counter the rising trend of urban land prices. But in actual fact, very little was done by way of putting a brake on that trend. Finally, urged on by the mounting chorus of public opinion, the government decided to propose the "Fundamental Law on Land" and pass it through the Diet in December 1989, a kind of manifesto-type legislation which is to serve as the basis for concrete steps to be taken subsequently. It remains to be seen what fruits it will bear: but here are the five "Basic Ideas for Policy" enunciated in the Law:

1 On the use of land, the standpoint of public welfare is to be given priority.
2 Land should be utilized in a proper manner in accordance with the conditions obtaining in each region.
3 There should be a utilization plan for the use of land.
4 Land shall not be made an object of speculation.
5 When the value of land appreciates, a burden measured appropriately on the basis of gains is to be borne by the beneficiaries.

Although not explicitly stated in the "Basic Ideas," it is significant that one of the articles in the Law makes an affirmative statement on the need for the steps to promote the expansion of publicly owned land by the central and local governments (Article XII). It should also be noted that the legislative basis for the anti-speculation measures is clearly given in the "Basic Ideas" stated in the Law.

The "Fundamental Law on Land" constitutes only a beginning; therefore, my discussion of the land price revolution here is necessarily an interim report.

7. Macroeconomic mismanagement

In the discussion of inflationary episodes of a modern society I am aware that we should not underestimate the importance of macroeconomic policies of governmental and/or central-banking authorities. The foregoing discussion of the "double price revolution" has been deliberately focused on the problems of energy and urban land and has left incomplete the analysis, in particular, of the inflation of 1972–74 in Japan. A supplementary comment is called for especially in this regard inasmuch as the wholesale price index in Japan was recording already an 18.7 percent rise in September 1973 (compared with a year before), that is, before the first oil shock began. This could not be explained by the second high tide of urban land prices alone which had started in 1972. If we make a more comprehensive analysis of the period in question, we cannot deny the fact that a part of the responsibility lay with the monetary authorities which were continuing a positive policy of credit expansion roughly from the end of 1970 to the first quarter of 1973.[27]

Responsibility for the inflation of 1972–74

The key question here is to what extent the Bank of Japan was able to, and did, control the money supply at the time. In terms of the Marshallian k (measured by whichever ratio, M_1/GNP or M_2/GNP), monetary expansion began markedly from the last quarter of 1970; and the Bank of Japan was then explaining that this was *in response to* the market demand for liquidity. Although there might have been an element of truth in such judgment, what is important is *the extent of control* which the central bank *can exercise* over the volume of "high-powered money," or the monetary base of credit creation for deposit banks. "High-powered money" is the money used for the settlement between the central bank and deposit banks and consists of the latter's deposits in the former and the cash currency issued; and in the case of Japan it is subject, in a greater degree than in other countries, to control policies of the Bank of Japan through the notorious "window guidance," etc. The routes through which this "high-powered money" is supplied are:

a Net claims on the foreign exchange fund due to the surplus in international balance of payments.

b Net claims on the fiscal authorities other than (a).

c Credit granted to private business in the form of loans, bonds, etc., by the
  Bank of Japan.
The supply of such "high-powered money" and its components since the
first quarter of 1971 are shown in Table 6.7. From this table it can be seen
that in spite of the extraordinary increase in the surplus of the international
balance of payments in 1971, continuing into the first half of 1972, the net
increase of "high-powered money" outstanding was comparatively moderate, registering not more than 15 percent rate of increase at the end of 1971
compared with a year before. This result was achieved by the decline in net
claims on the fiscal authorities and the redeeming of central bank credit
from the private sector, in other words, the result of the neutralizing policy
by the Bank of Japan. The picture changes markedly if we look at Table 6.7
again, focusing upon the period which starts from the last quarter of 1972.
From then on, the component share of the item (c), or central bank credit to
the private sector, is definitely higher than that of the item (a), or the net
claim on the foreign exchange fund, in spite of the fact that the surplus in the
current balance of payments was maintaining its momentum until the
second quarter of 1973; and also it can be seen from the table that the rate of
increase of "high-powered money" outstanding compared with a year
before jumped to 30 percent or higher from the last quarter of 1972, and
through the entire year of 1973.
   The implication of the statistics summarized above is quite important in
view of the fact that the inflationary impact of the first oil-shock began only
after October 1973. The fact that the wholesale price index, after
maintaining a near stability since 1956 until the first half of 1972, definitely
started rising from the third quarter of the latter year and registered 18.7
percent rise by September 1973 compared with a year before must mean
that causes for the inflation have to be sought in factors unrelated to the
sudden rise of the oil price in the period after October 1973. No doubt, the
land price revolution, which we discussed in the earlier sections of this
chapter, was a factor; but, in a sense, it had been a continuing trend since
1960 and can hardly explain a rather marked upward trend of wholesale
prices from the latter half of 1972 onward. There was also an inflationary
impact of the US decision in August 1971 to abandon gold convertibility
with subsequent consequences of price rises of various internationally
traded commodities, about which a reference was made in an earlier section
of this chapter. Far more important, however, was the macroeconomic
policy of the monetary authorities which was causing a marked expansion
in the supply of "high-powered money." Why was it that such a policy was
taken? It is true that business trend was seen to be downward in the spring of
1971 and it was feared further that the expected appreciation of the yen
exchange rate subsequent to the US decision of August 1971 would cause in

Table 6.7. *The supply of "high-powered money" and its components – 1971–1974*

	Net increase of "high-powered money" outstanding compared with the same period a year before (in billion yen)	The rate of increase of the left column over one year (%)	Components of Sources of Increase					
			(a)* (in billion yen)	(%)	(b)* (in billion yen)	(%)	(c)* (in billion yen)	(%)
1971 (I)	76.9	15.3	67.6	(61)	−70.3	(−63)	114.4	(102)
(II)	80.3	15.9	168.0	(481)	−157.2	(−450)	24.1	(69)
(III)	97.0	19.5	391.7	(428)	−234.6	(−257)	−147.9	(−162)
(IV)	90.1	14.5	440.0	(518)	−163.2	(−192)	−192.0	(−226)
1972 (I)	78.5	13.5	435.6	(593)	−144.7	(−197)	−217.5	(−296)
(II)	100.7	17.2	317.4	(337)	−155.4	(−165)	−67.9	(−72)
(III)	112.0	18.9	160.6	(155)	−152.4	(−147)	95.6	(92)
(IV)	205.8	29.0	174.0	(88)	−198.1	(−100)	222.2	(112)
1973 (I)	222.1	33.7	178.7	(82)	−164.8	(−76)	203.7	(94)
(II)	255.6	37.2	122.9	(49)	−155.5	(−62)	281.2	(113)
(III)	265.6	37.6	23.0	(9)	−193.1	(−75)	429.2	(166)
(IV)	313.9	34.3	−188.4	(−62)	−78.1	(−25)	572.0	(187)
1974 (I)	241.1	27.4	−246.8	(−107)	−167.6	(−73)	645.1	(280)

Notes:

* Refer to the text for the notations of (a), (b) and (c).

Percentages given in brackets under (a), (b) and (c) are to the total of the three items, which agree only approximately with the figures in the first column on account of the omission of other negligible minor items involved.

Source: The Bank of Japan, *Economic Statistics Annual*, as tabulated by Ryūtarō Komiya, *op. cit.*, p.32.

Japan stagnation in exports and a decline of private capital formation. No doubt, such circumstances prompted the Bank of Japan to adopt a policy of "easy money" in order allegedly to turn the tide. This policy, while creating sizable excess liquidity in the hands of the private business sector, did not materialize in the recovery of capital formation until the fourth quarter of 1973; and the monetary authorities kept on encouraging the expansion of money supply through the year 1972 until they decided to raise the deposit reserve ratio in January 1973 and the official bank rate in April of that year. The effects of these measures, however, were slow to come, as can be seen in the continued high level of "high-powered money" through the year 1973, as shown in Table 6.7. It can hardly be doubted that the easy money policy of the monetary authorities, especially from 1972 to the spring of 1973, was responsible, to a significant degree, for the inflation of 1972–74. Were it not for the excess liquidity generated through this process, the "second high tide" of urban land prices starting in 1972 might not have been as extensive as it was.

The exchange-rate policy reviewed

It is necessary to add at this point a brief review of the exchange-rate policy of the Japanese government, which compounded the macroeconomic mismanagement just discussed. It may be recalled that the single exchange rate of 360 yen to the dollar was established in April 1949 while Japan was still under the Occupation and also that this rate was judged by many experts then as similar to a handicap given to a convalescent golfer. Quite soon after, the 360-yen rate turned out to be yen-cheap as Japanese manufacturing industries recovered their potential efficiency and further caught up with the front-ranking countries of the West. In Chapter 3 (Table 3.1) we compared the rate of growth of labor productivity in manufacturing industries among a number of developed countries between 1950 and 1973 and showed that with the 1950 level as 100 the index was 1,412 for Japan contrasted with 210 for the US, 210 for UK, and 411 for West Germany, namely about seven times more rapid in Japan compared with the USA or UK. If this was the case, it must have meant that the 360-yen rate established in 1949 would prove to be grossly undervalued against the dollar, for example, as the decades progressed. As a matter of fact, West Germany revalued her Mark upward in 1961 by 5 percent and again in 1969 by 9.3 percent. But the Japanese government was adamant in maintaining the old rate in the face of the evident disequilibrium in the balance of trade chiefly caused by the undervaluation of yen.[28] By the Smithsonian Agreement of December 1971, the yen was revalued upward by 16.88 percent to the dollar (with the central rate at 307 yen to a dollar). But even at this rate Japan's balance of trade recorded a big surplus in 1972, in fact, bigger than in 1971; and it was clear enough, even before the US decision to devalue the dollar by 10 percent in February 1973, that the'Japanese yen had been undervalued. In any case, the Smithsonian Agreement broke down in March 1973 and the second floating period was ushered in. As a result, the yen went up immediately to the 265-yen-to-a-dollar level. But, again, the intervention of the Bank of Japan was applied in the form of "reverse dirty float," as it were, to absorb the excess demand for the yen by selling the previously accumulated dollars, thus maintaining the yen exchange rate more or less fixed for about seven months until the first oil shock struck.

The relevance of this exchange-rate episode to the inflation of 1972–74, insofar as it is applicable to the period before the oil shock, consists of the rigid adherence to the fixed exchange rate of the yen at a cheaper than equilibrium rate, thus inviting the importation of higher commodity prices into Japan. If Japan had abandoned the Smithsonian system in June 1972 when the UK did, the situation might have been quite different. The fact of the matter was that during those critical months from the last half of 1972 to the spring of 1973, the delay in the exchange rate adjustment compounded the macroeconomic mismanagement in the attempt to offset the surplus of the international balance of payments.

It would not be fair to conclude this chapter without recording the fact that the Japanese government, and also the Bank of Japan, learned a valuable lesson from the experience of the 1972–74 inflation so far as monetary and exchange-rate policies were concerned, so that when the second oil shock struck in 1979 their policy reactions met the requirements of the contingency better.

7   The march of corporate capitalism

In this chapter I propose to introduce a concept of "corporate capitalism" of Japan, which has come to evolve since about the decade of the 1970s – a distinctive turn of events in the history of Japanese capitalism. But first, a brief sketch of "Japan as Number One" in her economic performance. Then, the definition is given for the concept of "net internal surplus" as a difference between the sum of retained earnings (S) and depreciation funds (D) and gross investment (GV), or (S + D) – GV. It used to be the case until quite recently (as was pointed out in earlier chapters) that this was generally a negative figure so that a fairly large amount of borrowing from outside (L) was needed to fill the gap. But as empirical studies have shown, the ratio of (S + D)/GV gradually rose for Japanese manufacturing corporations from around 60 percent in the early high-growth period (1956–60) to over 100 percent in the latter part of the 1970s and maintained that level into the decade of the 1980s. Not that indirect financing was entirely absent; but the growth of net internal surplus led to the latest evolving pattern of the intra-firm division of labor, expanding the theater of operation of, and control by, a single firm to cover more than one industry (conglomerate creation) and beyond the national boundary (globalization). These trends brought to the fore at the same time the renewed importance of ownership control, often with networks of mutually associated corporate organizations. Thus the stage of "corporate capitalism" as I have termed it.

The remainder of this chapter is devoted to the discussions of (1) the globalization trend citing examples from one particular industry (the household electric and electronic industry) and one region (Japanese capital in Australia), and (2) the privatization trend in Japan as a reflection of the confident march of corporate capitalism, giving a specific example of the National Railroad in some detail.

Table 7.1. *Comparative figures of per capita GNP – 1950 to 1988*

	Japan	USA	UK	West Germany
1950	131	1,897	744	468
1955	273	2,446	1,068	825
1960	468	2,852	1,390	1,302
1965	919	3,629	1,877	1,942
1970	1,949	4,952	2,254	3,041
1975	4,475	7,401	4,254	6,784
1980	9,103	11,996	9,567	13,296
1985	11,098	16,760	8,134	10,355
1988	19,905	18,570	12,107	18,373

Note:
In US dollars, converted each by current exchange rates respectively.
Source: IMF, *International Financial Statistics* as tabulated by R. Komiya,
Gendai Nihon Keizai, p.157, except the figures for 1988, which were taken from
The Bank of Japan, *Comparative Economic and Financial Statistics – Japan and
Other Major Countries*, 1989.

1. Capitalism "triumphant"?

"Japan as number one"?

The performance of the Japanese economy as reflected in the unparalleled
growth of per capita real GNP over the forty years after the end of the war
bespeaks of a success story of modern capitalism or, more accurately, of a
mixed economy capitalism. Table 7.1 gives comparative figures among
several developed countries on per capita GNP in US dollars.

It is remarkable, indeed, that within about forty years Japan attained the
152-times growth in per capita GNP (in dollar terms) while the next best
performance was that of West Germany, namely 39 times, and that even
basing our comparison on 1970, the year which was pretty close to the end
of the high-growth period in Japan, we find that the growth in Japan over
the following 18 years was more than 10 times in contrast to West
Germany's 6 times. Alarming perhaps, from the standpoint of the
competing developed countries, was the impressive growth of Japan's share
in world export markets, as can be gleaned from Table 7.2. Such *relative* rise
of Japan's share, which occurred in fact during the interval when the yen
was appreciating by almost 100 percent,[1] must have been viewed abroad
both with envy and as a potential threat.

No wonder, therefore, that numerous commentaries and books began to

Table 7.2. *Japan's share in world export markets**

(Unit: %)

	Total exports	Manufactured goods	Machinery and equipment
1955	2.4	4.2	1.7
1960	3.6	5.9	3.9
1965	5.1	8.1	6.7
1970	6.9	10.0	9.8
1975	7.0	11.3	12.5
1980	7.1	11.9	16.3
1985	10.1	15.5	22.0

Note:
* Does not include communist countries.
Source: R. Komiya, *Gendai Nihon Keizai*, p.157.

appear outside Japan, raising the question of how to explain such an achievement and/or predicting a still brighter future for Japan. The first of such predictions was by the famed futurologist Herman Kahn;[2] but more typical in this regard was a book by Ezra Vogel, professor of sociology at Harvard University, entitled: *Japan as Number One*, in which he summarized his observations in the following words:

At present, in political and cultural influence and even in gross national product Japan is not the number one power in the world. Yet in the effectiveness of its institutions in coping with the current problems of the post-industrial era Japan is indisputably number one. Considering its limited space and natural resources and its crowding, Japan's achievements in economic productivity, educational standards, health, and control of crime are in a class by themselves. This success is more striking when one considers how far behind Japan was in many of these areas not only in 1945 but even in the middle 1950s, after recovery from World War II was essentially complete.[3]

More recently, a somewhat droll vision of the future, probably not intended seriously, was depicted by Australian critic, Murray Sayle, who wrote:

The outline of a future Japanese empire is plain: Britain and Ireland could respectively be Japan's Hong Kong and Macao, well-placed for the European *entrepôt* trade, the United States will be Japan's fabulously wealthy India, *terre des merveilles*, while Australia can be Japan's Australia, land of rugged adventure and heavy drinking, the appropriate place of exile for Japanese dissidents and remittance men. This would leave only table scraps for the others: Holland, perhaps for the Indonesians; France for the Vietnamese.[4]

Gavan McCormack, professor of Japanese History at the Australian National University, who quoted this passage, contributed an article to a US magazine, with the title: "Capitalism Triumphant? The Evidence from 'Number One' (Japan),"[5] and analyzed, in effect, the relevance of the *institutional* aspect of Japanese society to its economic success in the postwar period. Vogel also was interested in "the effectiveness of [Japan's] present-day institutions"; and these commentaries naturally lead us to take up the evolving transformation of Japanese capitalism, whether triumphant or not, as it has gone through the most successful high-growth period in its modern history.

2. A new stage of corporate capitalism in Japan

If one were asked what peculiarities, if any, could be mentioned of Japanese capitalism in the prewar era, one would have pointed to (a) its *zaibatsu* structure, or the octopus-like control of major industries by family-based holding companies and (b) the heavy reliance on *indirect financing* by manufacturing corporations for expansionary activities.

When the war ended and Japan came to be subjected to the Occupation reforms, the first of the above peculiarities was considered to have been "as responsible for Japan's militarism as the militarists themselves" (Edwin W. Pauley) and a thoroughgoing dissolution of the *zaibatsu* structure was initially proposed. However, as we have discussed in an earlier chapter, with a major shift in US policy on Japan from about 1947, the dissolution program itself became half-hearted; and soon after the Occupation ended in 1952, the prewar *zaibatsu*-like structure was resuscitated, though in a slightly modified, less aggressive, form. As for the second of the peculiarities mentioned above, or the heavy reliance on external debt in the capital structure of Japanese industrial corporation, the postwar reforms remained entirely unconcerned; and, as was touched upon in Chapter 4, the peculiarity continued more or less as a typical situation well into the high-growth decade of the 1960s.

Evolving changes of economic institutions, however, often become visible to naked eyes only after a number of years. Thus in retrospect, we do recognize significant changes in certain aspects of Japanese capitalism, in particular in relation to the mechanism of supply and use of corporate funds. In short, one is here reminded of the statement often repeated in the United States to the effect that the corporate internal reserve is the American way of providing investment funds[6] – the business creed which was only infrequently shared in Japan until recently, but which has now become a solid fact of life through evolving changes in the high-growth period. This section is to deal with this changing picture; and introductory remarks are in order, for the purpose of elucidating, in a somewhat schematic fashion, conceptual, and partly causal, relations among the relevant factors involved.

Sources and uses of corporate funds – a schematic overview

Let us think of a representative firm, *à la* Marshall, in the manufacturing sector and set it in the context of the two-decade-long high-growth period that was observed in Japan. The typical *modus operandi* for this firm as a going concern in the early postwar years was to obtain its net investment fund from banks and to attempt to expand its share in the product-market in which it specialized. Maximum efforts were made to reduce the cost of production through productivity improvement and to enhance its profit position so that internal reserve could be gradually expanded. When the firm is on a growth path, its depreciation allowances (D), however calculated, are necessarily greater than its replacement needs (R); and an element of surplus ensues here, or $D - R > O$. This surplus plus the internal reserve earned after the payment of dividends (S) in a particular year may not yet be sufficient to cover the projected cost of net investment (V), or $D - R + S < V$; and the firm still continues to rely on long-term loans from banks (L), or $V = D - R + S + L$. This is the stage where indirect financing is prevalent, of which we made a special point in Chapter 4, as characterizing the investment fund structure of Japanese corporations.

As the favorable high-growth period continues, the firm in question grows to a significant size in the industry, soon to enjoy an oligopolistic position which enables it to adopt the entry-preventing price policy. Naturally it follows then that the firm's profit expands, generating a much larger internal reserve (S) than before, so large in fact that the net investment cost (V) may be more than covered, or $S - V > O$. Once the firm attains this position, a new type of surplus arises to the extent of $(D + S) - (R + V)$, which we shall designate as "net internal surplus of the firm" (NS).

Then the firm becomes confronted with the problem of how to make use of this NS. There are several possibilities, namely:

a To repay its debt to banks.
b To increase R&D expenditures.
c To launch upon direct investment abroad.
d To spread out its business activities beyond its original speciality.
e To engage in speculative investment in securities and land.

Not all of these possibilities are seized upon at once by the firm in question; but when we view the entire economy, composed of numerous firms, the aggregate of NS found its destinations in all these directions as the high-growth period progressed.

Each one of these developments, of course, is bound to have far-reaching consequences. Firstly, if bank loans are paid back on a large scale, banks will have to face the problem of finding alternative outlets for their loanable funds. This they did by shifting the direction toward purchasing stocks and bonds. But what about the intimate relations, within the *zaibatsu*-type multi-enterprise structure, between the leading bank and the associated enterprises which used to rely heavily on that bank? This is a problem in itself, and we will have to deal with it later.

On the second of the developments mentioned above, that is, the increase in R&D expenditures, it may suffice to say that a new dimension was in fact accorded to such expenditures, supporting the high growth itself in the period under review. As for the fifth point, that is, speculative investment in securities and land, we have essentially dealt with the problem in the last chapter. On the third and fourth points however, it is worth paying special attention to evolving patterns of the division of labor under capitalism.

To begin with, there are four types of textbook-style division of labor, as follows:

a The intra-firm division of labor, the classical example being Adam Smith's pin manufacturing plant, amenable to planning control by a single firm.

b The inter-firm, but intra-industry, division of labor, with no central controlling agent under competitive conditions and presumably subject to the reign of "The Invisible Hand."

c The social, or inter-industry, division of labor within one country, often interfered with by deliberate state policies.

d The international division of labor, presumably based on the conditions of comparative advantage, but occasionally distorted, for example, by infant industry policies.

It is true that in the actual course of capitalistic development various kinds of modifications to the above formulation have occurred; for example, the development of monopoly which amalgamated (a) and (b), or the imperialistic exploitation which forcefully defied the economic rationality implied in (d) above. But probably much more significant is the latest evolving pattern of the *intra-firm* division of labor, expanding the theater of operation of, and control by, a single firm to cover more than one industry and beyond the national boundary. The implication is that private capital, the basic unit of economic activities under capitalism, as it becomes bigger and bigger, tends to embrace within itself the *inter-industry* division of labor creating a *conglomerate* multi-industry structure on the one hand, and further ushers in an era of *globalization* through the formation of multinational corporations on the other. These trends are both rooted in the growth of "net internal surplus of the firm" (NS), mentioned above, and constitute at the same time manifestations of the inherent dynamics of private capital to embrace within itself one after another of spheres of social institutions and functions, the market itself for one[7] and also other smaller units of private capital. In other words, what was once a representative firm, "a tree in the forest" in Marshall's simile, concerned mainly with the intra-firm division of labor, maximizes profits, but it does so "primarily through attempting to alter precisely those parameters taken as exogenously determined in the neoclassical model: tastes, state policy, technologies, the structure of competition."[8] Of the four types of the textbook style division of labor we have referred to earlier, the first one, i.e. the intra-firm "pin factory" type, was the only type which can be said to be amenable to planning control by a single firm. This limitation remains under capitalism even after a single firm becomes a giant one. It is, therefore, cogent to argue, as Galbraith did, that "the part of the modern bimodal economy that is dominated by the large corporations and where these, as an essential aspect of their planning, take markets under the control"[9] had better be referred to by the term "planning system."

Still in pursuit of a schematic picture of the changing pattern of capitalistic development, in particular in the context of Japan's postwar high-growth period, we are naturally led to ask the question: what is the relevance of the famed thesis of Berle and Means in their 1932 publication *The Modern Corporation and Private Property* where they, noting the undeniable trend of ownership dispersion of corporate shares, assumed that mature corporations were effectively becoming controlled by their management while the power of the owners was to that extent eroded? Their basic thesis of "managerial control," which they reaffirmed in the postwar edition of their book (1968), may still be valid; but in the case of Japan, as we shall observe through empirical evidence, the consequences of the notable expansion of the net internal surplus (NS) of giant corporations spreading out into conglomerate creation and globalization are bringing to the fore the renewed importance of ownership control, thus compounding the two aspects, management and ownership, into an integrated pattern.[10] Berle and Means spoke of the wide dispersion of corporate ownership; but what is increasingly happening in Japan is the inter-corporate ownership of corporate equity shares either through mergers and acquisitions or as the continued legacy of the erstwhile *zaibatsu* ties. This trend is further reinforced by the shifting emphasis of financial institutions toward investment in bonds and shares and away from long-term loans to manufacturing corporations, this too being a consequence of the expansion of the net internal surplus (NS) of giant enterprises. Inevitably there have ensued networks of mutually associated corporate organizations which have become the dominant units of economic activities – a structural mode which may best be referred to as "the stage of corporate capitalism." The

Table 7.3. *Relative growth of internal funds of manufacturing corporations (in quinquennial averages)*

(Unit: billion yen)

	Internal reserve (S)	Depreciation (D)	Gross investment (GV)	$\frac{S+D}{GV}$ (%)
1956–60	77.5	181.3	442.2	59
1961–65	92.6	502.9	940.2	63
1966–70	353.8	934.4	1,950.7	66
1971–75	463.8	1,696.9	2,864.0	75
1976–80	811.4	2,354.2	2,903.1	109
1981–85	1,193.4	3,605.7	4,744.5	101
1986–89*	1,907.5	4,671.8	5,976.2	110

Note:
* The 4-year average. The 1990 figures were not yet available.

Source: Tabulated by Yoshikazu Miyazaki in his *Gendai Kigyō-ron Nyūmon* (Introduction to the Theory of the Firm in the Present-day), Yūhikaku, 1985, pp.358–9, from the Bank of Japan, *Shuyō Kigyō Keiei Bunseki*. Updated by the author from the same source.

institutional motive force ingrained in this stage of capitalism is the self-aggrandizement through the maximization of internal reserves destined for the expansion of spheres of control multi-industry-wise and beyond national borders. In this way, individuals, instead of being master of economic activities, become subservient to the self-perpetuating organization called "corporate body."

The schematic picture depicted above is in the nature of theoretical abstraction, somewhat simplified and also in need of qualifications at a number of points. In what follows, therefore, we shall offer some empirical evidence for the evolving pattern of capitalistic structure in Japan through the high-growth period and beyond.

Empirical evidence on the net internal surplus

The first point to be discussed empirically is the expanding trend of the net internal surplus (NS) of mature corporations, that is to say $(D+S) - (R+V)$ in our earlier notations. In Table 7.3 we have added R (replacement) and V (net investment) together and designated the sum by GV (gross investment). The trend is clearly marked, confirming the thesis that while the high-growth period started with a fairly high degree of dependence on outside funds as a source of gross investment in manufac-

Table 7.4. *The ratio of internal funds to gross investment for specific industries*

	1960 ratio	1970 ratio
Construction industry	58	146
Precision machinery	34	154
Cement manufacturing	47	107
Food processing	50	103
Electric machinery	29	109
Wholesale industry	64	115

Source: Yoshikazu Miyazaki, *Nihon Keizai no Kōzō to Kōdō* (The Structure and Performance of the Japanese Economy), Vol. II, Chikuma Shobō, 1985, p.220.

turing industries as a whole the ratio of S + D to GV, or the internal funds to gross investment, steadily rose in the decade of the 1970s and finally exceeded the 100 percent level by 1976–80, which level was maintained more or less in the decade of the 1980s.[11]

If we examine such ratios for each of the specific industries, we find that a number of them had already exceeded the critical 100 percent level by 1970, as shown in Table 7.4. The number of such industries increased further by 1974, extending to chemical fertilizers (121), metal manufacturing (136), rubber manufacturing (104), mining (117), etc.

The other side of the coin, so to speak, of this greater dependence on internal funds by corporations has been the changing pattern of investment by financial institutions as evidenced by a marked increase of stock-holdings by them. The relative share of such holdings in the total rose steadily from 12.6 percent in 1950 to 32.6 percent in 1971, while the share held by individuals declined from 61.3 percent in 1950 to 37.2 percent in 1971.[12] Such a changing pattern was naturally reflected in the interlocking network of equity holdings among corporations to a greater extent than used to be the case, where financial institutions often kept their dominant position. This was typically the case with the *zaibatsu*-type groups which were resuscitated in the post-occupation period. One example may suffice to show the extent of *intra*-group holding of equity shares in the case of *zaibatsu* firms. The top 10 shareholders of Sumitomo Shōji (trading company) in 1967 were headed by Sumitomo bank (with 8.06 percent holding) followed by 9 other companies all identifiable as belonging to the Sumitomo group, with the 10 of them together holding 42.5 percent of the total capitalization of Shōji Company.

If we add all the capitalizations of each of the newly resuscitated *zaibatsu*-

Table 7.5. *The trend of the mutually holding ratios within* zaibatsu *groups*

(Unit: %)

	1963	1965	1968
Sumitomo	14.26	15.13	18.62
Daiichi	10.18	10.26	15.84
Fuji	9.85	10.41	13.57
Mitsubishi	12.91	13.93	16.35
Mitsui	8.27	9.51	11.20
Sanwa	6.96	7.73	9.60

Source: Yoshikazu Miyazaki, *Nihon Keizai no Kōzō to Kōdō*, Vol. I, Chikuma Shobō, 1985, p.241.

type groups and calculate the percentages of *intra*-group holdings in the total of each group, we find the generally increasing trend as the high-growth period progresses, as shown in Table 7.5. The matrix-type mutual holding among the companies within each *zaibatsu*-type group has been statistically tabulated by Miyazaki[13] and presents to us an impressive picture of interlocking which exists today among manifold industrial corporations within each group. It is only logical, in such circumstances, than an intimate degree of interlocking directorship prevails within each group, bolstered by monthly meetings of the presidents concerned, as mentioned earlier in Chapter 3.

Institutionally, this matrix-type interlocking is different from the prewar *zaibatsu* structure; but in practical terms it functions almost identically with the latter and it resembles quite closely what came to be called "conglomerates"[14] in the postwar period. While the growth of individual firms independently, or through mergers and acquisitions in earlier periods, notably during 1895–1907 and 1920–39 in the United States, took the forms of horizontal and/or vertical expansion, the post Second World War period witnessed the prominent growth of diversified, or conglomerate, types of expansion in the western countries. For example, "between 1961 and 1969, ITT, already a very large multinational telecommunications company, acquired amongst other concerns, the largest US bakery, the largest US hotel chain, and the largest US housebuilder, the second largest US car rental service and a number of large insurance and finance companies."[15] In the case of Japan, a network of this type had been an accustomed pattern for the former *zaibatsu*-group companies; and it was for independent giant corporations like Toyota Motor Company to emulate the agglomeration steps taken by US corporations like ITT.

Toyota's case

Toyota Motor Company, which headed the list of big corporations in declared income in Japan for 1989 and was ranked as the sixth biggest industrial corporation of the world by the 1990 "Fortune" survey, was established in August 1937 as a kind of subsidiary to the Toyota Jidō Shokki (automatic loom) Company, which was a brain child of Sakichi Toyoda,[16] an independent inventor-entrepreneur without any connection with *zaibatsu* groups initially or thereafter. Sakichi Toyoda, one year before he died (1930), obtained £100,000 from a British company, Pratt Brothers, as royalty income for his patents on the automatic loom and handed this entire sum over to his son, Kiichirō, telling him to make use of it as R&D funds for founding a new venture of manufacturing automobiles; and, thus, a tradition was established in the Toyota Motor Company not to rely on external finance for investment purposes. True, resort was made to debenture bonds in an earlier period; but even these were redeemed entirely by 1978 and the accumulated net internal surplus (NS) was big enough for the company to engage in semi-banking activities, earning as much as 36 billion yen as loan-interest income in that year.

The times were such in the latter 1930s that the expansionary militarism of Japan was on its ascendancy and the Toyota Motor Company was constrained by army order to concentrate on the production of trucks for military purposes. This constraint naturally remained throughout the war; and it was not until after 1959, when the name of birthplace of the company was changed from Koromo to Toyota City, that the manufacturing of automobiles was seriously launched. The meteoric rise of the Toyota since then is well known. Rationalization *à la* Toyota was harsh on its employees and on subcontracting shops in the vicinity; and numerous reports came to be published with such titles as "The Factory of Despair" and "Gloomy Darkness of the Auto Kingdom." But a single statistic is sufficient to attest to the unmatched position which Toyota attained in the value productivity of automobile production by 1976. The following figures (in yen) compare the per employee profit earned (after tax) of leading auto-makers in that year:

Toyota	2,570,000
Nissan	1,340,000
GM	1,140,000
Ford	650,000[17]

In this way, Toyota went on to become the top auto producer of the world, increasing its net internal surplus which was utilized, in the first instance, in setting up a finance company for loaning to its own customers and then was channeled into the establishment of branch factories abroad. Finally, however, the company decided to become a conglomerate, changing its

Table 7.6. *Quinquennial averages of Japan's direct foreign investments*

(Unit: billion dollars)

1956–60	0.09
1961–65	0.13
1966–70	0.53
1971–75	2.47
1976–80	4.13
1981–85	9.43

Source: The Ministry of Finance. These statistics are based on the permits given by, and the applications to, the Ministry; but quite often investment actions are not finalized, and even if they are, the timing may be delayed for more than a year. However, these statistics are useful since they are classified by industries and the countries of destination. There is another set of direct foreign investment statistics published by the Bank of Japan in its international payments series. These show smaller absolute amounts (40 to 60 percent) compared with the Ministry of Finance figures.

articles of incorporation to extend its activities into aeroplane production and servicing as well as marine-related activities and housing construction. Such has been the logical consequence of the prodigious growth of the net internal surplus of a giant corporation in Japan's high-growth period.

3. The globalization trend

Increase in direct foreign investment

Among the possibilities of the use made of net internal surplus (NS) as the amount grew in the high-growth period, we have referred, in the preceding section, to that of launching direct investment abroad. We can verify this trend easily in terms of statistics, as shown in Table 7.6. The latest figure available is for the year 1986, which was 22,320 million dollars, almost twice the amount for 1985. We may recall that manufacturing corporations' internal reserve (S) plus depreciation (D) turned out to be larger than their gross investment (GV) in the five-year average of 1976–80 (109 percent) compared with 1971–75 (75 percent); and this turn of events is clearly reflected in the marked increase of the flow of direct foreign investment (DFI) in the decade of 1970s.

Needless to say, Japanese capitalism engaged in fairly extensive DFI in the prewar days; but they were mainly the exploitative arms of Japan's imperialism in the Far Eastern region. Whatever assets remained abroad after the war, such as in China (including what used to be called Manchuria), were sequestered or liquidated; and Japan was to begin her external adventure entirely anew from zero after the war as an equal, or subaltern, partner with any region of the world. Moreover, it was not until 1951 that still-occupied Japan was allowed to promote direct investment projects abroad. Even then, however, her international payments position was such that the government had to restrict severely the issuing of permits for the external ventures that would drain the meager foreign-exchange holdings of the country. Thus, the spheres of DFI initially attempted upon reopening in the early 1950s were restricted to:

a The setting up of branch offices of trading companies and banks in foreign countries for the purpose of facilitating, in particular, export sales abroad, and

b The promotion of big investment projects related to the development of natural resources, such as the Alaskan pulp (1953), the Brazil's Minas Gerais Iron Works (1957) and the Arabian Oil (1958).

These spheres were soon followed, in the 1960s, by the setting up of production sites for labor-intensive light manufacturing industries (such as textiles and food-processing) mainly in South-East Asian developing countries. The motivating factors here were evidently the latter's protectionist policies as well as the shifting comparative advantage. Still, the total amount of DFI was fairly limited; and it was only after the government took steps, from 1969 to June 1972, to liberalize almost completely the exporting of funds for direct investment abroad that the real impetus was given. Whereas the total DFI during 21 years between 1951 and 1971 amounted to 3.6 billion dollars only, such flow of funds shot up to 5.8 billion dollars in the mere two years of 1972 and 1973 – the first high tide in the postwar period.

Conditioning factors behind this high tide were: (a) the appreciation of the yen exchange rate (from 360 yen to the dollar in 1971 to 265 yen in 1973) which made Japanese export goods dearer abroad; (b) the marked rise of real wages in Japan as the high-growth period progressed, shifting the comparative advantage of labor-intensive products further to less developed Asian countries; and (c) the emergence of pronouncedly favorable current balance of payments at least until the first oil shock of 1973–74. Although the oil shock had some depressing effects on the economy, as was discussed in the preceding chapter, these same conditioning factors continued to operate essentially through the decade of the 1970s to sustain the high level of DFI until the second high tide visited Japan as the decade of the 1980s approached. Especially from the year 1981 the annual flow began rising conspicuously to the level of nine billion dollars; and the 2 year total for 1985 and 1986 (34.5 billion dollars) was equivalent to the 30-year total for 1952 and 1981. By this time a new conditioning factor was in operation. That was the increasing friction which began to plague the Japanese government in relation to the countries where Japanese exports came to be regarded as unfairly competitive. Trade frictions had existed in an earlier period especially in connection with Japan's textile exports. But the target commodities this time were new – basically the consequences of superior performance of high-technology industries in Japan during the decades of the 1960s and 1970s compared with most other developed countries.[18] It was unavoidable that the countries affected began resorting to various measures of import control against Japanese goods, such as the raising of tariff rates, the instituting of "antidumping" measures, the proposing of "voluntary" export restriction by Japan, etc. Faced with such developments in regard to foreign trade and fearing that the trend was likely to continue in a more aggravating form, Japan's manufacturing firms with big enough interests in export trade began seriously to launch upon the establishment of branch factories abroad, especially in those countries where specific trade frictions were causing problems. In a survey made by the Ministry of International Trade and Industry among the Japanese corporations which had set up their subsidiary firms in advanced countries since 1980, it is significant to note that the motives for such actions were indicated for relevant industries in the percentage breakdowns as shown in Table 7.7. We can see from this table how the second high tide of DFI from the late 1970s to the early 1980s was characterized by new dimensions: that of (a) the primary motivation being to cope with the trade friction problems, (b) the industries concerned being generally those of high-technology ones, and (c) the countries of destination being advanced ones.[19]

It was in the course of such development that the growth of DFI was accompanied by the globalization trend in the case of Japan also, resulting in the cropping up of multinational corporations (MNC) in various fields of manufacturing. Along with these, however, it is to be noted that especially since the first half of the 1980s the wave of globalization began spreading into the spheres of finance and insurance as well as of real estate, often with the motivation of seeking tax havens.[20]

Thus we can now speak of Japanese capitalism as having joined, though

Table 7.7. *The motives for establishing subsidiary firms in advanced countries – by industries*

Industries	In order to cope with the trade friction problems (%)	In order to maintain or increase the share in the market within the country concerned (%)
Office machinery	96.7	negligible
Machine tool	77.1	14.3
Household electric apparatus	53.6	13.6
Electronics	30.0	32.1
Automobiles	66.0	24.0

Source: Tsūshō Hakusho (White Paper, MITI), 1986, p.182. The motives other than the two referred here are not reproduced.

somewhat belatedly, the front rank of world capitalism which now has the intimate network of multi- and trans-national corporations dominating over a large part of market-oriented economies of the world. That Japan has been a newcomer in this race for globalization can be verified by Table 7.8 which gives, for the year of 1981, the ratios of the value produced by subsidiary firms of each country's MNCs as divided by the total volume of ordinary exports of that country. It is significant that in the case of the United States, for example, MNCs' subsidiaries abroad produced more than twice the total export volume of that country. Japan, as can be seen, is listed at the bottom of the table, with the lowest globalization ratio of 12.2 percent and with only 20.3 percent of exports being the values produced by her MNCs' subsidiaries abroad.

After 1981, however, the picture did change considerably as the dynamic of Japanese capitalism kept on making headway farther afield, as has been indicated earlier in terms of the growth in DFI. This trend shows no sign of abating at the time of this writing (September 1990), and it may be appropriate to trace here the globalization pattern of two representative cases: one, a particular industry – the household electric goods and electronics – that has been running at the top of the globalization trend in Japan, and the other, a particular region – Australia – that has been a favored hunting ground for Japanese capital in recent years.

The globalization pattern illustrated – the case of E-E industry

The history of the growth and development of the household electric goods and electronics industry (E-E industry) in Japan illustrates vividly so many

Table 7.8. *The volume of sales by MNCs compared with the total exports from each country – 1981*

| Country | No. of firms | Multinational Corporations | | | Country's exports (million $) (C) | Production abroad divided by exports (%) (B)/(C) |
		Volume of sales (million $) (A)	Values produced by subsidiaries abroad (million $) (B)	Globalization ratio (%) (B)/(A)		
USA	239	1,427,819	483,286	33.8	233,677	206.8
Switzerland	10	42,934	34,044	79.3	27,049	125.9
UK	67	263,320	128,133	48.7	102,201	125.4
Sweden	16	39,512	28,166	71.3	28,401	99.2
France	20	144,031	57,632	40.0	106,425	54.2
West Germany	33	218,517	80,447	36.8	176,090	45.7
Netherlands	8	45,436	29,261	64.4	68,715	42.6
Japan	62	251,832	30,831	12.2	152,030	20.3

Source: Tabulated from Yoshikazu Miyazaki, *Gendai Kigyōron Nyūmon*, p.346, which made use of J.M. Stopford, *The World Directory of Multinational Enterprises*, 1983 and The Bank of Japan, *Gaikoku Keizai Tōkei Nempō* (Statistical Yearbook of Foreign Country Economies), 1981.

Table 7.9. *Export components of electric–electronic industry 1960–1985*

(Unit: percent of total exports)

	1960	1965	1970	1975	1980	1985
Heavy electric machinery	8.3	8.2	10.0	15.4	14.7	10.9
Household electric appliances	4.2	4.0	4.9	4.8	5.5	5.2
Lighting fixtures	9.0	6.8	3.0	1.7	1.9	1.4
Home electronic goods	61.1	54.6	55.8	43.9	36.8	31.5
(radio receivers)	(53.3)	(23.9)	(12.6)	(4.8)	(1.2)	(0.5)
(monocolor television)	(1.1)	(11.1)	(6.8)	(2.4)	(1.6)	(0.2)
(color television)	—	—	(5.5)	(7.8)	(5.1)	(5.4)
(tape recorders)	(3.6)	(10.4)	(22.0)	(19.0)	(13.4)	(7.1)
(video tape recorders)	—	—	—	—	(8.0)	(14.2)
Industrial electronic goods	3.4	7.8	13.1	15.8	14.8	24.4
(Electronic computers)	—	—	(0.6)	(1.5)	(2.2)	(9.9)
Electronic parts	14.6	18.6	13.1	18.4	26.3	26.6
Total (in billion yen)	93.6	276.7	1,051.4	2,154.6	5,566.5	11,169.4

Source: Yasuo Okamoto, (3), p.46, based on The Ministry of Finance, *Customs Statistics.*

of the important features of the globalization trend as well as the nature of high-technology industries that it actually calls for a volume-sized treatment.[21] But here, we have to be satisfied with a bare outline of the essential points involved.

The growth of the E-E industry in the postwar period in Japan has been truly phenomenal. Its production, which amounted to 192.4 billion yen in 1955, had increased 124 times by 1986 to 23.9 trillion yen, occupying 39.6 percent of the machinery industry as a whole, larger than transportation equipment (including automobiles and shipbuilding) which was in the second position with 32.6 percent. A summary picture may be given in terms of growth of *exports* of that industry classified by component categories, as shown in Table 7.9. The table reveals vicissitudes of several divisions of the E-E industry clearly enough, with lighting fixtures and radio receivers, added together, declining from 62.3 percent in 1960 to 1.9 percent in 1985 while the sum of three items – video tape recorders, industrial electronic goods and electronic parts (semiconductor devices, integrated circuits, etc.) – rising from 16.0 percent in 1960 to 65.2 percent in 1985. Such a radical shift in the composition, as well as the apparent stability in weights of some other items – such as household electric appliances and color television – reflect, on the one hand, the technological development and the competitive market conditions abroad and, on the other, deliberate policy measures of foreign governments and the globalization moves by the industry itself over the quarter century since 1960.

As was mentioned earlier, it was only in 1951 that Japan, still under occupation, was allowed to launch direct investment projects abroad, and that the earliest attempt in this regard was the setting up of branch offices of trading companies for the purpose of facilitating, in particular, export sales abroad. Such was the case in connection with the E-E industry also. The burgeoning production sites with Japanese capital could be found in the 1960s especially in South-East Asian countries, usually in the form of joint ventures with local capital. The motivations behind these ventures were, generally speaking, (a) to circumvent the protectionist measures of those countries, and (b) to take advantage of the lower wage rates prevalent there. Products taken up then were still limited mainly to household electric appliances and radio receivers.

Although trade frictions with the United States began as early as 1959 when the EIA (Electronic Industries Association) brought a case before the OCDM (Office of Civilian Defense Mobilization) against the "flooding" of Japanese transistor radios in the US market, it was not until Japan's exports of television sets, first the monocolor and then the color models, began showing big potentials from the middle 1960s onwards that trade frictions became serious enough to motivate the major suppliers of Japan to set up production bases abroad. In retrospect we may say that the turning point came in 1976 so far as color television sets were concerned when the Sylvania Company appealed to the US government over the alleged violation of Article 337 of the Customs Tariff Act by five Japanese manufacturers. The upshot was the US–Japan governmental agreement in March 1977 for the maintenance of "orderly market conditions" and the instituting of voluntary restriction of exports by Japan. Such a turn of events naturally led to greater efforts by Japanese companies for the expansion of foreign production bases and already in 1979 exports of color television sets from Japan to America were overtaken by their supply from the production bases there. From then on, the ratio of Japanese color television sets produced abroad to those produced at home kept on rising from 41 percent in 1979 to 95 percent by 1987. By this latter date, however, Japan could no longer rely on a big share in the US import market of color television sets, occupying only 6 percent compared with 31 percent for Formosa, 22 percent for the Republic of Korea and 19 percent for Mexico.

Another field within the E-E industry where the sharp increase of Japan's share in the world supply led to trade frictions and, in due course, motivated Japanese producers to globalize their production bases has been the electronic parts, or the semiconductor industry in particular.

In 1965, the world top five semiconductor makers (with their relative shares in brackets) were: Texas Instruments (32), Fairchild (18), Sygnetics (15), Westinghouse (12) and Motorola (6); but, by 1982, two Japanese firms, NEC and Hitachi, thrust themselves into the top five list; and, in 1987, the list read in the order of NEC, Toshiba, Hitachi, Motorola and Texas Instruments. The rapid shift which came to pass in this competitive field is eloquently told by the replacement of the US by Japan as the top supplier of IC (integrated circuits) in the world in 1986. Whereas the US share in 1985 was 48.5 percent against Japan's 39.9 percent, the positions were reversed in 1986, with Japan occupying 46.1 percent against America's 42.0 percent. In a more sophisticated sector of DRAM (dynamic random-access memory) Japan shot up to the top position a little earlier, i.e. in 1981, with the share of 66 percent of the world in the supply of 64K·DRAM (led by Hitachi, Fujitsu and NEC) against America's 31 percent. It was inevitable, we may say, that the SIA (Semiconductor Industry Association) of the United States, which was organized in 1977, started quite early in its career to seek measures to fend off the Japanese encroachment, through, for example, an appeal to the Office of USTR (The United States Trade Representative). But such steps did not bear fruit until 1985, by which time the evident competitive superiority of Japan's 256K·DRAM came to be regarded with concern by the military and space-science quarters in the United States and the dumping charge by the SIA was instituted against Japanese suppliers. This led to the official confrontation between the two countries, resulting in the conclusion of the Japan–US Semiconductor Agreement of 1986 with a 5-year time limit. In effect, this agreement entailed voluntary export restriction by Japan.[22]

Against such a background evolved gradually the globalization trend in Japan's semiconductor industry. Production units abroad were first set up in the middle 1970s in the South-East Asian countries, such as Malaysia and Singapore, and then spread in a bigger fashion into Western developed countries as the decade of the 1980s began. It was characteristic in almost all these cases that the local companies set up were 100-percent-owned subsidiaries of their mother companies, bespeaking of the special import-ance attached to such ventures by the latter. Thus, for example, as the one-mega bit DRAM entered the stage of quantity production in Japan, which was around 1986, the subsidiaries abroad followed suit almost immediately – apparently a strategic move for the industry as a whole. At the same time it is to be noted that the globalization trend in the E-E industry is not limited to widening the scope of operations on the national base, such as NEC of Japan extending its production units into several foreign countries, but increasingly we find a tendency to explore a competitive coexistence among leading producers on a global scale, either through agreement on co-operative ventures, as in the case of Hitachi with Texas Instruments for the development of 16M·DRAM, or through a deliberate division of labor with emphasis on respective specialities, as in the case of the big three in Europe: Philips (The Netherlands) for SRAM, Siemens (Germany) for DRAM, and Thomson (France) for EPROM (erasable programmable read-only memories). Is it that world capitalism is now capable, at least in one sphere, of conducting itself in a much more organized fashion than used to be the case? A big question that remains to be answered in years to come!

In concluding the discussion on the US–Japan trade friction problems related to the semiconductor industry, let me quote R.V. Ramachandran:[23]

Over the longer history of human civilization, one sees the centers of economic power shifting around. The last phase began with industrial revolution in England, which spread to geographically and culturally contiguous areas of Europe and North America. The inability of the rest of the world to absorb the new industrial technology acted as a barrier, protecting the industries in these countries. The striking achievement of postwar Japan seems to have been its ability to break this barrier and compete with Western nations in areas where they were traditionally dominant. Now other countries like Korea are following the Japanese lead in absorbing highly productive technology into a low-cost economy. Traditional international trade theory would suggest that the resulting expansion in trade would permit the Western and Asian nations to enjoy a new era of prosperity. But one is left to wonder whether the growth of the Pacific region is another orderly expansion of the international economy or the prelude to one of those historic swings in economic power.

Reading this passage, one recalls a farseeing dictum of Brooks Adams who predicted almost a century ago that: "For upward of a thousand years the tendency of the economic center of the world has been to move westward, and the Spanish War has only been the shock caused by its passing the Atlantic. Probably, within two generations, the United States will have faced about, and its great interests will cover the Pacific, which it will hold like an inland sea."[24] The subsequent history vindicated Adams' prescience and after the defeat of Japan in the last war the era of *Pax Americana* dawned in the Pacific. US leadership was undisputed at the beginning, with, however, a paternalistic attitude toward Japan as a junior partner and at the same time as a bulwark against a communist China. It was around that time (in 1952) that Sir Robert Menzies, the Australian Prime Minister, wrote: "it would come as a shock to most Australians to be told that, as a punishment for the Japanese, Australian troops were in future to defend Japan while the Japanese themselves went smiling and bowing about their affairs of production and commerce."[25] In fact, the Japanese did go "smiling and bowing about their affairs of production and commerce" most energetically after they regained their independence in 1952 and, before long, Japan became an equal partner when the Pacific Basin Economic Council was formed in 1967 by corporate executives from the USA, Japan, Australia, Canada and New Zealand, followed in 1968 by the proposal of a formal Pacific Basin Organization. By the time what is known as "the Pacific Rim Strategy" was developed at a meeting in Kyoto in May 1975, Japan had gone through two decades of unsurpassed rapid economic growth and the position of leadership in the Pacific passed from the United States to Japan. The impact of such a turn of events on the Australian economy has been considerable, to say the least. Although Murray Sayle wrote, as was quoted earlier in this chapter, that "Australia can be Japan's Australia, land of rugged adventure and heavy drinking, the appropriate place of exile for Japanese dissidents and remittance men," the influx of Japanese products and capital in recent years has been of a much more substantive character. Captains of industry now residing in Australia are far from resembling the erstwhile "remittance men" of the British Empire period. We may recount here some concrete evidence of the inroads which Japanese capital has made into Australian society in recent years.[26]

Japanese capital in Australia

What is most striking is the extremely rapid pace in which Japanese investment in Australia has grown. By the end of the financial year 1986–87 the United States was still at the top in the list of foreign investors in Australia followed by the UK and Japan; but over the five years between 1981 and 1986 Japan increased its amount more than five times while British investment merely doubled and American investment increased only two and a half times. And, in terms of annual inflow, Japan overtook both the USA and the UK in 1987–88 as the largest source of foreign investment in Australia; and it is significant that 60 percent of Japanese investment in that year went into Australian real estate.[27] It has been indeed characteristic of the manner of Japanese capital moving into Australia in most recent years to extend its control over real estate primarily for the purpose of developing resort bases, complete with hotels and golf courses, to lure affluent Japanese tourists. It has even been commented that "a Japanese business consortium with unlimited funds wants to buy every privately owned golf course in the Sydney metropolitan area . . . The ambitious plan would link ownership of the golf courses with major international city hotels already owned by the Japanese."[28] This is a kind of vertical integration by Japanese capital, encompassing further department stores and some of the infrastructures such as harbor facilities and power stations. The Japanese government itself joined in the developmental boom by proposing a giant project to set up a High-technology City, or what is known as "Multi-function Polis" (MFP), an integrated work and residential community emphasizing consumerism and incorporating, amongst other features, "high-tech" R&D industries, leisure facilities and housing for 100,000 people. The capital cost involved is estimated to amount to five trillion yen.

Although such projects as the MFP and a number of conspicuous real estate purchases by Japanese capital have attracted a great deal of public attention in Australia, often highly critical,[29] the infiltration of Japanese capital, riding on the globalization wave, into other sectors of the Australian economy has been going on much more quietly and steadily.

To begin with, it is to be noted that Australia has one of the highest levels of foreign ownership in the country's industries. Sectorwise, percentages owned by foreign interests in the middle 1980s were recorded as shown in Table 7.10. It is further reported that "one estimate is that by 1990 about 300 of the top 500 Australian companies will have been involved in mergers or takeovers."[30] Japanese participation in this state of affairs has been quite manifold, broadening its coverage considerably as time goes on. The early inroad that was made by Japanese capital was, characteristically, in the form of trading companies handling exports from, and imports into, Australia. By 1988, nine Japanese trading companies, such as Mitsui, Mitsubishi and Itochū, accounted for over one-fifth of all exports, dominating, in particular, trade in agriculture and mineral commodities out of Australia. Above all, mineral resources are of special importance; and naturally, as well as buying Australian raw materials, the Japanese have been moving towards buying out Australian suppliers. Thus, Idemitsu-Kōsan, one of Japan's biggest energy companies, has been buying up Australian coal mines, now holding 49 percent of Ebenezer Steaming Coal and 22.5 percent of Ensham Steaming Coal in Queensland. Other Japanese companies have followed. Another resource field of special importance for Japan is forestry products, in particular woodchips for the pulp and paper industry. Australia is the world's largest exporter of woodchips, and Japan is the largest importer, buying about 75–80 percent of world supply. In 1985, for example, of some 14 million cubic meters traded in the world, Japan took 11.8 million, of which Australia supplied 6.8 million. Here again, Japanese capital went in to control the source of supply. Daishōwa, the second biggest pulp and paper company in Japan, won as early as 1969 a tender to build a A$35 million pulp and paper plant in Eden NSW but, instead of doing so, took out the controlling stake later in a company originally established by Harris Holdings, to become a guaranteed buyer of the woodchip output of the firm.

As for the sector of manufacturing, the automobile industry tops the list of Japanese participation. General Motors and Ford had been in Australia

Table 7.10. *The extent of foreign ownership in Australian industries*

Sector	Year	Foreign ownership (%)
Mining	1984–85	44.7
Mineral processing	1981–82	46.3
Manufacturing	1982–83	31.9
Life insurance	1983–84	40.3
General insurance	1983–84	34.9
Financial corporations	1986	38.1
Banking	1986	21.0
Agricultural land	1983–84	5.9
Transport	1983–84	5.1

Source: Federal Investment Review Board Report, 1987–88, p.22, as reproduced by David and Wheelwright, p.102.

since before the war; but with the coming in of three Japanese makers (Toyota, Nissan and Mitsubishi) after the war, there now exists no independent local maker in the country. The landscape of the industry, however, is somewhat complex. Toyota operates a joint venture with GMH, and Nissan is merged with Ford on a project basis. The federal government took steps to encourage exports, for example, by exempting from tariff imported components to the amount of the export of fully built cars accomplished, and further abolished the quantitative restriction on the importation of passenger cars from April 1988. Still, any export plans of the Australia-based plants must be first cleared by head office either in Tokyo or Detroit. Furthermore, what might be called "the conglomerate propensity" of Toyota inspired the company to sign up advertising and sponsorship deals with a couple of television networks in Australia, eliciting a somewhat sarcastic comment to the effect that "television viewers could be forgiven for thinking that Australia has only one motor vehicle manufacturer on television since January [1989] – Toyota Motor Sales of Australia."[31]

According to the annual survey made by the Ministry of International Trade and Industry of the Japanese government,[32] there were 61 Japanese controlled manufacturing firms in Australia as of March-end 1989, covering virtually every important field. Other than automobile production, the fields of telecommunications equipment and electronic goods are also rapidly becoming a major tributary arm of Japanese capital, with such companies as NEC, Fujitsu and San'yō already firmly entrenched. Financial services also, linked in particular to Japan-based property and construction activities, have grown markedly in recent years, with a number of Japanese banks having obtained full banking licenses in Australia. Nor are other types of financial institutions, such as securities companies and insurance, absent from this picture.

Altogether, one gets the impression, at stated earlier, that Australia has been a favored hunting ground for Japanese capital in recent years, including, alas, "the sex industry" with the infamous gangs known as the *Yakuza* operating as middle-men.[33]

Theories on globalization

In concluding this section on the globalization trend, it may be appropriate to make a brief comment upon theoretical issues related to foreign direct investment. As is well known among specialists in the field, controversy started with the advancing of the product-cycle hypothesis by Raymond Vernon in 1966,[34] which admittedly was quite relevant to US experience during the decades of the 1950s and 1960s. Products go through the stages of innovation, maturation and standardization; and in the early innovation stage the front-running firm would naturally attempt to exploit profit possibilities abroad through both exports and direct investment abroad. IBM was a typical example in this regard. Vernon's hypothesis was soon followed by a theory emphasizing superiority through oligopolistic differentiation, championed by Hymer, Kindleberger and Caves.[35] The essential element in this theory attributed any success of direct foreign investment to the monopolistic superiority of the investing firm. As the globalization progressed in the decades of the 1970s and 1980s, however, attention came to be drawn more and more to *the inner motive force* of oligopolistic firms to internalize externalities through the exporting of "managerial resources" in a broad sense which would subsume not only capital itself but also technological know-how, managerial skills and market-expanding capabilities. One of the pioneers advocating this type of explanation was Ryūtaro Komiya[36] who incorporated into his theory the basic idea of managerial resources advanced by E.T. Penrose.[37]

Komiya's theory actually harmonizes quite well with the observation presented earlier in this chapter concerning the expanding trend of net internal surplus under corporate capitalism with the inevitable consequence of the intra-firm division of labor to encompass broader dimensions (as far as the international division of labor) under the planning control of a single firm. The march of corporate capitalism, we may say, has come to this stage. What implication this may have for hegemonic strifes, or the dissolution of contradictions, among dominant international capitals is a problem to be dealt with separately.[38]

4. Privatization

Background for the privatization moves

Confidence gained with the march of corporate capitalism in the decades of high-growth period prompted the political and business leaders of Japan to proceed to emulate the privatization programs of Mrs Thatcher's government, a trendsetter in this regard. The occasion provided was what was called the "3-K deficit" in government finance – Kokutetsu (National Railroad), Kome (rice subsidy), and Kempo (health insurance), which called for a fairly bold program of fiscal retrenchment. Thus the government decided to set up the Temporary Administrative Reform Commission in March 1981, ostensibly for the purpose of general rationalization of administrative functions, but with a specific (unrevealed) mandate to consider the question of privatizing public enterprises.[39] As the Commission started undertaking its work, it became undeniably clear that the clandestine auxiliary purpose of privatization in the mind of the establishment was the undermining of the strength of the recalcitrant unions among public enterprise workers. At the time, Japan's largest nationwide federation of labor unions was Nihon Rōdō Kumiai Sō-Hyōgikai, abbreviated as Sōhyō, politically closest to the left wing of the Japan Socialist Party. The total membership of this federation then numbered some 4.5 million, of which, significantly, about 70 percent was occupied by public officials and public enterprise workers, among whom the Kokurō (National Railroad Workers Union) was reputedly the most radical.

But one may ask the question, how could they weaken the strength of this railroad workers' union through the privatization of the National Railroad? The answer is somewhat complex and we have to go back to the history of the National Railroad in the postwar period. It may be recalled that Blaine Hoover, who came to Japan to advise on civil service reforms in 1947, was convinced that the crux of his problem was discipline of all the public service unions, including those in public enterprises; and thus a natural conclusion for him was to prohibit by law collective bargaining and strikes for all the public service workers irrespective of the type of activities they were engaged in. Hoover's reform ideas were opposed by the Labor Division of the occupying authorities; but in the end they were approved by General MacArthur in July 1948. However, to ameliorate the drastic nature of Hoover's proposal, MacArthur wrote to Prime Minister Ashida at the same time, instructing him to split off the government railways and monopoly enterprises to form separate public corporations and let their employees bargain collectively, although *not strike*. Instead, mediation and arbitration procedures were to be set up. Thus was born the Japan National Railroad Public Corporation in June 1949 with the entire capital subscribed by the state.

The concept of "public corporation" was quite attractive in those days as combining public accountability with managerial autonomy in day-to-day decision-making. Apparently, the successful performance of the Tennessee Valley Authority in the United States with the much heralded slogan of "Democracy on the March" was to be studied and emulated. But transplanting the western concept of "public corporation" onto Japanese soil was no easy matter. In particular, "managerial autonomy," in the case of the National Railroad Public Corporation, for example, was highly restricted by legal, bureaucratic and political prescription and interference to such an extent that Fumio Takagi, president of the corporation from March 1976 to December 1983, once complained that his predicament was similar to a swimmer whose arms and legs were tied. Restrictions ranged from (a) legislative control of the rates and fares; (b) political interference in investment programs; (c) bureaucratic control of personnel policy and pay scales, to sundry other cramping rules, such as disallowance of retaining cash-sales intake for more than a day in station offices.[40] By way of offsetting these restrictions, the fiscal authorities of the government have habitually looked after the financial difficulties of the Corporation, covering partially the annual deficit on the record book only, not clearing it in each year. Such circumstances nurtured the prevalent sense of what came to be known as "Oyakata-Hinomaru" (Our Boss is the National Flag), or the generally permissive attitude over the lack of discipline and some excesses on the side of both management and labor. The excesses on the union side were basically related to the legal restriction of the "no strike" imperative. The management having no power to negotiate the wage rate with the union, which in turn was prohibited from striking, workers' discontent and grievances tended to be aired in numerous directions, such as the refusal to cooperate in the productivity-raising campaign and the field-consultation system. But, most paradoxically, strikes were called more frequently in this strike-forbidden industry than in other private industries where they were not banned. Finally, "the strike for the right to strike" was called on November 26, 1975, mobilizing close to one million workers employed in public enterprises. In the case of railroad workers the strike continued for eight days – the longest complete stoppage of operations in the history of Japan's national railroad. The upshot was not only a losing game for the strikers, with more than five thousand railroad workers penalized and damage compensation to the amount of 20.2 billion yen demanded against the unions, but had the effect of arousing an anti-railroad-unions attitude in a large section of the general public at the time. The government utilized this occasion to take the offensive against Kokurō in particular, blaming the "Oyakata-Hinomaru" permissiveness which was alleged to have prevailed, and started, in effect, the preparation for privatizing the national railroad.

The case of the National Railroad

The actual move for privatization began, as stated earlier, in the spring of 1981 and took four (for the Nikon Telephone and Telegraph Company) to six (for the Nikon National Railroad) years for consummation. The government's striving toward the privatization of the National Railroad, however, was by no means plain sailing. Major problems which were debated heatedly in the process in parliament and in public in general were: (a) the causes of, and responsibility for, the bankrupt condition of the public corporation, and (b) the controvertible aspects of the proposed plan of dismembering the integrated network into a number of independent regional companies along with privatization. Here we shall take up only the first of these problems.

The basic question for the National Railroad Public Corporation was how to harmonize the efficiency-seeking business principle with public interest commitments. If the latter, which necessarily would involve specific cost, could be clearly specified and accompanied by governmental subsidies for the purpose, the Corporation could accept them as a given datum in its operation. But it was very often the case that even when the specific cost could be ascertained as in the cases of the rate-discounting for the transportation of rice and for student commuting tickets – matters of public policy – the relevant ministries did not cover the consequent shortfall in the Corporation's revenue. Much more important were the shouldering by the Corporation of the extraordinary cost of absorbing more than 100,000 repatriates from the Japan-controlled railroads in Mainland China immediately after the war, and also the cost of running the politically sponsored local lines for which there was no hope of making ends meet. In both of these cases the business principle had to be compromised; but the quantitative share of the cost attributable to the contribution for public interest was impossible to measure. Furthermore, the Corporation's competence in setting rates and fares was legally circumscribed by the National Railroad Rates and Fares Act of 1948, which prescribed such conditions as: (a) they should aid in promoting the development of industries; (b) they should contribute to the stability of wages and prices; (c) they should cover the cost adequately; and (d) they should be uniform throughout the country. These prescriptions could in actual fact contradict each other and were often a source of conflict with the business efficiency principle.

In other words, it was extremely difficult for the Corporation to

harmonize the business efficiency principle with the imposed commitments
for public interest, and the net result was like making the room appear to be
clean by sweeping the dust under the carpet – the carpet hiding the
accumulated debt of considerable size.

The accumulated deficit at the time the cabinet decision was made for
privatization in 1985 amounted to 16.7 trillion yen, or approximately
140,000 yen per capita of the Japanese population. And the amount of
deficit in a single year of 1985 was 1,847 billion yen with the following
composition (unit – billion yen):

(A) Deficit in the General Account	317.8
(B) Deficit due to the Extraordinary Separation payments	762.1
(C) Deficit due to the Extraordinary Pension Payments	355.8
(B) + (C)	(1,117.9)
(D) Capital cost for the "Bullet Train" development	412.1
(B) + (C) + (D)	(1,530.0)
Total	1,847.8

The two items, (B) and (C), in this table are the consequences of the
unilateral command by the government to the Corporation to absorb into
its manpower upward of 100,000 repatriates from Mainland China and
therefore constitute the burden which, the Corporation could say, was
independent of its operation. Item (D), on the other hand, was not in the
nature of a deficit and was a part of usual net investment expenditures
which could be recouped in the future. The critical deficit item was (A), for
which the Corporation could be held responsible. It was big enough in the
1985 settled accounts as shown above. But it is to be noted that the amount
of this deficit item was steadily declining from 1983 on, to the extent of
having been halved in two years. Advocates of privatization spoke loudly of
the "deficit-prone propensity" of the Corporation by citing the total figure
of 1,847 billion yen; but clearly this was not fair. For one thing, railroad
operation was becoming increasingly unprofitable in almost all advanced
countries; and it has been customary for the state to cover the deficit *each
year* in West European countries.[41] In Japan's case, however, the annual
deficit in the general account was allowed to accumulate to an unmanage-
able sum. Furthermore, the legal prescription on the rates and fares
prevented the Corporation from adjusting the price schedule in step with
the inflationary trend of the economy. Each time, the revision had to go
through the Diet deliberation and the appropriate timing was missed.[42]
Table 7.11 shows the distinct lag in the railroad-related prices compared
with other prices over the forty years between the prewar base and
December 1976.

Table 7.11. *Comparative price increases between 1934–36 and 1976*

	1934–36 Average	December 1976	Multiple
Newspaper (one month)	98.4 sen	1,750 yen	1,779
Public bath (for adult)	5 sen	120 yen	2,400
Postcard	1.5 sen	20 yen	1,333
Consumer Price Index (Tokyo)	1	1,128	1,128
Wholesale Price Index	1	675	675
National Railroad			
Passenger rate (first region fare rate)	1.6 sen	7.9 yen	506
Freight rate (on ton on km)	1.6 sen	7.54 yen	471
Parcel rate (20kg, second region)	1.75 yen	7.50 yen	429

Source: The Bank of Japan Statistical Monthly.

The need for a comprehensive plan for the transportation industry

The extenuating circumstances cited above were not sufficient to explain the deficit-prone character of the railroad industry in Japan. More basically, the erstwhile semi-monopoly position of the railroad has come to be definitely undermined by the effective competition provided in recent years by aeroplanes and road transport. This has been an inevitable trend in all developed countries and Japan could hardly be an exception. Let us see, first, how the relative shares of major transport media have changed in Japan in the course of four decades since 1950. Table 7.12 summarizes the notable changes that have taken place. The drastic decline in the share of the railroad and the concomitant rise in that of motor cars in both passenger transport and freight transport are impressive enough. A question can be raised, naturally then, to what extent such changes were the consequences of genuinely fair competition among different media of transport. Thus arose the controversy over the so-called "equal footing" between the railroad on the one hand and the motor and air transports on the other. The major issue in this controversy was the comparative degrees of government support for the provision of infrastructure and other facilities for each of the transport media. For example, the construction of highways – an essential condition for the expansion of motor transport – has been financed not only by the fuel tax revenues paid by drivers but also by governmental subsidies from the general account; and as for the airport construction, the initial outlay has been taken care of entirely by the government. But the comparable infrastructure for the railroad has always been the product of self-financed project and the capital cost for the

Table 7.12. *Relative shares of the major transport media – changes between 1950 and 1987*

(Unit: %)

Passenger transport (in man-km)

	Railroad	Buses	Automobile	Ships	Aeroplanes
1950	90.0	7.1	0.6	2.2	0.0
1965	66.8	21.0	10.6	0.9	0.8
1975	45.6	15.5	36.3	1.0	2.7
1987	31.1	9.3	55.6	0.5	3.5

Freight Transport[a] (in ton-kg)

	Railroad	Trucks Commercial	Owner driven	Total	Coastal shipping
1950	52.3	3.7	4.7	8.4	39.4
1965	30.7	12.0	14.0	26.0	43.3
1975	13.1	19.2	16.8	36.0	50.9
1987	4.6	34.6	15.8	50.4	44.8

Note:
[a] The share of air transport is omitted here, as being negligible.
Source: Un'yu-Keizai Tōkei Yōran (Handbook on Transport Economy Statistics), The Ministry of Transportation, 1989.

purpose often occupied a sizable portion of the Corporation's expenditures.[43] Freight transport by rail is further handicapped by the fact that the express services to and from rail stations are handled by an independent company which is also engaged in long-distance truck transport.

What has been lacking is the working out of a comprehensive plan for the transportation industry as a whole, with a systematic appraisal of costs and benefits of competing and often complementary means of transportation. After all, rail transport is the safest, the most energy efficient, the relatively most space-saving, and environmentally least damaging mode of carrying people and goods. In addition, as an executive of the German Federal Railroad once remarked,[44] the railroad is an important component of the culture of a nation – an opinion shared by many of us in Japan as well. The country's comprehensive plan for the transport industry will have to be broad enough to take all these matters into account, going beyond the simplistic concern over a monetary deficit in a single sector of the industry.

Thus we come to the final question of whether the privatization of the National Railroad Public Corporation can be expected to solve its major deficiencies of the past and to answer the societal objective of improving the welfare content of Japan's transportation sector as a whole. At the time of this writing (September 1990) it is still premature to give definitive answers to these problems. But it is at least certain that the privatization drive of Japan's conservative government, thus far successful in the case of railroads, telephone and telegraph, and tobacco and cigarettes, has been of a piece with the confident march of corporate capitalism in the wake of the high-growth period.

8   Whither Japan?

On the basis of the analysis given above, it is proposed in this chapter to discuss the direction in which Japanese capitalism might hopefully evolve with positive programs of nation-building. The nature of the topic is such that the concluding part of this chapter reflects necessarily my personal views which, I am aware, may not be shared by some of my compatriots.

First, however, a brief discussion is presented on the fact of capitalism undergoing a transformation toward the mixed economy type of socio-economic organization, thus travelling the road of convergence with socialism. The prime mover of this transformation is identified as technological progress, giving birth to the planning system within the private sector itself. The mixed economy can be regarded as a new mode of production; but, by its very nature, mixture of social motive forces is unavoidable. Thus the question arises of how we may be able to "vitalize the social economy" as an aspiration of such a society. The concrete answer to this question in the case of Japan is couched here in terms of two main pillars of nation-building: that is: (1) "Restoration of Man" and (2) "The Peace Constitution." More concretely, a summarizing sentence at the end of this chapter may be reproduced: "A Japan that takes the lead in pressing for world disarmament, is assiduous in the fight against disease by making the country the health-care center of the world, lays emphasis on tourist facilities at sites of scenic beauty, is active in international exchange in the fields of cultural and aesthetic life, is willing radically to increase the country's contribution to the United Nations University, and works hard, through both aid and trade, to wipe out the poverty which plagues the Third World, would be a Japan where the people would feel assured of holding in common positive values worth defending." And it may be added that such a prospect, I am certain, will have sobering as well as vitalizing effect on the spirits of Japan's younger generation.

1. The trend toward convergence of the two systems

Prewar opinions

The symbolic significance of the tearing down of the Berlin Wall as opening the door to a new stage of the rapprochement between East and West, and the widespread homage accorded to the market principle by socialist countries in recent years make us recall inevitably that prescient remark of Maxim Litvinoff some sixty years ago on the occasion of his encounter with Franklin Roosevelt, the then newly installed President of the United States. We had occasion to quote it earlier (in Chapter 2); what Litvinoff said was essentially that US capitalism and Soviet socialism were, though poles apart in 1920, coming closer to each other and would, before long, approach to the extent of "60 percent capitalism" in the US and "40 percent capitalism" in the USSR, with, however, the gap of "20 percent" remaining unbridged.

On the American side, there had been a somewhat similar prediction of rapprochement voiced in the early 1930s by journalist, Lincoln Steffens, who visited the Soviet Union after the revolution and summed up his impressions by saying that "Russia is the land of conscious, willful hope." To this remark he added: "But the United States of America, which the Russians recognize as their chief rival, is, however unconsciously, moving with mighty momentum on a course which seems not unlikely to carry our managing, investing, ruling masters of industry, politics, and art – by our blind method of trial and error – in the opposite direction around the world to the very same meeting-place, as they, some of them, are beginning to see and say."[1]

Litvinoff's remark must have been diplomatic, and Steffens' judgment intuitive. But economists, too, have been talking about the likelihood of *convergence* of the two rival socio-economic systems since as early as the late 1920s. The most prominent among them was Joseph Schumpeter, who wrote in an article published in 1928:

Capitalism, while economically stable, and even gaining in stability, creates, by rationalizing the human mind, a mentality and a style of life incompatible with its own fundamental conditions, motives and social institutions, and will be changed, although not by economic necessity and probably even at some sacrifice of economic welfare, into an order of things which it will be merely a matter of taste and terminology to call socialism or not.[2]

Schumpeter, as a social scientist, sided with the basic philosophy that there do exist *objective laws* of socio-economic development amenable to scientific formulation; and he held on, till the end of his life, to the view that "the capitalist process not only destroys its own institutional framework but it also creates the conditions for another."[3] Such a view, however, partakes the nature of a theory of social evolution in the historical process, and does not necessarily lead to the idea of convergence. But it at least prepared the ground, from the standpoint of capitalism, for the recognition that a major transformation of the system was in order.

Approach from the socialists' side

From the standpoint of socialism, on the other hand, a new vista was opened by Oskar Lange,[4] who, as early as in the 1930s, developed a theoretical framework for "the liberal socialism" which would retain the parametric function of prices under the control of the Central Planning Board with the system of social ownership of the means of production. In other words, according to Lange, the Central Planning Board would perform the functions of the market, establishing "the rules for combining factors of production and choosing the scale of output of a plant, for determining the output of an industry, for the allocation of resources, and for the parametric use of prices in accounting."[5] Once the parametric function of prices is adopted as an accounting rule, the price structure would be established, through the method of trial and error, by the objective equilibrium condition. Thus, it was claimed that there would be no fundamental inconsistency between social ownership of the means of production and rational economic calculation.

Lange, however, was a minority among Marxist economists then; and it was not until 1943 that Soviet economists came to embrace a doctrine basically akin to the position which Lange pioneered. It was in the midst of the grueling, exhausting battles against Hitler's invasion of the country that the Soviet official Marxist journal *Under the Banner of Marxism* (July/August 1943) published an article with authorization by its editors[6] affirming the relevance of "the law of value" to the Soviet socialist economy. This meant, in effect, in terms of modern economic terminology, that resource allocation, in the interest of efficiency, can and should follow the dictate of non-arbitrary, objectively determined valuation in the market. If expressed in this fashion, the new position taken appears to contradict squarely the orthodox Marxist doctrine of "the law of value," which can be summarized, according to Paul Sweezy, as "those forces at work in a commodity-producing society which regulate (a) the exchange ratios among commodities, (b) the quantity of each produced, and (c) the allocation of the labor force to the various branches of production. The basic condition for the existence of a law of value is a society of private producers who satisfy their needs by mutual exchange."[7] And in Marx's own words, "only as an internal law, and from the point of view of the individual agents as *a blind law*, does the law of value exert its influence and maintain the social equilibrium of production in the turmoil of its accidental fluctuations."[8] In other words, "the law of value" for Marxists used to be regarded as the antithesis of "the planning principle"; and thus it was inevitable that a heated controversy erupted both in the Soviet Union and the United States centering around the question of whether or not the new position advanced by the editors of *Under the Banner of Marxism* meant an undeniable revision of the basic tenet of Marxism.[9] As expected, Lange came to the rescue of the journal's editors,[10] giving incidentally what he considered to be corroborating evidence from Marx's own writings, which read: "After the abolition of the capitalism mode of production, but with social production still in vogue, *the determination of value* continues to prevail in such a way that the regulation of the labor time and the distribution of the social labor among the various groups of production, also the keeping of accounts in connection with this, become more essential than ever."[11] It is problematical if Marx used the expression "the determination of value" (die Wertbestimmung), nearly in the same sense as "the law of value." But in the light of the position Lange held, namely that the parametric function of prices was to be under the control of the Central Planning Board, "the law of value" under socialism was subject to determination by the planning authority and yet could perform the market function.

Debates inside the Soviet Union continued until what appeared to be the official summary was given by K. Ostrovitianov in the Communist Party organ *Bolshevik*,[12] in which he reviewed first the orthodox position on socialism[13] and then conceded a *subservient* role of "the law of value" to the planning principle on the ground that Soviet socialism still "retained, and had to make use of, the commodity-money relations." His article, undoubtedly, was a compromise gesture to all the participants of the debate within the country, attempting to avoid a sharp division of opinion in the midst of war. In fact, it is significant to note that Ostrovitianov, before concluding his article, made a special point of emphasizing the imperative need for drastic economizing of resources, both men and materials, in "the momentous war for the fatherland" as occasioning serious reflection over a number of economic principles including "the law of value."[14] It stands to reason that such a reflection arose in the minds of Soviet leaders in the circumstance of severest pressure on the manpower supply inasmuch as a planned economy which relies on the bureaucratic controls and calculation to the minutest detail would require a prodigiously large corps of manpower. This reflection, no doubt, was one of the factors in later years for the Soviet Union to become inclined to place positive significance on the market principle. But in any case, it can be stated that a door was opened, already in the decades of the 1930s and 1940s, for the adoption of a more liberal principle for the conduct of economic affairs under socialism – a trend for convergence towards a "40 percent capitalism" in Litvinoff's prescient remark of the early 1930s.

Postwar comments

In other words, there were historical trends toward convergence from both sides of capitalism and socialism even before the war. Such trends became more apparent in the postwar period and a large number of economists on the Western side began speaking about them, so that Paul Samuelson, even in his general textbook, had to go as far as to say that "with some exaggeration, John Kenneth Galbraith and Jan Tinbergen can point to a convergence, all over the globe, to a single modern industrial state – not capitalism, not socialism, but *a mixed economy*."[15] In fact, the argument for convergence was further strengthened in the postwar period by the introduction of a normative standpoint, notably by Tinbergen,[16] into the subject matter. Tinbergen starts with the premise that the common objective of all the societies, which ever socio-economic system they may be characterized by, should be the maximization of welfare of their contemporary citizens and the attainment of the optimum rate of growth for the benefit of their future generations. For this objective, according to him, policy measures will have to be of two kinds: (a) for the spheres of activities in which diminishing returns to scale prevail and external effects are negligible (such as in retail trade), the reign of the market will attain the optimum; and (b) for the spheres of activities in which increasing returns to scale prevail, with the possibility of emergence of monopolies, and external effects are likely to be considerable (such as in railroads), governmental interference is indicated. Such being the case, any society aiming at an optimum regime will have to converge towards a mixed economy type of organization. Tinbergen himself is aware that there could be various qualifications to this thesis; but it can hardly be gainsaid that he now represents a majority among theoretical economists on the Western side.

2. The mixed economy as a mode of production

Trends toward privatization and globalization assessed

The trend toward privatization, started by Mrs Thatcher's government of Great Britain after her election victory in May 1979, gradually gained momentum throughout the world in the 1980s. Japan, too, jumped on this bandwagon, as noted in the last chapter, by setting up a special commission in March 1981 with a specific mandate to consider the question of privatizing public enterprises. The highlight of this worldwide trend was an international conference on privatization sponsored by the United States Agency for International Development (USAID), held in Washington, DC, in February 1986, where nearly five hundred delegates from forty-six countries assembled. They were addressed by Secretary of State George P. Schultz, who explained that the conference symbolized a "revolution in economic thinking. It has been an unusual revolution in that it is a *return to principles we once adhered to, but from which we had strayed.* They are principles of individual freedom and private enterprise that have changed the world more in 200 years than all the changes in the preceding 2,000 years."[17] Although the longer term assessment has to wait for future historians, there seems to be a general agreement that "the British privatization program has been widely acclaimed as an economic and political success of the first order. It has led to a massive expansion in the number of shareholders, billions of pounds have been raised for the Exchequer, and state involvement in industrial decision-making has been drastically reduced."[18]

Another significant trend in recent decades has been the globalization of giant capitalistic enterprises in the form of multi- and trans-national corporations. We have given some concrete account of this trend mainly as related to Japan; but an additional comment may be given here with respect to its implication for world capitalism as a whole. In the prewar days also, we observed a kind of globalization in the sense of major capitalist countries expanding their spheres of influence abroad through direct foreign investment and otherwise. That was the era of imperialism, which Lenin characterized as the highest stage of capitalistic contradiction. But the table has been turned; and the colonies which used to be the object of exploitation by imperialist powers have become, almost all of them, politically independent and the erstwhile practice of armed intervention in the interest of capital is no longer condoned. Does it mean, then, that the globalization of private capital today, while strengthening the hegemonic rule by world capitalism, need not create its own contradictions? In other words, is it an aspect of "triumphant" capitalism, hardly calling for concession to the socialistic pattern of society?

Both of these recent trends, privatization and globalization, appear to support a view, which is touted in various quarters, to the effect, in the words of Robert Heilbroner, that "less than 75 years after it officially began, the contest between capitalism and socialism is over: capitalism has won."[19] If this is the case, the convergence hypothesis also has to be revised; and even Schumpeter's words of wisdom on the evolutionary transformation of capitalism are contradicted. We cannot, therefore, shy away from facing this contentious question squarely.

It may be agreed that George Schultz's dictum, quoted earlier, was in the nature of a rallying call for a like-minded partisan group. And although the "shareholders' democracy," championed by Mrs Thatcher, has been honored by authors like John Naisbitt and Patricia Aburdene as heralding a major "megatrend" for the twenty-first century,[20] consensus among experts appears to be that the worldwide fashion of privatization has been more of a political than economic action "structuring [its] strategies to build political constituencies."[21] Theoretical problems involved here are quite complex, and we can touch only on a few basic points relevant to our discussion. The variables involved are (a) the question of *ownership*, i.e. private or public; (b) the market power and the degree of *competition*; (c) the nature of *planning* and regulations; and (d) several dimensions of *efficiency*. All these are closely interrelated determinants of corporate incentives and behavior and simple generalizations will be out of place. Nevertheless, Assar Lindbeck's summarizing statement, which follows, may be considered as representing a majority opinion of theoretical economists today:

Central economic planning presumably has its main strength in the mobilisation, accumulation and rapid reallocation of resources . . . Competition between independent firms, in the context of a market system, by contrast, may be quite successful in terms of static allocative and technical efficiency, *provided* some kind of central planning is implemented to take care of collective goods and externalities, as well as to guarantee full utilisation of resources – a Keynesian stabilization policy as a minimum.[22]

It is important to note that the dichotomy in ownership (private versus public) is not parallel with the dichotomy in market relations (competition versus monopoly). Thus, for example in Britain's case, whereas in markets where effective (actual or potential) competition prevailed, such as Amersham, British Aerospace, Enterprise Oil, etc., it was found, empirically also, that private ownership – hence privatization – was efficient and suitable, "policy dilemmas became sharper when the Government's ambitions to privatize grew to embrace firms with extensive market power. Where monopoly exists – that 'great enemy to good management' in Adam Smith's words – the case for preferring private ownership to public ownership weakens considerably: privately efficient profit seeking can no longer be expected to lead to socially efficient results."[23]

In other words, it may be safe enough to conclude that the privatization boom of the 1980s does not necessarily mean an unqualified return to "principles of individual freedom and private enterprise" as George Schultz suggested, nor an irreversible evolution toward "people's capitalism" as Naisbitt and Aburdene predict.

What about, then, the globalization trend? Here, too, the problems
involved are far from simple. Although it is certain that the era of
imperialism is now a thing of the past and also that wars among major
powers with nuclear capability are highly unlikely, we have to keep in mind
the fact that multinational corporations, most of them, are giant
oligopolies normally exercising sophisticated planning strategies on an
international scale. "The borderless economy" is the term commonly used
nowadays, with the implication that policies of nation states often do not
constitute any constraint on their activities except when such policies can be
taken advantage of. At the same time, however, rivalries do exist among
trade-and-currency blocs which are being formed, such as the US–Canada
"free trade" treaty, the moves to eliminate internal barriers in the European
Community now with unified Germany as a dominant force, and the
increasing dominance of Japanese trade and finance in South-East Asia.
We had occasion to relate in the last chapter a concrete instance of such
rivalry in connection with the electric-electronic industry. What portends
for the future as each of the present trade-and-currency blocs becomes
further solidified is uncertain; but we may at least conclude that world
capitalism today is far from being characterized by atomistic competition
among myriads of free private enterprises and also that the bloc-rivalries
which exist today are not yet harmoniously contained. It is against this
background that the problem of convergence of socio-economic systems
emerges as a genuine issue.

The role played by technological progress

Reviewing the trends of privatization and globalization has given us, if
anything, a confirmation that the capitalist mode of production has had its
own way of modifying itself institutionally in the course of history in a
number of significant respects. A question arises, therefore, as to the basic
conditioning factors which have lain in the back of this evolutionary
process. Numerous economists have addressed themselves to this question
in the past; and a significant number of them seem to have agreed with
Veblen who held that technology was the prime mover of socio-economic
development. Veblen's thesis was that technology's progress was cumulative and independent of the will or actions of businessmen and further that
technical progress would bring in its wake institutional changes leading at
first to a state of chronic depression, then to a monopolized economy in
which profits are protected but human and material resources are
persistently underutilized.

Among the more modern economists, J.K. Galbraith in particular
followed the Veblenian tradition in emphasizing the role of technology in

transforming the institutional pattern of capitalism. His oft-quoted dictum that "the enemy of the market is not ideology but the engineer"[24] summarizes most succinctly the position he has taken. What he called "the theme of the imperatives of technology" was developed further under the following six headings:

a "An increasing span of time separates the beginning from the completion of any task . . . The more thoroughgoing the application of technology . . . the farther back the application of knowledge will be carried."

b "There is an increase in capital that is committed to production aside from that occasioned by increased output. The increased time, and therewith the increased investment in goods in process costs money."

c "With increasing technology the commitment of time and money tends to be made ever more inflexibly to the performance of a particular task. That task must be precisely defined before it is divided and subdivided into its component parts."

d "Technology requires specialized manpower . . . Organized knowledge can be brought to bear, not surprisingly, only by those who possess it."

e "The inevitable counterpart of specialization is organization. This is what brings the work of specialists to a coherent result . . . So complex, indeed, will be the job of organizing specialists that there will be specialists on organization."

f "From the time and capital that must be committed, the inflexibility of this commitment, the needs of large organization and the problems of market performance under conditions of advanced technology, comes the necessity for planning."[25]

These points, combined, are persuasive enough to suggest an appreciable impact of technological progress on the institutional behavior patterns of front-running business enterprises, especially in the context of the "scientific-industrial revolution" to which we had occasion to refer in Chapter 3.

Technological progress, which belongs to the realm of the real-wealth aspect as distinguished from the socio-institutional aspect, does impinge upon the mode of production in such a way that this latter undergoes qualitative changes often of major dimensions. Galbraith's thesis on technology illustrates this historical process. But it was Karl Marx who dwelled on this point repeatedly, venturing even a longer-run prediction which postulated advances in the use of automation. We may give here a relevant quotation from him:

As large-scale industry advances, the creation of real wealth depends less on the labor time and the quantity of labor expended than on the power of the instrumentalities set in motion during the labor time. These instrumentalities, and their powerful effectiveness, are in no proportion to the immediate labor time which their production requires; their effectiveness rather depends on the attained level of science and technological progress; in other words, on the application of this science to production . . . Human labor then no longer appears as enclosed in the process of production – man rather relates himself to the process of production as supervisor and regulator . . . He stands outside of [*neben*] the process of production instead of being the principal agent in the process of production.[26]

From here, Marx goes on to suggest the emergence of a "societal individual" or the man "whose knowledge and mastery of nature are acquired through his societal existence" with the consequence that labor time ceases to be the measure of wealth and therefore that "the exchange value must of necessity cease to be the measure of use value . . . The mode of production which rests on the exchange value thus collapses."[27]

The implication here is quite far-reaching. For one thing, the conditions for the atomistic attribution of labor's contribution to final products would inevitably disappear as automation and other advanced forms of application of science to production progressed and the "societal individual" comes to be developed. Then the determination of basic factor prices will lose the market objectivity of impersonal character and may become the product of power relations. As a matter of fact, we are already in such a stage in the evolving mode of production so that private firms (at least in the "planning system" in the Galbraithian sense) can more or less determine the size of their mark-up ratio, and the organized workers, if strong enough, can successfully obtain their scheduled wage demands from their employers.

The mixed economy as a mode of production

Such considerations as above, both Galbraith's and Marx's, point to an inevitable transformation of market-oriented free enterprise capitalism into something else, which, for want of a better terminology, may be called "socio-capitalism" or "the mixed economy," that is, a system of economic organization where the price mechanism functions in a limited way with a variety of public controls intervening to achieve the desired objectives of society. In a happy simile used by Wassily Leontief, it may be likened to a sail-boat with sails (the motive of self-interest) capturing the wind and the rudder (public control) guiding the direction. Since the standard textbook of Paul Samuelson and William Nordhaus defines the mixed economy as "the dominant form of economic organization in non-communist countries,"[28] I have no reason to hesitate in calling the mixed economy a mode of production in the social scientific sense.

Now, the underlying reasons which have justified the conception of the mixed economy are not limited to the impact of latter-day technological progress. The phenomena called "market failure" occur on a significant scale in modern capitalist societies and we know that in many instances devices to correct the existing imperfection of markets cannot solve the negative consequences which occur. Most egregious in this respect, in the case of Japan, have been the instances of environmental disruption, about which we gave detailed accounts in Chapter 5 (Section 3). Theoretically more basic, however, is the existence of value objects which defy any market valuation, such as natural beauty and the diversity of wild species. Value standards in this regard may be personal; but one can hardly take issue with an old lady, who, residing in the vicinity of a projected regional development plan area (the Shibushi coast in Kagoshima), commented in opposition to the project that "I would rather be sucking a pickled plum under a clear sky than be feasting on beef steak in the smog-filled atmosphere."

Possibly more important as an argument in favor of the mixed economy is the changing role of profits in the capitalist system. In the classical situation, profits constituted a source of, as well as an index of contribution to, economic growth under capitalism. They do constitute, even now, an important source of investment funds which are *sine qua non* for economic growth. In the last chapter (Section 2) we dealt with this aspect fully in connection with present-day corporate capitalism in Japan. What is in doubt now, however, is whether profits can still be regarded unequivocally as "an index of contribution to economic growth." It is generally agreed that under imperfect competition it pays people to limit the supply of their factors somewhat and that a positive profit can be earned as the return to a contrived or artificial scarcity. In the classical model of capitalism, on the other hand, profits were *temporary* excess returns to innovators or entrepreneurs; they were temporary because they were, in due course, competed out by rivals and imitators. But, of course, as one source of innovational profits was disappearing, another was born; and economic progress continued with profits accruing to successive, successful innovators as a reward. In the latest stage of capitalism, however, giant corporations with oligopolistic power are capable of perpetuating excess returns to themselves through oligopolistic price maintenance and various other devices such as privatizing particular innovations as well-guarded know-how. In other words, in such cases profits have become an index of the degree of success in *not* making others share the progress in productivity which in the nature of things should redound to the benefit of all. It is not easy for the mixed economy to cope with this type of situation. But if it can be stated that net internal surplus under corporate capitalism does not reflect truthfully the socially desired innovative activities, Lester Thurow's suggestion of setting up "the national equivalent of a corporate investment committee to re-direct investment flows from our 'sunset' industries to our 'sunrise' industries"[29] becomes quite germane in the context of the mixed economy.

Finally, to the points mentioned above, we will have to add, as an established characteristic of the mixed economy, the positive functions of the government in macroeconomic management of the economy to guarantee full utilization of resources, as well as those in instituting basic welfare measures to aid the weak and the underprivileged.

In summary we may say that:

a Capitalism has been undergoing a transformation toward the mixed economy type of socio-economic organization or "socio-capitalism," thus traveling the road of convergence with socialism.

b The prime mover of this transformation has been technological progress, or the development of productive powers, giving birth to the planning system within the private sector itself.

c But market failure, or external diseconomies in particular, has become often so flagrant that public intervention had to be countenanced – a common feature of the mixed economy.

d Along with the strengthening of oligopolistic power of giant corporations the role of profits has also been changing, to the extent that public intervention in the economy's investment direction has come to be proposed.

e Public policies for macroeconomic management and the welfare-oriented redistribution of income continue to be established features of the mixed economy.

Thus we have moved, in most capitalist countries of the world, into an era of the mode of production called "the mixed economy." Whither we go from here is, of course, uncertain. We shall discuss the case of Japan in the next section. But one general point may be mentioned here. That is in relation to the basic characterization, or the *differentia specifica*, of each socio-economic system. I have held that *the form of surplus* distinguishes one system from another, such as, for example, the land rent under feudalism and the profit for private capital under capitalism. Now the question is, what is the form of surplus under the mixed economy if this is to be understood as a distinct mode of production? The answer cannot be unequivocal inasmuch as it is, by definition, a mixed system. Here, the surplus consists, admittedly, of profits for private capital as well as of the social fund under public control. But it is significant that the dividing line between these two types of surplus can be movable depending on the consensus obtained in society. It is on this feature of the mixed economy that citizens can focus in their aspirations for the evolutionary development of their society in one way (further privatization) or another (toward socialism).

3. The prospect for the Japanese economy and Japan's role in the world

Two fundamental pillars of national policy proposed

Almost thirty years ago I wrote a short essay entitled "Is Japan a 'Big Power'?" at the beginning of which I related the following parable – a parable which used to be told to us when we were children.

Once upon a time, there lived in a certain village three brothers: Strong, Rich and Warmhearted. At first, Strong ruled the family with his muscular power. "Might makes right" was the rule. Years passed, however, and age began to tell on Strong, and he could not assert his authority as before. By that time, second brother Rich had amassed wealth, having built a number of warehouses. Now it was Rich who could hold hegemony in the family. In other words, the criterion of excellence shifted from strength to wealth. One day, there was a fire in the village, and it burnt down all the warehouses which Rich owned. Overnight he became penniless. An epidemic spread in the wake of the fire. The third brother, Warmhearted, had studied medicine and could tell immediately what kind of epidemic it was. He proceeded to take the necessary measures and saved many lives in the village. As the story goes, if you visit that village today, you will see a statue of Warmhearted standing in the center of the village. Warmhearted triumphed over Strong and Rich.

The transition of our criteria for individual excellence has more or less followed this course in the history of mankind. As for the criterion of national reputation, however, we may still be in the era of Strong and Rich. But I am certain that the time will come when the criterion for nations also will shift. Japan is not, at present, one of the "powers" as judged by the criterion of Strong. But it is generally agreed that Japan is now one of the "powers" as judged by the criterion of Rich. Where she goes from here is the problem we take up in this section.

As has been discussed in earlier chapters, the Japanese economy has displayed a remarkable performance as capitalism in the post-Second World War period. Though basically capitalistic, developing into "corporate capitalism" as I called it, Japan is nevertheless a mixed economy in the sense we defined above. The very high growth rate it achieved during the two decades after 1955 depended heavily on governmental stewardship in a number of respects; and offsetting measures against market failures became an accepted feature of public policy. But it remains true that a mixed economy implies a mixture of social motive forces, the profit motive on the one hand and the societal welfare motive on the other, which may, not infrequently, conflict with each other. Thus a question arises as to the controlling principle in vitalizing the economy.

When we speak of "vitalizing the economy," it is often understood to be with the rate of GNP growth. But this need not be the case, as could be inferred from our discussion of the welfare content of GNP growth in Chapter 5 (Section 4), and earlier by John Stuart Mill to the effect that: "It is scarcely necessary to remark that a stationary condition of capital and production implies no stationary state of human improvement. There would be as much scope as ever for all kinds of mental culture, and moral and social progress; as much room for improving the Art of Living, and much more likelihood of its being improved, when minds ceased to be engrossed by the art of getting on."[30] In other words, reorientation in the meaning of socio-economic progress is quite possible in the affluent stage of development which Japan has attained. As a matter of fact, in the years immediately following the high growth period, a number of Japan's highest ranking state officials already began speaking of such reorientation. For example, Kakuei Tanaka, Prime Minister from July 1972 to November 1974, wrote in his book *Plan for Remodeling of the Japanese Archipelago* (1972): "We are entering a new stage of 'restoration of man' in which man, the sun and green shall prevail and not the large cities or industries." Or, in June 1974, Takeo Miki, then the director of the Environment Agency and later the successor to Tanaka as Prime Minister, addressed the national convention for adoption of the "Charter for the Conservation of Nature" and said: "This Charter can be considered as exhorting a sharp change in values for our countrymen, particularly for those of us who are concerned with the administration of the government and local public bodies. At the least, it sets standards which differ from those that value mere economic efficiency, and places importance on aspirations for human health, happiness and beauty." Then again, Takeo Fukuda, Prime Minister from December 1976 to December 1978, in his address in Manila during the summer of 1977, made the following points: that (a) historically, economic powers have always been military powers as well, but Japan rejects the path of acquiring military might and, although it possesses the technical capabilities to make them, chooses not to keep nuclear weapons; that (b) this may be an "historically unprecedented challenge," but it is impossible for Japan to make any other choice, and that (c) Japan believes it can best contribute to the world by exercising all its energy to establish peace and prosperity at home and abroad, without resorting to military threats against other nations. These principles later came to be known as the "Fukuda Doctrine."

These statements have two underlying themes. One is what Tanaka termed "restoration of man," namely making respect for human beings the foundation of social and economic management. The other is that Japan's Peace Constitution, unique in the world, should be made the mainstay of the nation's foreign policy.

We need not question here whether these three successive Prime

Ministers exerted their full efforts to pursue the policies they advocated. The fact remains, at any rate, that the two fundamental pillars of national policy mentioned above do correspond with views held by a majority of the Japanese population; and it may well be that such views were reflected in the pronouncements of the political leaders. In what follows we shall discuss some concrete issues related to the future of Japanese society with orientation towards basing its policies on "respect for human beings" and the Peace Constitution. The discussion will concern itself with topics broader than the sphere of economics, but it will, incidentally, have the effect of portraying, as it were, the characteristic features of the type of mixed economy to which Japan should aspire. Since the matter concerns the future, there can be divergent views depending on the basic position one takes; and I must caution the readers that the remainder of this treatise partakes more of the nature of my personal manifesto than do the analyses and discussions which have preceded it.

The peace constitution and the issue of defense

First, we shall consider the issue of defense. It is a matter of common sense that Japan's survival depends on a peaceful international environment. With about 55 percent of basic foodstuffs (in original caloric terms) being imported and the greater part of its major industrial raw materials, let alone primary energy sources, coming from abroad, Japan would be forced to surrender by a blockade of its sea lanes. If this is true, is Japan capable of holding enough military power to keep those sea lanes secure? Right now, the answer is "No." And if even this defense is beyond her military capacity, how could Japan ever defend herself against an insane military aggression, such as was launched by Hitler? It is an illusion to think that Japan could do so with its own military forces.

As Ryūtaro Komiya wrote: "The principal aims of Japanese self-defense should be to avoid getting Japan involved in conflicts and to maintain a peaceful posture toward the region surrounding Japan and also toward the entire world. Our supreme goal in order to enjoy peace should be to work to prevent wars from occurring. And for this purpose, military defense power would have no positive significance."[31] A similar opinion was expressed more recently by Kenneth Boulding while visiting Japan: "Every yen you put into national defense I would say diminishes your national defense . . . Security for Japan lies in not being a threat to anybody, and the more you build up your 'offensive' defense force the more threat you are to somebody who has a bigger threat than you have . . . Even in the cowboy era in the West, the unarmed Methodist missionary had probably a much better chance of survival than the armed cowboy."[32] It is also edifying to recall the dictum of Shōjirō Kawashima in a press interview[33] on his return as a special envoy from the tenth anniversary of the Afro-Asian Assembly held in April 1965 in Jakarta, who said: "What I was especially impressed with was that the fact that Japan does not possess arms constitutes, in fact, her major qualification. Southeast Asian nations apparently feel that a strongly armed Japan cannot be relied upon as an arbiter in disputes, but that Japan without armed forces can play the role of a peacemaker in this area." Such an impression may still linger on in Asia. But it is ironic that within 25 years, the size of the Japanese armed forces has grown, in spite of its Peace Constitution, to a level ranking the third biggest in the world in terms of annual budget expenditures.[34]

There have been three constraints on the rearmament of Japan, i.e. (a) the Peace Constitution, which specified that "land, sea, and air forces as well as other war potential will never be maintained"; (b) the "Three Non-nuclear Principles" of not to produce, not to possess, and not to have nuclear weapons brought in; and (c) the ceiling of "1 percent of GNP" for defense expenditures.

Historians in the future may wonder how all these three constraints could have been breached in spite of the fact that Japan has not faced a threat from any country since the end of the war. But the fact of the matter is that they were;[35] and the dominant factor in the process has been the military alliance with the United States under the terms of the US–Japan Security Treaty. The rationale of this military alliance has been the alleged "Soviet threat" – a theme impressed on the mind of Japanese public both by US and Japanese political leaders to the extent of Yūkō Kurihara, one-time Minister of Defense, saying in public that "it is my duty as a statesman to make Japanese people recognize the threat of the Soviet Union." It has not been easy, however, for the military establishment to evoke popular support for the Security Treaty with the United States even at the height of the cold war. It was in March 1959 that the famous Daté judgment in Tokyo District Court ruled that "the American troops stationed in Japan on the basis of the US–Japan Security Treaty constitute a violation of the Constitution and that the Special Criminal Law based on the above Treaty is void." The relevant passage of the judgment is significant enough to be quoted here:

The US troops stationed in Japan will not only be used to support the suppression of internal disturbances and for self-defense against external attacks on Japan, but also they will be deployed into areas outside Japan if the strategic necessity arises in a situation where military intervention becomes necessary to maintain international peace and security in the Far East. In such a case, the military facilities in Japan made available to the US troops will be used as a matter of course, thus involving Japan in the whirlpool of a military conflict with which Japan has no direct concern. There is definitely a chance that the ravages of war may spread into our country.

These were truly prophetic words. However, in December of the same year, the Daté Case was appealed to the Supreme Court, which overturned the lower court's decision. Still, public sentiments gradually became more and more disenchanted with the military alliance with the United States and voices for at least rethinking the Security Treaty grew as time went on.

That the defense of a country involves more than just the military dimension is common sense. In particular, the defense debate becomes meaningless when separated from the question of what is to be defended, or what is the kind of country that has to be defended. Many publicists started speaking in this vein quite early; for example Shintarō Ryū, editor-in-chief of the *Asahi Shimbun* at the time, wrote: "As Japan does not have power in the sense of military force, what will protect Japan should be a strength of mental composure which cannot be slighted by other countries."[36] And Masanori Kikuchi, a specialist on comparative socialism, wrote: "Defense debate lacking the sense of love for your country is dangerous. If so, should not the discussion first of all deal with the problem of how to make Japan a country which is really loved by the Japanese people?"[37]

Concrete policies for Japan's nation-building proposed

Thus, inevitably, we are made aware that of the "two fundamental pillars of national policy" mentioned above, i.e. the Peace Constitution and the policies for "restoration of man," the discussion on the former leads us logically to the consideration of the latter. The answer to the question of how to vitalize Japan's mixed economy will also be provided by concrete policy suggestions which follow. The nation-building oriented toward "respect for mankind" will not only evoke a sense of patriotism among the people, i.e. an awareness of having a "mother country worth defending," but also will impress upon potential invaders the meaninglessness and inhumanity of attacking Japan.

In more concrete terms, what does founding a country on the basis of respect for mankind imply?

Respect for mankind entails respect for life, and therefore the maintenance and improvement of health. It is also linked to improving the quality of life and the working environment. It further urges valuing of goals more than means and setting store by those things, such as the beauty of nature, to which no market price can be attached. Respect for humankind should also imply rethinking the nature of human labor. Economists have been wont to equate human labor with toil, thus identifying it as "disutility" or "negative utility," and have regarded wage payments, as compensations, for such "disutility." But, from the standpoint of respect for mankind, work should not be all pain and sweat.

Rather it should be an essential part of purposeful life, in fact comple-
mented by leisure and not opposed by it. In general, a country which is
oriented toward respect for mankind is expected to rate cultural values
highly. In other words, what is being urged on Japan from now on is a
"change in values," as described in the quotation from former Prime
Minister Miki cited earlier, namely: "more important than standards that
value economic efficiency are those which prize aspirations to human
health, happiness and beauty."

A comprehensive program to satisfy these requirements would be so
massive, entailing a kind of social revolution, that it probably could not be
placed on the agenda at one stroke for the nation as a whole. It is vital, and
in fact sufficient, however, clearly to set forth the direction of reform and to
make advances wherever possible. Toward these ends, I propose the
following concrete ideas to form the basis of Japan's national policy.

(1) *Japan should strive, as part of her policy of placing emphasis on human
lives and health, to become the "health care center" of the world; expanding
and improving her medical personnel and medical facilities while putting
greater effort into the development of medical technology.*

Because there is still considerable room for improvement in the medical
services now offered to the Japanese public, it may seem presumptuous to
speak of becoming the "health care center" of the world. Improvement of
public medical services in Japan, of course, is an urgent matter. But
planning for such improvement can be done within a broader context,
encompassing the world, as suggested above. Japan has, to use an economic
term, a comparative advantage in medicine. In cardiac surgery, for
example, Japanese medical skill leads the world; and a number of patients
who require especially delicate surgery come to Japan from foreign
countries to receive treatment. Also, the nurturing and caring qualities of
Japanese women in general could be an excellent qualification for the
profession of nurses. The dedication, humility and sensitivity of the nuns
who work in religious charity hospitals abroad receive frequent praise. But
I feel that the keen awareness of their mission is high enough among the
Japanese nurses, although they are grossly underpaid at present. If Japan
were to become the "health care center" of the world, it would be certain
that the morale of medical and paramedical personnel would be heightened
still further.

In addition, the recent development of medical equipment in Japan has
been most striking. Computerized tomographic analyzers (CT scanners),
for example, used in many of the nation's hospitals, presently cost about
¥100 million for the models designed for full body analysis – the lowest
price in the world. Recent news reports tell of the development of a
computerized positron scanner for the diagnosis of brain tumors and

apoplexy. This device was developed at the National Institute of Radiological Sciences of the Science and Technology Agency. Japan, as a nation of peace, should concentrate its energies on research and development in the expanding field of such medical instruments. Rather than recommend the export and technological development of "instruments of death" such as weapons, we should find our role in breaking new ground in the field of medical equipment – the "instruments of life."

(2) On a theme related to our first point above, *Japan should work to develop more facilities for use at places of scenic beauty (and hot spring areas) which can be visited by many people, both native and foreign, for tourism and health.*

Fortunately, Japan possesses a rich variety of climatic regions spread over its 3,000 kilometer length from north to south and is blessed with areas of hot springs and natural beauty in which to enjoy the changes of the four seasons. The Inland Sea of Seto, for example, is designated by law as "something which should be passed on to future generations and whose blessings should be enjoyed equally by the public as a storehouse of priceless marine resources and as a scenic area which boasts a beauty not seen elsewhere in Japan and unmatched in the rest of the world."[38] It is a treasure unique in Japan, suited as a multidimensional national park; or perhaps we should say "*was* a treasure." For, during the postwar period of rapid economic growth, factories multiplied on reclaimed land along the Inland Sea shore, which is now over one-third human-made coastline. Within an unbelievably short period this National Park area has come to contain facilities for crude steel production equivalent to the combined capacity of France and West Germany and oil-refining and petrochemical capacities matching those of Great Britain. No wonder that damage from red tides and cases such as the Mizushima oil-spill incident have plagued the area.

Japan in the period of her rapid economic growth chose to "expand the kitchen at the expense of the garden." However, beautiful "gardens" are still preserved in many places across the country and can be enjoyed as resort areas. Compared with such places in foreign countries, it cannot be denied that Japanese resorts lack good facilities, their vulgarity is often conspicuous and they fall short of satisfying the varied demands of the visiting public. It is against this background that it is proposed that the government should take this opportunity to change its basic stance (as described by former Prime Minister Miki above) and devise concrete policies which will allow the people of the world to enjoy these really outstanding aspects of Japan.[39]

(3) *Japan should exert its full efforts to promote international exchange in the spheres of cultural and aesthetic activities.*

It is not widely known, but recently Japanese-made musical instruments have been sweeping Europe. At the end of February 1980, a musical instrument fair was held in Frankfurt, West Germany and, according to a French music magazine, *Disque*, distributed at that time, Japanese-made products accounted for 60 percent of the French market for electric guitars, 85 percent for synthesizers and 34 percent for pianos. Among West German orchestra musicians also, there are many who favor horns, trumpets, piccolos, and trombones made in Japan. Performers say that the reason these instruments enjoy such a high reputation is that Japanese manufacturers listen carefully to requests from musicians and work hard to continue to improve the sound of their instruments.[40] It is reassuring that Japan is able to make such contributions to the sensitive world of music and sound. Here again is the welcome possibility of exporting the "instruments of life" instead of weapons.

There are in Japan many other cultural activities which have attracted the minds of Westerners. Ceramic art is one example. Bernard Leach (1887–1979), who helped to spread Japanese ceramic art around the world, once said: "All my life I have been a courier between East and West. I believe in the interplay and marriage of the two contemporary branches of human culture as the prelude to the unity and maturity of man." Japan's cultural tradition, which has laid emphasis on aesthetic sensibility in all the items handled in daily life, certainly should hold the key to present-day international cultural exchange.

Not long ago, former Prime Minister Ohira, in an administrative policy address, referred to "transition in the country's orientation from that of economic expansion to that of cultural concerns," and emphasized the need for "nation-building in that direction as the 21st century approaches." If so, he also would have approved wholeheartedly the present proposal.

(4) *Japan should take long strides in increasing its aid to the United Nations University, making it a world center for education, research, and technical innovations that contribute to the social and economic development of the Third World countries.*

At present, Japan's funding of the United Nations University is the highest in the world. The university was founded with certain high ideals; but most other so-called large countries did not show much enthusiasm for this enterprise, and circumstances induced Japan also to take a somewhat lukewarm attitude in the past. Thus it is still hard to say whether the anticipated results will be achieved by the UNU. However, Japan need not consider balanced national quotas in funding. Instead, Japan should expand its commitments decisively at this juncture in order to revitalize this unique institution for fulfilling the original high ideals.

The "three problem areas" singled out by UNESCO in October 1970 when announcing its plans for an international United Nations University were: (a) Research on war and peace; specifically, questions of how to take decisive action toward arms reduction, the prevention of war and conflict resolution; (b) the problems of economic cooperation among nations and the security in livelihood for them; the question of how to bring about reversal of the "vicious cycle of poverty"; (c) the questions of the world's resources and technology; in particular, questions of how to treat technology as means in the social context in view of the fact that science and technology are not ends in themselves but are to serve the enhancement of the supreme values, namely those of nature and humankind.

The importance of the above questions is greater now than ever, but in general the existing universities cannot effectively carry out education and research specifically focused on these points. The United Nations University, above all, could function primarily to answer the demands of the Third World nations. Since it is now based in Japan, is not this an excellent opportunity? The Japanese government, as well as academic circles and the business world, should take this opportunity to invest on a redoubled scale in the activities of the United Nations University which, at long last, twenty years after its inauguration, will have an independent building of its own by 1991, but not yet a campus befitting its high-priority role.

(5) Continuing the list of priority policies, *Japan should raise the level of its financial and technical aid for developing countries, and, probably more important from a longer-run standpoint, should open her markets more widely for those manufacturing products of the Third World countries which are bound to gain comparative advantage in them.*

Currently, a little over 1 percent of Japan's GDP (gross domestic product) goes for defense spending. The United States spends about 6 percent, the United Kingdom 4.4 percent, France 3.8 percent and West Germany 3 percent.[41] Compared to other developed countries, therefore, the Japanese percentage is relatively low. On the other hand, the third UNCTAD Conference in May 1972 set targets for international economic cooperation. It fixed 0.7 percent of GNP as the agreed goal for government development aid, the so-called ODA (Official Development Assistance).[42] This was to have been met by the mid-1970s. By 1977, however, Japan's actual performance remained at 0.21 percent. In more recent years, this ratio rose to 0.32 percent in 1988,[43] but is still nowhere near the goal demanded by UNCTAD. Japan should proceed quickly to reach the 0.7 percent target. But more important is the content of Japan's ODA. For one thing, the United Nations did specify 42 countries as "least-developed countries" (LDC) and advised that priority should be given to them in the distribution of the assistance fund. Japan's performance in this regard has also been problematical. Of the top ten receiving countries of Japan's ODA in 1988, there were only two (Bangladesh and Myanmar) which were in the category of LDC. Furthermore, many of the projects sponsored by Japan's ODA have been the target of criticism, even of protest, by the residents of the region as involving shady deals with local politicians and not redounding to the benefit of the people for whom the aid was intended.[44]

Third World problems, even if limited to the economic, involve more than just the magnitude of aid. As regards a set of proposals for the New International Economic Order, Japan more than any other country is in a position to take the leadership in promoting the interests of the non-oil-producing developing nations. A few years ago, an international commission of inquiry on development problems, popularly known as the Brandt Commission, submitted its report titled *North–South: A Program for Survival* to the Secretary-General of the United Nations. It contains many proposals which deserve attention (including the implementation of a system of automatic transfer of resources from rich to poor nations), but there is no doubt as to whether the Japanese government has been treating the report seriously. A number of advanced nations, including the United States, has acted to protect their vested interests which have been built up over the years in the Third World countries, and sometimes control these nations through military aid and the export of arms. The basic historical tendency of the Third World people, however, has been to react strongly in resisting these colonialist policies. Japan, which does not possess such vested interests abroad, is in a position to use its Peace Constitution as a backbone of policy and to cooperate actively with such historical movements in the Third World.

Properly designed unilateral transfer of purchasing power from the rich countries to the poor is, no doubt, urgently needed in the present juncture of the world economy. But, from a longer-run standpoint, what is essential is the opening of markets of advanced countries to the products of less-developed ones which are bound increasingly to gain comparative advantage in many of the manufacturing industries of less technological sophistication in the near future. Aid is a temporary solution and trade is a permanent one. And unless a country like Japan keeps on widening the entrance gate for the exports of the Third World countries, the North–South economic disparity cannot be narrowed in the long run. One is reminded of an incisive reply made by a famed Indian economist, V.K.R.V. Rao, some years ago when he was asked by a visiting team of American officials: "what can we do by way of helping your country to come out of the present deadlock?" Rao said: "Stop giving us aid!" Dynamic adjustment of trade relations between the North and the South will inevitably imply, even in a short run, the need for transformation of industrial structures in advanced countries. Japan, in particular, having been a late-comer in her industrial maturity and having had the painful experience in the past of overcoming the high threshold of export markets abroad, should be the first to appreciate the importance of freer trade for less-developed countries and to take steps deliberately to carry out structural transformation of her industries in accordance with changing patterns of comparative advantage.

Incidentally, Japan continued to be the target of criticism from abroad, as being "cold to refugees." When the UN Conference on Refugees was held in Geneva in July 1979 to discuss the relief problem of Indonesian refugees numbering 350,000, the Japanese Foreign Minister, Sunao Sonoda, had to participate, representing the sole country among advanced nations which had not yet ratified the Treaty Relating to the Status of Refugees. Thus the UN High Commissioner for Refugees gave a report, a shameful one for Japan, in September of that year, to the effect that by that time the acceptance of Indo-Chinese refugees numbered 130,000 for the United States, 57,000 for France, 25,500 for Canada, 9,300 for Hong Kong, and a mere 62 for Japan. The reason for the protracted ratification of the Treaty was ostensibly that the related ministries were unable to make the necessary adjustments among themselves. The Treaty became finally effective in Japan from January 1, 1982. It is urgent that Japan catch up with the rest of the world in this humanitarian task.

Concluding remarks

The above five concrete proposals, founded on the Peace Constitution and respect for humankind, I believe, are far from wild dreams. Naturally, they require time; but to bring a shift in the direction of state policies in itself is of paramount importance. And these policies require expenditures as well: 1 percent of Japan's GNP now is ¥4,000 billion yen; to those who advocate raising defense spending by this 1 percent, I make a plea that the sum be used for the government programs proposed above. Considering Japan's economic strength, I am certain that it is an entirely feasible proposition.

Constructing national policies in the way I have described is in accord, to my mind, with what Michio Morishima has called the "software" approach, relying on "diplomacy, economics or cultural exchange."[45] A Japan that takes the lead in pressing for world disarmament, is assiduous in the fight against disease by making the country the health-care center of the world, lays emphasis on tourist facilities at sites of natural scenic beauty, is active in international exchange in the fields of cultural and aesthetic life, is willing radically to increase the country's contribution to the United Nations University, and works hard, through both aid and trade, to wipe out the poverty which plagues the Third World, would be a Japan where the people would feel assured of holding in common positive values worth defending and also would be a Japan upon which an attack from abroad would appear meaningless and inhuman.

There would be much constructive work to be done which should rouse the spirits of young people. Ardor for the country would also come naturally. I said earlier that the defense debate becomes meaningless when separated from the question of what is to be defended. When asked "what" is to be defended, that "what" is the homeland which is intent on carrying out the proposals above. Needless to say, there is an intimate relationship between the "what" and the "by what means" we defend; and if the "what" is defined in this way, answering the question of "by what means" is straightforward; it is not by enlarging and strengthening the armor for ourselves. Within the meaning of the "what" is provided directly the answer to the question of "by what means."

When we consider the defense of Japan in this way, we are logically led to feel that things such as the US–Japan Security Treaty must lose their *raison d'être*. It is most likely that public opinion in Japan will then gradually come around to supporting the eventual liquidation of the Security Treaty, in the same manner that the sun, not the north wind, may make the traveler take off his coat. In other words, the age of Warmhearted is certain to come in Japan, while at the same time the GNP growthmanship in the reign of Rich will be placed properly into a secondary role. Will it be a wishful thinking to concur, in concluding this treatise, with John Maynard Keynes, who wrote sixty years ago – "The day may not be all that far off when everybody would be rich . . . We shall then be able to rid ourselves of many of the pseudomoral principles which have hag-ridden us for two hundred years, by which we have exalted some of the most distasteful of human qualities into the position of the highest values . . . [Then] we shall once more value ends above means and prefer the good to the useful"?[46]

Notes

Introduction

1. *The Economist*, August 17–23, 1991, pp. 13–14.
2. Peter Drucker, "The Changed World Economy," *Foreign Affairs*, Spring 1986, pp. 768–91.
3. "Review of the Month," *Monthly Review*, March 1988, p.9.
4. The Bank for International Settlements, *Survey of Foreign Exchange Market Activity*, February 1990.
5. J.K. Galbraith, *A Short History of Financial Euphoria*, Whittle Direct Books, Knoxville, Tenn., 1990, p.80.
6. Michel Anglietta and André Orléan, *La Violence de la Monnaie*, Presses Universitaires de France, Paris, 1982.
7. As reported in the *Asahi Shimbun*, August 16, 1991.
8. Paul A. Samuelson and William Nordhaus, *Economics*, McGraw-Hill Book Company, New York, 1989, 13th edn, p.863.
9. Shigeto Tsuru, "The Effects of Technology on Productivity" in E.A.G. Robinson, ed., *Problems in Economic Development*, Macmillan, London, 1965.

The growth accounting equation cited above can be rewritten in terms of per capita Q and K, as Samuelson and Nordhaus did, thus:

$$\% \ Q/L \ \text{growth} = \tfrac{1}{4}(\% \ K/L \ \text{growth}) + \text{T.C.}$$

or, if we would like to estimate the extent of contribution by T.C. in the growth of per-labor output (Q/L), we may write:

$$\frac{\text{T.C.}}{\% \ Q/L \ \text{growth}} = 1 - \tfrac{1}{4}\left[\frac{\% \ K/L \ \text{growth}}{\% \ Q/L \ \text{growth}}\right]$$

This equation, incidentally, is exactly the same as the one I derived in my 1965 essay, though with my own notations. The result of empirical calculations will turn on the ratio on the right-hand side of the equation, or the ratio between the growth rate of capital–labor ratio and the growth rate of labor productivity, inasmuch as the fraction $\tfrac{1}{4}$, which represents the relative share of capital, can be considered as relatively stable. If [% K/L growth] and [% Q/L growth] move more or less in a parallel fashion, as a limiting case, the solution of the above equation (the extent of contribution of T.C. in the growth of per-labor output) is quite simple, namely, the answer is $1 - \frac{1}{4}$, or $\frac{3}{4}$, which is the relative share of labor. It is, of course, possible that [% Q/L growth] is greater than [% K/L growth], in which case the role of technical change becomes still larger. I questioned the practical significance of such growth accounting approach for policy purposes, entirely aside from the theoretical assumptions of the Cobb–Douglas production function on which the accounting is based.

10. This distinction is not the same as the one Drucker makes between the "real" economy and the "symbol" economy. On other occasions I used the contrasting terms of the "physical" aspect and the "institutional" aspect. In Drucker's concept of the "real" economy, or "the flows of goods and services," the "value" aspect in my terminology is inextricably involved.

11. Shigeto Tsuru, *Institutional Economics Revisited*, Cambridge University Press (forthcoming).

12. E. Denison, "Growth Accounting" in *The New Palgrave Dictionary of Economics*, Macmillan, London, 1989, Vol. 2, p.572.

1 The defeat and the Occupation reforms

1. Japan Resources Association, *A Key To Japan's Recovery*, 1986, pp.77–8.

2. Cf. Economic Stabilization Board, *Taiheiyō Sensō ni yoru waga Kuni no Higai Sōgō Hōkokusho* (Comprehensive Report on Damages to Japan from the Pacific War), April 1949.

3. The budgeted figure of "Extraordinary War Account" for the fiscal 1945 (April 1945 to March 1946) was 85 billion yen, of which 29.3 billion yen was disbursed during 4 months of April to July-end. But during one month of August alone the disbursement amounted to 12 billion yen – no doubt, a major contributing factor to the net increase of the Bank of Japan notes in circulation from 30.2 billion yen on August 15, 1945 to 42.3 billion yen on August 31, or the rise of 40 per cent in a half month.

4. Reprinted in *A key to Japan's Recovery*, edited by Japan Resources Association, 1986, p.132.

5. Reprinted in *ibid.*, p.75.

6. *Basic Problems for Postwar Reconstruction of Japanese Economy*, Ministry of Foreign Affairs' Special Survey Committee, September 1946 (English translation published by the Japan Economic Research Center, 1977). Sabro [sic] Okita writes as editor of this English translation that "the work was secretly prepared before the end of the war. If it was discovered, the people who participated in the work would have been arrested by military police." (p.iii). But the fact of the matter is that the work itself was begun after the end of the war: and there was no secrecy involved.

7. Notable among them were six Marxist economists: Hyōe Ouchi, Hiromi Arisawa, Kōzō Uno, Moritaro Yamada, Yoshitaro Wakimura and Yasuo Kondō; five modern economists: Ichiro Nakayama, Seiichi Tobata, Tokutaro Yamanaka, Yūzo Morita and Seijiro Kishimoto: two natural scientists: Naoto Kameyama and Kōichi Aki; seven publicists: Shūzo Inaba, Teizo Taira,

Yoshitake Sasaki, Haremaru Inoue, Chifuyu Masaki, Hisao Tomooka and Kiyoshi Tsuchiya; one business man: Ichiro Ishikawa; and several government officials, including myself.

8. *Basic Problems for Postwar Reconstruction of Japanese Economy*, September 1946, p.136.

9. Quoted directly from the verbatim translation of the original, the entire translation having been completed overnight on the request of the Occupation authorities. Thus some clumsiness in translation remains.

10. Quoted in Jerome B. Cohen, *Japan's Economy in War and Reconstruction* (University of Minnesota Press, 1949, p.427) from Pauley's Report on Japanese Reparations, November 1945 to April 1946.

11. In my private conversation with him at the time he emphasized this point to me; and I agreed with him.

12. Eleanor Hadley, "Trust Busting in Japan," *Harvard Business Review*, July 1948, pp.425 and 431.

13. *Contemporary Japan*, Vol. XVII, Nos. 1–3, January–March 1948, p.97.

14. In fact, General MacArthur was quite proud of his efforts in this respect and remarked in his *Reminiscences* (McGraw-Hill, New York, 1964) in later years as follows: "One of the most far-reaching accomplishments of the occupation was the program of land reform. Japan's feudalistic regime was most evident in the matter of landholding. As late as the end of the war, a system of virtual slavery that went back to ancient times was still in existence. Most farmers in Japan were either out-and-out serfs, or they worked under an arrangement through which the landowners exorbited [*sic*] a high percentage of each year's crops. The occupation was only a few months old when I attacked this problem. I felt that any man who farmed the land should, by law, be entitled to his crops, that there should be an end to sharecropping, and that even more fundamental, perhaps, was the need to make land itself available to the people. Under the system then in use it was practically impossible for a farmer to buy his own land" (pp.313–14).

15. A.J. Grad, *Land and Peasant in Japan*, Institute of Pacific Relations, New York, 1952, p.219.

16. R.P. Dore, *Land Reform in Japan*, Oxford University Press, London, 1959, p.148.

17. Quoted by Dore, *ibid.*, p.148, from Ladejinsky's unpublished MS.

18. In FEC deliberations, there was some conflict between the USA–UK group on the one hand and the USSR–Australia group on the other, the latter attempting to put in a clause on the role of unions in encouraging the democratization process of the society.

19. A detailed personal account on this incident by an Occupation official in charge of labor problems is given in Theodore Cohen, *Remaking Japan: The American Occupation as New Deal*, The Free Press, New York, 1987, pp.240–59; and the account is very revealing of the entanglement in which the Occupation administration found itself.

20. Again, a most detailed account of this episode is given by Theodore Cohen, *ibid.*, pp.277–300.

21. *Ibid.*, pp.299–300.

22. *Political Reorientation of Japan, September 1945 to September 1948*, report of the Government section of SCAP, US Government Printing Office, Vol. I, p.246.

23. T. Cohen, *Remaking Japan*, p.382.

24. Herbert Passin, *Society and Education in Japan*, New York: Columbia University Teachers College Press, 1965, p.129.

25. Quoted by Cohen, *Remaking Japan*, p.394. A most detailed and well-documented discussion in Japanese on the GHQ labor policy can be found in Eiji Takemae, *Sengo Rōdō Kaikaku* (Postwar Labor Reform in Japan), Tokyo: Tokyo Daigaku Shuppankai, 1982.

26. R.K. Hall, *Education for a New Japan*, New Haven, Yale University Press, 1949, p.iii.

27. The full text in the official English translation is as follows:

Know ye, Our Subjects:
Our Imperial Ancestors have founded Our Empire on a basis broad and everlasting and have deeply and firmly implanted virtue; Our subjects ever united in loyalty and filial piety have from generation to generation illustrated the beauty thereof. This is the glory of the fundamental character of Our Empire, and herein also lies the source of Our education. Ye, Our subjects, be filial to your parents, affectionate to your brothers and sisters; as husbands and wives be harmonious, as friends true; bear yourselves in modesty and moderation; extend your benevolence to all; pursue learning and cultivate arts, and thereby develop intellectual faculties and perfect moral powers; furthermore, advance public good and promote common interests; always respect the Constitution and observe the laws; should emergency arise, offer yourselves courageously to the State; and thus guard and maintain the prosperity of Our Imperial Throne coeval with heaven and earth. So shall ye not only be Our good and faithful subjects, but render illustrious the best traditions of your forefathers.
   The Way here set forth is indeed the teaching bequeathed by Our Imperial Ancestors, to be observed alike by Their Descendants and the subjects, infallible for all ages and true in all places. It is Our wish to lay it to heart in all reverence, in common with you, Our subjects, that We may all thus attain to the same virtue.

28. R.K. Hall, *Education for a New Japan*, p.162.

29. *Ibid.*, p.167.

30. For one thing, the immediate implementation of this reform plan was unrealistic in view of the extreme shortage of school buildings at the time relative to the requirements under the plan. In my capacity as vice-minister of the Economic Stabilization Board, I had to negotiate with the Economic and Scientific Section of the SCAP for permission to allocate the minimum necessary funds for the construction of needed school buildings under the suggested plan of the Mission; and it was a revelation to me to be told by a responsible officer of the Occupation that it was up to the Japanese government to decide autonomously whether they really wanted to follow the Education Mission's recommendation for the reform of the school system.

31. Quoted in R.K. Hall, *Education for a New Japan*, p.357.

32. Quoted in *ibid.*, p.359.

2 The road to recovery

1. There was a concern in the minds of persons like Herbert Feis and Percy Johnston, who came to Japan in March 1948 with W.H. Draper, jr. to review the Occupation's economic policies, that in the milieu of uncertainty then existing the Japanese economy might not be able to recover along capitalistic lines. Johnston, in particular, expressed his apprehension, in a conference with myself and Hiroo Wada (both about to resign from the Socialist-led Katayama cabinet), that Japan might be forced to feel that her future path had to be a socialistic reconstruction if the Allies continued to pursue harsh policies toward her.

2. This statement declared in part: "The Japanese government, under the supervision of SCAP, must prepare and implement plans under which Japan can become self-supporting at the earliest possible time. Progress has already been made in this direction. Although the primary responsibility for the preparation and execution of such a plan rests on the Japanese government and people, SCAP must take the requisite steps to ensure that the Japanese government and people energetically and effectively discharge that responsibility." For reasons unknown to us, this paragraph was omitted from the Japanese language press release at the time.

3. Robert A. Fearey, *The Occupation of Japan – Second Phase: 1948–50,* The Macmillan Company, New York, 1950, p.65.

4. Part of this report was published in *Newsweek,* December 1, 1947, pp.36–38.

5. Quoted in T. Cohen, *Remaking Japan,* p.367, from *The Forrestal Diaries,* New York, Viking, 1951, pp.328–29.

6. George Kennan, *Memoirs,* Little, Brown, Boston, 1967, p.409.

7. In a statement intended for the House and Senate Appropriations Committees, quoted by T. Cohen, *Remaking Japan,* p.371.

8. Howard Schonberger, "Ideologies of Reform and the Japanese Response," a paper presented at the 8th International Symposium of Hosei University: *The Allied Occupation of Japan in World History,* November 30, 1983.

9. Robert A. Fearey, *The Occupation of Japan,* p.69.

10. *Ibid.,* p.70.

11. *Ibid.,* p.75.

12. Robert A. Scalapino, *Democracy and the Party Movement in Prewar Japan – The Failure of the First Attempt,* Berkeley, University of California Press, 1953. Cf., in particular, p.396.

13. The index as compiled by the Research and Programs Division of Economic and Scientific Section of the Occupation authorities in co-operation with the appropriate Japanese government offices. I myself was involved in this work.

14. The government had promised to pay this "living-cost subsidy," totaling 3.4 billion yen, by the end of January 1948; and there was a conflict within the Japanese government between the Ministry of Finance and the Economic Stabilization Board over the question of revenue-source. The former proposed as new revenue raising the National Railroad passenger rates by 150 percent from March 1, and tele-communication rates by 200 percent from February 15,

whereas the latter, mainly led by myself, took the position that automatic increases in tax revenues due to inflation, not scheduled in the original budget, could easily cover the cost. In the end, the Ministry of Finance won out; and the draft proposal by the administration to the Diet was turned down by the Lower House Budget Committee, then chaired by Mosaburō Suzuki, a left-wing socialist, thus forcing Katayama to resign. The conflict within the Japanese government was much more complex than it appeared on the surface; and for those readers who may be interested in more detail, I refer to my own article, written in 1948, with the title of "Zaisei Minshuka no tameni" (In Search of Democratization in Public Finance) in Shigeto Tsuru, *Collected Works of Shigeto Tsuru*, Kodansha, Tokyo, 1976, Vol. 7, pp.209–24. Cf. also an account by Finance Ministry's chief liaison officer Takeshi Watanabe in his *Senryōkano Nippon Zaisei Oboegaki* (Memorandum on Japanese Public Finance under the Occupation), Nihon Keizai Shinbunsha, Tokyo, 1966, pp.87–99.

15. Martin Bronfenbrenner, "The American Occupation of Japan: Economic Retrospect," in Grant K. Goodman, *The American Occupation of Japan: A Retrospective View*, Lawrence, Kansas: Center for East Asian Studies, The University of Kansas, 1968, p.17. The other failures according to Bronfenbrenner were the *zaibatsu* dissolution program and the trade-union policy.

16. *Ibid.*, p.18. It was James Lee Kauffman who, on his return from Japan in September 1947, issued a blistering report on the Occupation's program in which he referred to the excessive salaries and luxurious mode of living of Occupation personnel (cf. T. Cohen, *Remaking Japan*, p.367). It was only in the autumn of 1949 that SCAP personnel lost the privilege of free travel on Japanese railroads, buses and street railways; and then, during the succeeding winter (1949–50), they lost a 10 percent pay differential when Japan ceased to be classified as a "hardship area."

17. See Kōichi Emi, *Government Fiscal Activity and Economic Growth in Japan, 1868–1960*, Tokyo, Kinokuniya Shoten, 1963.

18. With the institutionalization of the Marshall Plan, all foreign and budget requests were required to go through a new national Advisory Council, represented by Commerce, Treasury, and the Federal Reserve as well as State and the Army.

19. T. Cohen, *Remaking Japan*, p.419.

20. As for the price inflation, the rate of increase was declining from an average of 7 percent a month in the first four months of 1948 to 5 percent in the middle four and then to 3 percent in the last four. As for industrial activity, indexes were registering a rise of 55.6 in November 1947 to 83.0 in November 1948. See, T. Cohen, *ibid.*, p.522.

21. Orville MacDiarmid, who attended most of the Dodge consultations with the Finance Ministry, said many years later that "it is to Mr. Ikeda . . . that I give most credit for the accomplishments of the Dodge Mission." (*The Occupation of Japan Economic Policy and Reform*, Proceedings of a Symposium Sponsored by MacArthur Memorial, April 13–15, 1978, MacArthur Memorial, Norfolk, Virginia, p.68.)

22. T. Cohen, *Remaking Japan*, p.430.

23. Cf. Takeshi Watanabe, *Memorandum on Japanese Public Finance under the Occupation*, p.209.

24. Revenue of the Special Account consists of yen-proceeds of the sale of imported goods and expenditure out of the Account consists of yen-payment to exporters. Since the former is calculated on the basis of yen-dear ratios and the latter on the basis of yen-cheap ratios, such a discrepancy arises.

25. F.M. Tamagna, "The Fixing of Foreign Exchange Rates," *The Journal of Political Economy*, March 1945.

26. *Ibid.*, p.63.

27. G. Haberler, "The Choice of Exchange Rates after the War," *The American Economic Review*, June 1945, pp.308–18.

28. Tamagna, "The Fixing of Foreign Exchange Rates," p.69.

29. Taking the prewar average (1934–36) as 100, the index of industrial production in 1948 was at the level of 58.5, that of agricultural production 91.1, that of quantity exported 7, that of quantity imported 18, and that of urban family consumption level 63.8. And wholesale price index was still showing a galloping rise from 48.2 (1934–36 = 1) in 1947 to 127.9 in 1948 to 208.8 in 1949.

30. Whereas the percentage of budget balance was 58 percent in 1946–47, 88 percent in 1947–48, and 92 percent in 1948–49, it went up to 108.7 percent of expenditures for 1949–50, the surplus amounting to almost one billion dollars, as a consequence of drastic measures dictated by Dodge.

31. Saburo Shiomi of Kyoto University, Han'ya Ito of Hitotsubashi University and myself.

32. A most comprehensive appraisal of the Shoup tax reforms in English is given in "The Aftermath of the Shoup Tax Reforms" by M. Bronfenbrenner and Kiichiro Kogiku in *National Tax Journal*, September 1957 and December 1957. In the Japanese language, a most convenient summary discussion is given in *Shoup Kankoku to Wagakuni no Zeisei* (The Shoup Recommendations and the Japanese Tax System) compiled and published by Nihon Sozei Kenkyū Kyōkai (Japan Tax Research Association), 1983.

33. If we take, for example, the 1947–48 fiscal year figure, the budget estimates of income tax revenues were (a) 19.3 billion yen for the collected-at-source group, based on the average monthly salary or wage of 1,600 yen and (b) 49.2 billion yen for the self-assessed group, based on the average monthly income of 2,000 yen for farmers and 5,000 yen for other proprietors. But the paid-in amounts by the end of December 1947 were 15.4 billion yen (5.4 percent of the estimated total income of the group) for the former and 6.3 billion yen (1.2 percent of the estimated total income of the group). It was at this point that the political crisis arose on the issue of finding a revenue source for the promised payment of "living-cost subsidy" of 3.4 billion yen (as mentioned in the note 14 above). It was clearly the case where the Ministry of Finance deliberately underestimated the income of the self-assessed group in the original budget figure, coupled with the extreme delinquency of that group's compliance with the law, and the flagrant degree of inequity resulting.

34. I discussed this problem in detail in "Zeihōjō no Kōsei to Tekiyōjō no Kōsei" (Fairness in the Tax-law and Fairness in its Application) in Shigeto Tsuru, *Collected Works*, vol. 7, pp. 225–34.

35. The weights occupied by loans by RFB in the total loans by all the financial institutions, as shown by percentages in loans outstanding at the end of March 1948, were 70.6 percent for the coal industry, 87.4 percent for the electricity generating, 65 percent for the ship-building industry, and 23.3 percent for all the industries combined (Source: *Nihon Kaihatsu Ginkō 10-nen Shi* [Ten-year History of Japan Development Bank, 1963]).

36. Cf. T. Cohen, *Remaking Japan*, p.437.

37. *Ibid.*, p.441.

38. In the 1949 election, the Socialists' 1947 total of 7.2 million popular votes fell to 4.1 million; the Communists' rose from 1 million to 3 million; and the Farmer-Labor Party, which had not existed in 1947, collected 600,000.

39. *Nippon Times*, January 26, 1949.

40. Cf., in particular, *Shōwa Keizai Shi* (History of the Shōwa Era Economy), editorially supervised by Hiromi Arisawa, Tokyo: Nihon Keizai Shimbun, 1976, pp. 326–29; and also Hisao Kanamori, *Taiken Sengo Keizai* (My Experience in the Postwar Economy), Tokyo: Tōyō Keizai Shimpō Sha, 1985, pp.55–61.

41. T. Cohen, *Remaking Japan*, p.440.

42. Frederick S. Dunn, *Peace-Making and the Settlement with Japan*, Princeton: Princeton University Press, 1963, p.54.

43. Robert Menzies, "The Pacific Settlement Seen from Australia," *Foreign Affairs*, January 1952 (pp. 188–96), p.190.

44. There seems to be no clear evidence available that at the time of Dulles' appointment as Foreign Policy Adviser there was any intention to assign to him the task of negotiating a treaty with Japan. But on May 18, 1950, he was assigned to handle the treaty.

45. Cf. F.S. Dunn, *Peace-Making and the Settlement with Japan*, pp.99–102, for more detail.

46. John Gunther, *The Riddle of MacArthur*, New York: Harper and Brothers, 1951, p.166.

47. *The New York Times*, June 26, 1950.

48. Cf. John Foster Dulles, *War or Peace*, New York: Macmillan, 1953, pp.5–16.

49. Cf. George R. Packard III, *Protest in Tokyo: The Security Treaty Crisis of 1960*, Princeton: Princeton University Press, 1966.

50. *Ibid.*, p.313.

51. Japan signed the Treaty of Peace and Friendship with the People's Republic of China in August 1978; but this was not a full-fledged peace treaty. As yet, there was no peace treaty with USSR.

52. For example, "Peace Treaty with Japan" in *New Statesman and Nation*, April 29, 1950 – the article was apparently written shortly before the American and Commonwealth Foreign Ministers' Conference on the treaty with Japan.

53. This was the phrase used in his address at the Japan United Nations Society (Nippon Kokuren Kyōkai) on April 23, 1951.

54. Although George Packard III refers to them, saying that "almost all these scholars accepted the Marxist principle" (Packard, *Protest in Tokyo*, p.27), it can hardly be said that such leading members in the group as Yoshishige Abe (President of Peers College), Yoshirō Nishina (Director of the Science Research

Institute), Yasaka Takagi (Professor of Tokyo University), Tetsuro Watsuji (Professor Emeritus of Tokyo University), Kiyoko Takeda (Secretary of YWCA in Japan), Tadeo Kuwabara (Professor of Kyoto University), and also some others, were Marxists.

55. Cf. Hadley Cantril (ed.), *Tensions That Cause Wars*, Urbana: The University of Illinois Press, 1950.
56. A summary of their January 1950 statement is given in Baron E.J. Lewe Van Aduard, *Japan: From Surrender to Peace*, New York: Frederick A. Praeger, 1954, p.149. A fuller document in English is *Three Statements for World Peace*, compiled by the editorial staff of *Sekai*, detached appendix of *Sekai*, April 1950; a more complete one (in Japanese) is *Senso to Heiwa ni kansuru 9-shō* (nine chapters concerning War and Peace), detached appendix of *Sekai*, September 1962.
57. Dunn, *Peace-Making and the Settlement with Japan*, p.93.
58. Dated November 12, 1942. Quoted from *The Roosevelt Letters*, edited by Elliot Roosevelt, George G. Harrap & Co., Ltd, London, 1949–52, volume 3, p.444.

3 The period of high growth rate

1. J.M. Keynes, Galton Lecture before the Eugenics Society in 1937, *The Eugenics Review*, April 1937, p.16; reproduced in *The Collected Writings of John Maynard Keynes*, vol. xiv, "*The General Theory* and After," Pt. II, pp.124–33, Macmillan, St. Martin's Press, 1973.
2. Kenneth E. Boulding in his address to a Foreign Relations Dinner held at the International House of Japan on January 30, 1984, reproduced in *IHJ Bulletin*, Vol. 4 No. 2, Spring 1984 (pp. 1–7), p.6.
3. Denoting GNP by Y, labor force by N, the amount of capital in existence by K, and using subscripts to indicate time periods, we may write:

$$G = (Y_1 - Y_0)/Y_0, \quad x = (N_1 - N_0)/N_0, \quad y = \left(\frac{Y_1}{N_1} - \frac{Y_0}{N_0}\right)\bigg/\frac{Y_0}{N_0}$$

$\alpha = (K_1 - K_0)/Y_0$, and $\beta = K_1/Y_1 = K_0/Y_0$ (assuming tentatively that the capital coefficient remains constant)

Then,

$$y = \frac{Y_1}{N_1}\bigg/\frac{Y_0}{N_0} - 1 = \frac{Y_1}{Y_0}\bigg/\frac{N_1}{N_0} - 1 = \frac{G+1}{x+1} - 1$$

$$\therefore \ G + 1 = (x+1)(y+1)$$

$$\text{or } G = x + y + xy \doteqdot x + y$$

$$\text{(xy being negligibly small)}$$

Next,

$$\alpha = (K_1 - K_0)/Y_0 = \left(\frac{K_1}{Y_1}\cdot Y_1 - \frac{K_0}{Y_0}\cdot Y_0\right)\bigg/Y_0$$

under the assumption that $\dfrac{K_1}{Y_1} = \dfrac{K_0}{Y_0} = \beta$

$$\alpha = \beta\left(\frac{Y_1 - Y_0}{Y_0}\right) = \beta \cdot G$$

$$\text{or } G = \alpha/\beta$$

4. Cf. *The Scientific-Industrial Revolution*, Model, Roland & Stone, New York, 1957. The author remained anonymous, but later it became known that this small volume was written by P.M. Sweezy.

5. Mitsubishi Economic Research Institute, *Mitsui-Mitsubishi-Sumitomo: Present Status of the Former Zaibatsu Enterprises*, Tokyo, 1955, p.19. Thus, for example, Sumitomo Bank went back to its old name from Osaka Bank in December 1952, Mitsubishi Bank from Chiyoda Bank in July 1953, and Mitsui Bank from Teikoku Bank in January 1954.

6. The revision came into effect as of September 1, 1953.

7. Cf. Seiji Keizai Kenkyūsho, *Nihon Keizai no Ugoki* (Trends of the Japanese Economy), No.21, May 1955.

8. Cf. The Bank of Japan, *Comparative Economic and Financial Statistics: Japan and Other Major Countries* (bilingual).

9. Cf. Economic Stabilization Board, *Annual Economic Survey for Fiscal Year 1952* (in Japanese), 1952, p.39.

10. "Nimoku-kai" means "meeting on the second Thursday of the month." The meeting is for the benefit of the members of the group; but the charitable role it occasionally plays may be worth mentioning. When I served as President of Hitotsubashi University and was trying to obtain contributions from private corporations in order to purchase the "Bert Franklin Collection" of rare economic history books and documents for the university library, all I had to do was to make one visit to the "Nimoku-kai" to explain the value of the collections and in one stroke, as it were, the sum of 300 million yen was voted for by some twenty presidents of the Mitsui-group for donation to the university. I have reason to believe that I was not a lucky exception.

11. Cf. Daniel I. Okimoto, *Between MITI and the Market*, Stanford: Stanford University Press, California, 1989, pp.134–5.

12. That was the reason why the so-called "new *zaibatsu*" groups (e.g. the Nissan group) burgeoned forth to take up the then new industries like chemicals and automobiles.

13. Y. Miyazaki (*Business Groups in the Postwar Japan*, pp.268–78) gives a detailed analysis of the realignment process through which the "one-set" principle was further effectuated in the decade of the 1960s.

14. I am aware that a complete story of the rejuvenation of Japanese capitalism in the postwar period should contain a discussion on the role played by the working class which after all is a major factor in any mature capitalist society. Here is a topic that can be focused upon for an extensive study. But for the purpose at hand I considered it peripheral for a number of reasons. Reference has already been made in an earlier chapter to the excess of supply over demand in labor force in the early postwar period, enabling the capitalist class to maintain a strong bargaining power against labor. True, there occurred episodes of labor's activism on a number of occasions. But, more important, labor unions in Japan have essentially been *enterprise unions* and the psychology of "*Mitgefangen, Mitgehangen*" has been prevalent among union members. Even when the confrontation between capital and labor approached an embittered showdown, labor realized in the end that their well-being was coterminous with the prosperity of their employer. For example, Japan's

performance in "quality control" (QC), which has been the object of emulation by foreign enterprises, could succeed only through the willing cooperation of union members. It has also been characteristic of Japanese industrial relations that so many of the presidents and executive members of private corporations were previously union leaders of their own corporations. Union radicalism in postwar Japan was confined largely to public enterprises and offices, where the market incentive was absent.

15. The account in this paragraph is based on the reminiscences of Dr Shintaro Hayashi who served as director in charge of light machinery in the JETRO from the beginning of 1961 to August 1964, published in *Ekonomisuto*, June 8, 1976, pp.82–89.

16. Cf. Takeshi Uno, *Medium-term Prospect and Shift in Structure of Japanese Industries* (in Japanese), The Industrial Bank of Japan, 1976, p.4.

17. "Conflicts in National Economic Objectives," *Economic Journal*, March 1971, pp.1–6.

18. It has been mentioned above that at the promotional stage of sewing-machines the price quoted for export was actually less than one-half of the price in the domestic market. Another instance of dual pricing was the steel industry in the critical period of its growth in the middle 1950s. It was customary at the time that the industry would make sizable profits through their sales at home, and, when confronted by the contingency of excess supply, would try to sell the products abroad at a price one-third lower than that to domestic buyers. The case of chemical fertilizers, especially of ammonium sulphate, was still more flagrant; the ratio of the export price to the domestic price having been around 75 percent between 1959 and 1967 and reduced thereafter to a figure as low as 39 percent in 1971. It is significant to note that the share of export in the total demand for ammonium sulphate in those years was consistently about one-half and that by far the biggest buyer then was China – a country which proved itself to be a hard bargainer.

19. Richard E. Caves, "Export-Led Growth and the New Economic History," in Jagdish N. Bhagwati and Others (eds.), *Trade, Balance of Payments and Growth*, North Holland, 1971, pp.403–42.

20. "Japan and World Economy" in Hugh Patrick and Henry Rosovsky (eds.), *Asia's New Giant – How the Japanese Economy Works*, The Brookings Institution, 1976, p.400.

21. *Ibid.*, pp.401–02.

22. Masahiro Takemoto, "Stabilization Policy in Japan and its Relations to Economic Instability in the World" (a paper presented at the International Seminar in Public Economics, Williamstown, Mass., June 10, 1974).

4 The role of the government in the high-growth period

1. Quoted in Yūjiro Hayashi, *Nihon no Keizai Keikaku* (Economic Planning in Japan), Tokyo, 1957, pp.144–45. Here, this passage was retranslated into English from Japanese.

2. The rapid growth period of 1955–57 was referred to in Japan as the "Jinmu

Boom" with the implication that it was unprecedented since the days of Emperor Jinmu, the first of Japan's mythological emperors. The GNP growth rates of 1959 and 1960 were still higher (8.9 percent and 13.3 percent) than those of the "Jinmu Boom" period. Thus reference had to be made to a still earlier myth of Amaterasu-Ōmikami (the Sun-Goddess) coming out of the Gate of the Celestial Rock Cave, which briefly could be rendered as "Iwato." When the economy experienced another sustained high-growth period during the latter half of the 1960s, we had to resort to the "Izanagi Boom," Izanagi being the name of the male character in the genesis of the Japanese archipelago.

3. Gardner Ackley and Hiromitsu Ishi, "Fiscal, Monetary, and Related Policies" in Hugh Patrick and Henry Rosovsky (eds.), *Asia's New Giant – How the Japanese Economy Works*, The Brookings Institution, 1976, pp.236–7.

4. Philip H. Trezise and Yukio Suzuki, "Politics, Government, and Economic Growth in Japan," in Patrick and Rosovsky (eds.), *Asia's New Giant*, p.785.

5. That is: No.2, No.3, No.6, No.7, No.8, No.9, etc. From the data provided by the Federation of Steel Industry in Japan (Nihon Tekkō Renmei), reproduced in M. Shinohara, *A Treatise on Industrial Structure*, 1976, p.258.

6. In the *Fortune* directory of the 100 world's biggest industrial companies (outside the United States) in 1963, these six companies were ranked as follows: Yawata 31st, Fuji 57th, Nihon Kōkan 65th, Kobe 70th, Sumitomo 86th, and Kawasaki unranked.

7. See the interview article with Mitsuharu Itō in *Ekonomisuto*, July 6, 1976 (pp.76–83), p.79.

8. This episode is recounted by Shintarō Hayashi in his interview article in *Ekonomisuto*, June 22, 1976 (pp.78–85), p.80. Hayashi was at the time in charge of agricultural and marine products (which would include sugar) in the MITI. This subsidy measure was so effective that many of the ships "exported" were actually bought by Japanese shipping companies.

9. Ackley and Ishi, "Fiscal, Monetary, and Related Policies," p.239.

10. Organization for Economic Co-operation and Development, *Revenue Statistics of OECD Member Countries, 1965–72*, Paris, OECD, 1975.

11. By way of illustration we may enumerate here a list of tax-free reserves as a part of inventory of tax incentives as of 1975:
    1. Reserve for Bad Debts
    2. Reserve for Loss on Returned Goods Unsold
    3. Bonus Reserve
    4. Reserve for Retirement Allowances
    5. Reserve for Special Repairs
    6. Reserve for Repairs and Guaranteeing Certain Products
    7. Reserve for Price Fluctuations
    8. Reserve for Overseas Market Development
    9. Reserve for Overseas Investment Loss
    10. Reserve for Investment Loss in the Free Trade Zone in Okinawa
    11. Structural Improvement Project Reserve for Small- and Medium-sized Enterprises
    12. Reserve for Prevention of Mineral Pollution of Metal Mining, etc.

13. Depreciation Reserve for Specific Railway Construction
14. Depreciation Reserve for the Construction of Atomic Power Generation
15. Depreciation Reserve for Specific Gas Construction
16. Forestation Reserve
17. Reserve for Pollution Control
18. Stock Transactions Loss Reserve
19. Drought Reserve
20. Unusual Risks Reserve
21. Default Loss Compensation Reserve
22. Security Transactions Responsibility Reserve
23. Commodity Exchange Responsibility Reserve
24. Reserve for Losses Caused by Repurchase of Electronic Computer
25. Reserve for Guaranteeing the Quality of Computer-Programs
26. Reserve for Participation in the Okinawa International Ocean Exposition
Details of these Reserves are explained in *An Outline of Japanese Taxes, 1975* [in English], Tokyo: Okura Zaimu Kyōkai, 1975, pp. 87–94.
12. Joseph A. Pechman and Keimei Kaizuka, "Taxation," in *Asia's New Giant,* edited by Hugh Patrick and Henry Rosovsky, cited earlier, p.343.
13. Tokyo-to Shin-zaigen Kōsō Kenkyūkai, *Dai Toshi Zeisei no Fukōhei Zesei* (Rectification of Unfairness in the Tax System Relevant to Big Cities), January 1975; and Tokyo-to Shin-zaigen Kōsō Kenkyūkai, *Fukōhei Zeisei to Zaisei Kōzō no Kaikaku* (Unfair Tax System and the Reform of Fiscal Structure), August 1976. Both were later published as Masao Yamamoto (ed.), *Toshi Zaisei Kaikaku no Kōsō* (Proposals for Reforming of Fiscal Structure of Cities), Tokyo: Sinji Shobō, 1979.
14. *Hōjin Kigyō no Jittai* (Facts and Statistics on Corporate Enterprises), compiled by the Ministry of Finance, annual series.
15. Masu Uekusa, "Hōjin Zeisei no Jittai o Tsuku" (How is the Corporate Tax System Working Actually?), *Tōyō Keizai,* August 4, 1973, pp.52–59.
16. *Ibid.,* p.57.
17. Joseph A. Pechman and Keimei Kaizuka, in *Asia's New Giant,* p.361.
18. Ackley and Ishi, in *Asia's New Giant,* p.205.
19. Loans outstanding of city banks at the end of 1956 amounted to 1.4 trillion yen compared with GNP at current prices of 9.7 trillion in 1956, or 14.4 percent; but they rose to 32.3 trillion yen by the end of 1974 compared with GNP at current prices at 132.5 trillion yen of 1974, or 24.4 percent.
20. See, in particular, Zen'ei Imai's reminiscences in *Ekonomisuto,* September 14, 1976 (pp. 78–85), p.82. Imai was at the time chief of the International Trade Bureau of MITI.
21. Cf. Nihon Sangyō Kōzō Kenkyūsho, *An Analysis of Japanese Heavy and Chemical Industries on the Basis of the 1961 Input-Output Table* (in Japanese), 1964.
22. Cf. *Public Enterprises Yearbook for 1971* (in Japanese), compiled by Bureau on Fiscal Affairs of the Ministry of Home Affairs, annual series.
23. Takeo Sato, *Mizu no Keizaigaku* (Economics of Water), Tokyo: Iwanami Shoten, 1965, p.193.

5 A turning point cometh

1. Kakuei Tanaka, *Nihon Retto Kaizō Ron* (The Plan for Remodeling of the Japanese Archipelago), Tokyo: Nikkan Kōgyō Shimbun-sha, 1972, p.218.
2. *Ibid.*, p.124 and p.115.
3. Compared with the price at the end of 1970, which was $1.8 per barrel, this meant a rise of 6.47 times.
4. Cf. Phillis Deane and W.A. Cole, *British Economic Growth*, Cambridge: Cambridge University Press, 1962, pp. 329–30.
5. In Japan it has been customary to use the term "kōgai" for the phenomena which in the West are referred to variously by such terms as "pollution," "public nuisance," "Immission," or "les pollutions et nuisance d'origine industrielle et urbaine." "Kōgai" means literally "disamenities and damages inflicted on the public." It could be used in place of "environmental disruption" in English; therefore, we shall use this term frequently because it is conveniently short.
6. Cf. Hugh Patrick and Henry Rosovsky, *Asia's New Giant*, p.906.
7. The population of the three largest urban areas, Tokyo, Osaka and Nagoya, increased by more than ten million in ten years from 1960 to 1970, from 37,380,000 to 48,260,000.
8. The number of passenger cars owned per 1,000 population in Japan increased from 3.4 in 1959 to 154.0 in 1975; and already by 1969 the number of automobiles of all kinds per 1,000 hectares of flat land space was more than 1,300 in Japan, while in West Germany, the next congested country, it was 750.
9. Ashio is situated along the upstream of the Watarasé River, a major tributary of the Toné, one hundred kilometers directly north of Tokyo and twenty kilometers southwest of Nikko. Copper was discovered there as early as in 1610, and, with some vicissitudes, the Ashio mine remained as a top supplier of copper for two and one-half centuries under the direct management of the central feudal government of Tokugawa. After the Meiji Restoration, the mine was transferred to a private firm; and, from 1877 on, under the ruthless enterpreneurship of Furukawa, it was made into a major modern copper-refining center. With this modernization and the prosperity of the copper-refining industry there emerged inevitably spillover effects of an undersirable kind, first (around 1880) in the form of damage to fish in the Watarasé River, then (from 1888 on) affecting the rice crops which depended on the river for irrigation, and soon thenafter causing ill effects to the health of the people residing along the river.
10. It is true that the Ducktown problem was tackled in the 1930s, much later than the Ashio case in the history of world capitalism. But the keen awareness of welfare needs of citizens with which the TVA administrators coped with the environmental issues from the very beginning under the leadership of David Lilienthal is in sharp contrast with the cold-blooded indifference of the Japanese bureaucracy in dealing with the Ashio case.
11. Japanese Government, Environment Agency, *White Paper on Environment for 1976* (in Japanese), annual series, p.513.

12. Cf. Shin'ichi Takayanagi, "Michigan-shū Kankyō Hogo Hō" (Environment Law of the Michigan State), *Kōgai Kenkyū*, Summer 1971, Vol. 1, No.1, pp. 55–57; also Joseph L. Sax and Roger L. Conner, "Michigan's Environmental Protection Act of 1970: A Progress Report," *Michigan Law Review*, May 1972, Vol. 70, No.6, pp.1003–106.

13. F.J. Fisher, "The Sixteenth and Seventeenth Centuries: The Dark Ages in English Economic History?" *Economica*, February 1957 (pp. 2–18), p.3.

14. Lecture delivered at Bradford in March 1859. See J. Ruskin, *The Two Paths*, Smith and Elder, London, 1859, pp.109–10 (italics added).

15. In this connection, E.F. Schumacher's following dictum is quite germane: "Nature always, so to speak, knows where and when to stop . . . There is measure in all natural things – in their size, speed, or violence. As a result, the system of nature, of which man is a part, tends to be self-balancing, self-adjusting, self-cleansing. Not so with technology . . . Technology recognises no self-limiting principle – in terms, for instance, of size, speed, or violence. It therefore does not possess the virtues of being self-balancing, self-adjusting, and self-cleansing. In the subtle system of nature, technology and, in particular, the super-technology of the modern world, acts like a foreign body, and there are now numerous signs of rejection." (E.F. Schumacher, *Small is Beautiful*, London: Blond & Briggs Ltd., 1973, pp.136–7.)

16. Ivan Illich actually went so far as to suggest that transport cost might be deducted entirely from GNP. Cf. Illich Forum (ed.), *Illich Speaks in Japan – Hopes for Mankind* (in Japanese), Shinhyōronsha, Tokyo, 1981, p.177.

17. See *The New York Times*, August 16, 1970. In this connection, one cannot help recalling a discerning passage from writings of a "classical" economist a century ago, to wit: "A philosopher produces ideas, a poet poems, a clergyman sermons, a professor compendia, and so on. A criminal produces crimes. If we look a little closer at the connection between this latter branch of production and society as a whole, we shall rid ourselves of many prejudices. The criminal produces not only crimes, but also criminal law, and with this also the professor who gives lectures on criminal law, and in addition to this the inevitable compendium in which this same professor throws his lectures onto the general market as 'commodities.' This brings with it augmentation of national wealth, quite apart from the personal enjoyment which – as a competent witness, Herr Professor Roscher, tells us – the manuscript of the compendium brings to the originator himself. The criminal moreover produces the whole of the police and of criminal justice, constables, judges, hangmen, juries, etc.; and all these different lines of business, which form equally many categories of the social division of labor, develop different capacities of the human spirit, create new needs and new ways of satisfying them. Torture alone has given rise to the most ingenious mechanical inventions, and employed many honorable craftsmen in the production of its instruments . . . The effects of the criminal on the development of productive power can be shown in detail. Would locks ever have reached their present degree of excellence had there been no thieves? Would the making of bank-notes have reached its present perfection had there been no forgers? . . . Crime, through its constantly new methods of attack on

property, constantly calls into being new methods of defense, and so is as productive as strikes for the invention of machines." Probably few economists today can identify the author of this passage. It is from K. Marx, *Theories of Surplus Value*, Foreign Languages Publishing House, Moscow, 1964, Vol. 1, pp.375–76.

18. Here is the relevant passage as reproduced in R.F. Harrod, *The Life of John Maynard Keynes*, Macmillan, London, 1951, p.583: "I have been known to complain that, to judge from results in this lawyer-ridden land, the *Mayflower*, when she sailed from Plymouth, must have been entirely filled with lawyers. When I first visited Mr. Morgenthau in Washington some three years ago accompanied only by my secretary, the boys in your Treasury curiously enquired of him – where is your lawyer? When it was explained that I had none – 'Who then does your thinking for you?' was the rejoinder."

19. T. Veblen, *The Theory of Business Enterprise*, New York: Mentor Book, 1904, p.120.

20. I. Fisher, *The Nature of Capital and Income*, Macmillan, New York/London, 1906. As a matter of fact, Fisher developed this set of ideas much earlier and published them in "What is capital?," *Economic Journal*, December 1896. The idea dawned on him, according to his son, "in the summer of 1894 as he drove from Lauterbrunnen toward Zermatt: 'It suddenly occurred to me while looking at a watering trough with its in-flow and out-flow, that the basic distinction needed to differentiate capital and income was substantially the same as the distinction between the water in that trough and the flow into or out of it.'" See I.N. Fisher, *My Father Irving Fisher*, New York: Comet Press, 1956, p.123.

21. K. Boulding, "Income or Welfare," *The Review of Economic Studies*, 17, 1949–50, pp.77–86.

22. N. Kaldor, *An Expenditure Tax*, Allen and Unwin, London, 1955, pp.54–78.

23. A.C. Pigou, *The Economics of Welfare*, London: Macmillan, 1932, p.36.

24. J.S. Mill, *Principles of Political Economy*, New Impression, Longmans, Green and Co. Ltd, London, 1926, p.751.

6 The double "price revolution"

1. While the wholesale price index rose 1.88 times between 1956 and 1975, the urban land price (national average, and not that of six biggest cities) rose 24.1 times during the same period.

2. *International Encyclopedia of the Social Sciences*, Vol. 12, 1968, p.473.

3. *Ibid.*, p.474.

4. J.M. Keynes, *A Treatise of Money*, Macmillan & Co., London, 1934, Vol. II, p.158.

5. *Ibid.*, p.159.

6. It may be mentioned here that the second oil shock of 1979–80 witnessed the price rise from $13.34 per barrel in January 1979 to $32 in November 1980.

7. One important aspect of the immediate negative consequences which we did not touch upon was the widespread panic among city-dwellers concerning the

consequential non-availability of household necessities, such as toilet paper and detergents, illustrating a typical response of urban mass psychology in the context of the Japanese distributive system. An excellent socio-economic analysis of this panic episode is given in Yoshikazu Miyazaki's *Atarashii Kakaku Kakumei* (A New Price Revolution), Iwanami Shoten, Tokyo, 1975, pp.12–108.

8. In this connection, it should be mentioned, as was discussed at the end of Chapter 4, that the rates charged for industrial use were kept unduly low using cross-subsidization at the expense of household users. The ratio was 38 to 100 in 1962 in the unit rate per kWh in favor of industrial users, although it was adjusted to 53 to 100 in 1974.

9. Charles J. Hitch, "Energy in our Future," *The Key Reporter*, Summer 1978, p.3.

10. Imports occupy more than 99 percent of the supply of petroleum in Japan.

11. Reproduced in The Bank of Japan, *Chōsa Geppō* (Monthly Research Bulletin), April 1990, p.56.

12. Federal Reserve Board, *Balance Sheets for the U.S. Economy*, as reproduced in *ibid.*, p.57.

13. OECD, *Revenue Statistics*, as summarized by the Ministry of Finance, the Japanese government in *Sankō Shiryō* (Reference Materials), 1990, p.6. Illustrative of the fact of the increasing trend of the real estate tax burden in Tokyo is my personal experience of paying in 1989 38.2 times the amount I paid in 1956 for a small piece of land on which I have lived while the consumer price index rose 5.3 times.

14. The assessment of landed property for the inheritance tax is made on the basis of what is known as "route rates" compiled by the Internal Revenue Agency, which are generally ascertained to be about 30 percent of the market price. There are two other categories of officially assessed prices of land. One is the "posted prices" compiled by the National Land Agency once a year as of January 1 as "that price which is seen to reveal when the transaction is free and normal." The absolute level of these "posted prices" follows more or less the actually transacted price and is usually 50 to 70 percent of the latter. Another category is the "assessment-base price" for the real estate tax posted by the Ministry of Local Autonomous Bodies. This is as low as 5 percent of the market price at present. The urban land price index we have been using in this Section is the one compiled by Japan Real Estate Research Institute, which is mainly concerned with the *trend* (and fluctuations) of land prices; and as such it is rated highly as an index of actual price movements.

15. Cf. *Nihon Keizai Shimbun*, April 18, 1990.

16. *Bungei Shunjū*, August 1990, p.150.

17. *Mainichi Shimbun*, August 5, 1990.

18. It may be relevant to remind ourselves in this connection that the present Liberal-Democratic Party came into existence as the result of a merger, in November 1955, of two conservative parties, and ever since then it has continued to remain as the government party in power for more than thirty years.

19. In a dialogue with Hideo Aragaki of the Asahi Shimbun in *Hōsō Asahi*, January 1965.
20. *Jeremy Bentham's Economic Writings*, Vol. I, edited by W. Stark, George Allen & Unwin Ltd., London, 1952, p.332.
21. *International Encyclopedia of Social Sciences*, Vol. 12, 1968, p.592.
22. *Proceedings of the 13th Plenary Session of the Constitution Research Commission*, 1958, p.40.
23. The high cost of land in Tokyo did not escape the attention of *The Economist*, which commented in its October 3, 1987 issue (p.25): "If this page were a piece of prime Tokyo property, it would cost 1.8m yen (about $12,000) to buy. If, instead, this page had been part of a recent, headline-making property deal in the City of London it would have cost $3,400. Property, like much else in Japan, is outrageously expensive." We may append here an additional comment to say that the urban land price index rose by 73.8 percent in Japan between September 1987 and March 1990.
24. Income tax paid by Mr. I, who topped the list in 1990, was 3.2 billion yen.
25. Kazuyuki Hibino, *The Asahi Shimbun*, December 27, 1987, p.1.
26. For example, Ryūtaro Komiya in *Gendai Nihon Keizai Kenkyū*, Tokyo Daigaku Shuppankai, Tokyo 1975, pp.225–68, and Ken'ichi Inada in "Toshi to Tochi-Zeisei," *Sekai*, December 1987, pp.123–36.
27. A detailed discussion of this problem is given by Ryūtaro Komiya in his *Gendai Nihon Keizai* (The Japanese Economy Today), Tokyo Daigaku Shuppankai, Tokyo, 1988, Chapter 1: "Causes of the 1973–74 Inflation."
28. For eleven days after the Nixon announcement on August 15, 1971, Japan kept its exchange market open with the 360-yen rate and added 3.9 billion dollars to its foreign currency reserve during that time; and, further, during the first float period of August to December, the Bank of Japan exercised its policy of "dirty float" by going into the market to buy an additional 2.7 billion dollars, giving the impression that the value of yen would not go down.

7 The march of corporate capitalism

1. The yen exchange rate to the dollar was set at 360 to 1 in April 1949, and then it was upvalued to 308 to 1 by the Smithsonian Agreement of December 1971. Since that time, it has continued to strengthen and was quoted at 200.6 to 1 at the end of 1985. By 1987, it had appreciated to the level of 122 to 1.
2. See Herman Kahn, *The Emerging Japanese Superstate*, Prentice-Hall, Englewood Cliffs, NJ, 1970.
3. Ezra F. Vogel, *Japan as Number One – Lessons for America*, Cambridge, Mass.: Harvard University Press, 1979, p.22.
4. Murray Sayle, "Bowing to the Inevitable," *Times Literary Supplement*, April 28–May 4, 1989 (pp. 443–5), p.445.
5. *Monthly Review*, May 1990.
6. Cf. F.C. Crawford, *The American Triangle of Plenty*, New York, 1943, p.67.
7. An alternative formulation of this embracing process would be Galbraith's

concept of the "revised sequence," the replacement of the old economic proposition of consumers' sovereignty, of wants calling forth production, by a situation in which the large corporation "reaches forward to control its markets and on beyond to manage the market behavior and shape the attitudes of those whom it, ostensibly, serves." (Cf. J.K. Galbraith, *The New Industrial State*, Houghton Mifflin Company, Boston, 3rd edn, 1968, p.222.) The gluttonous embracing tendency of giant private capital is further illustrated by an incident recounted in an article in *Fortune* (July 1964) with the expressive title "Who Owns What's in Your Head?," a story which appears to be typical of the scientific mind itself becoming subservient to the dictate of profit-oriented private corporations.

8. Samuel Bowles and Richard Edwards, "Varieties of Dissent: Galbraith and Radical Political Economy," in *Unconventional Wisdom: Essays in Honor of John Kenneth Galbraith*, edited by S. Bowles, R. Edwards and W.G. Shepherd, Houghton Mifflin Company, Boston, 1989, p.48.

9. J.K. Galbraith, *The New Industrial State*, Houghton Mifflin, Boston, p.xviii.

10. Paul Samuelson, too, wrote recently: "Each new edition of my *Economics* and the Samuelson–Nordhaus *Economics* has had to move further away from the Berle–Means paradigm of corporate-bureaucrats-in-the-saddle and share-owners-sans-power." (Paul A. Samuelson, "Galbraith as Artist and Scientist" in Samuel Bowles, Richard Edwards, and William G. Shepherd (eds.), *Unconventional Wisdom: Essays on Economics in Honor of John Kenneth Galbraith*, Houghton Mifflin Company, Boston, 1989, p.125.)

11. The rising trend itself seems to have stopped in the 1980s; but the discussion of the most recent development requires a rather complex treatment and therefore is not attempted here. For example, the decline of the ratio to 101 during 1981–85 can be explained by a sharp increase in gross investment (by 63 percent, compared with the period of 1976–80) in those years.

12. Cf. Yoshikazu Miyazaki, *Nihon Keizai no Kōzō to Kōdō* (The Structure and Performance of the Japanese Economy), Chikuma Shobō, Tokyo, Vol.II, 1985, p.33.

13. Yoshikazu Miyazaki, *Nihon Keizai no Kōzō to Kōdō*, Chikuma Shobō, Tokyo, Vol.I, 1985, pp.238–9.

14. The standard formulation of this concept can be found in Machlup as follows: "Horizontal integration is the unification of the management of establishments producing the same products. Vertical integration unifies the management of establishments of which one uses (processes, fabricates, distributes) the products of the other. Diversification adds new lines of business to the production program of a firm. If the new product is so different from those previously produced that it is classified as belonging to a different industry – which is admittedly very arbitrary – one frequently speaks of the corporation as having become a 'conglomerate.' Acquisition of several firms engaged in very diverse industries is sometimes referred to as an 'agglomeration.'" Fritz Machlup, *The Political Economy of Monopoly*, Johns Hopkins Press, Baltimore, 1952, p.110.

15. Alan Hughes on "conglomerates" in *The New Palgrave: A Dictionary of Economics*, Macmillan, London, Vol.I, 1987, p.574.

16. The family name is "Toyoda"; but when the motor company was established in 1937, the spelling for the car model was changed to "Toyota" which was to be the company's trade mark. On the historical development of Toyota Motor Company, cf. Kōnosuke Odaka, Keinosuke Ono and Fumihiko Adachi, *The Automobile Industry in Japan: A Study of Ancillary Firm Development*, Economic Research Series No.26, The Institute of Economic Research, Hitotsubashi University, Kinokuniya Company Ltd., Tokyo and Oxford University Press, 1988, pp.111–30.

17. Cf. Satoshi Kamata, *Jidōsha Ohkoku no Kurayami* (Gloomy Darkness of the Auto Kingdom), Suzusawa Shoten, Tokyo, 1984, pp.107–8.

18. Readers are referred to Table 3.1, comparing the rates of growth of labor productivity in manufacturing industries among major advanced countries, where it was shown that with the 1950 level as 100 the relevant index for 1973 was 1412 for Japan, contrasted to 210 for the US, 210 for UK, and 411 for W. Germany.

19. The average DFI for five years, 1981–85, was 9.43 billion dollars, of which 2.38 billions were in the spheres of manufacturing. Of this sum, it was characteristic that more than 50 percent (1.36 billions) was destined to advanced countries.

20. DFI in the spheres of finance and insurance totaled 8.4 billion dollars during five years from 1981 to 1985 (the annual average being 1.7 billions), recording 3.8 billions in the year of 1985. Still bigger was the DFI in the spheres of other tertiary industries with the total of 13.2 billion dollars for the same five years. DFI in tertiary industries as a whole occupied 54.4 percent of the total in 1985 while the share of manufacturing was 22 percent in that year.

21. A recent, most detailed treatment of the subject by an economist can be found in Yasuo Okamoto, "Takokuseki Kigyō to Nihon Kigyō no Takokusekika" (Multinational Firms and the Multinationalization of Japanese Firms), (3) and (4), *Keizaigaku Ronshū*, Vol.55, No.2 (July 1989) and Vol.56. No.1 (April 1990). I am greatly indebted to this study for the following discussion of the E-E industry in Japan.

22. For the details of the trade friction between Japan and the US in connection with the semiconductor industry, cf. T.A. Pugel, "Limits of Trade Policy Toward High Technology Industries: The Case of Semiconductors" in *Trade Friction and Economic Policy* (ed. by R. Sato and P. Wachtel), Cambridge University Press, Cambridge, 1987, pp.184–223.

23. R.V. Ramachandran, "Discussion" on Chapter 11, Sato and Wachtel, *ibid.*, p.229.

24. Brooks Adams, *America's Economic Supremacy*, New York and London: Harper & Brothers Publishers, 1947, (reprint of the 1890 edition), p.104.

25. Robert Gordon Menzies, "The Pacific Settlement Seen from Australia," *Foreign Affairs*, January 1952 (pp.188–96), p.190.

26. For the detailed account of this subject, readers are referred to Abe David & Ted Wheelwright, *The Third Wave: Australia and Asian Capitalism*, Sutherland,

NSW, Australia: Left Book Club Co-operative Ltd., 1989.

27. According to the report of the Foreign Investment Review Board, as reported in *Sydney Morning Herald*, March 6, 1989.

28. Oscar Landicho in *Daily Mirror*, January 13, 1989.

29. The television "Channel 10" conducted a public opinion survey on January 23, 1990 on the question of whether the Japan-sponsored MFP should be established in Sydney, and the negative response to the question was as high as 91 percent (*Asahi Shimbun*, January 25, 1990). It has also been pointed out that the price paid by a Japanese developer for the purchase of Woodstream Golf Course in Sydney was 1,568 million yen, which was three times the value the owner expected (*Asahi Shimbun*, February 20, 1989). More generally, anxiety has been expressed over the inflationary impact of the real estate purchases by Japanese capital (cf. Max Walsh in *Sydney Morning Herald*, February 2, 1989).

30. David & Wheelwright, *The Third Wave*, p.229.

31. Lea Wright in *Sydney Morning Herald*, March 30, 1989.

32. *Wagakuni-Kigyō no Kaigai Jigyō Katsudō* (Business Activities of Japanese Firms in Foreign Countries), edited by the International Enterprise Section, MITI, March 1990. The survey was first conducted in 1970.

33. Cf. David and Wheelwright, *The Third Wave*, pp. 150–1.

34. Raymond Vernon, "International Investment and International Trade in the Product Cycle," *Quarterly Journal of Economics*, Vol. 80, May 1966, pp.190–207.

35. Stephen Hymer, *The International Operations of National Firms: Study of Direct Foreign Investment*, Cambridge, Mass., MIT, 1976 (Ph.D. dissertation, MIT, 1960); Charles P. Kindleberger, *American Business Abroad*, New Haven, Yale University Press, 1968; and Richard E. Caves, "International Corporations: The Industrial Economics of Foreign Investment," *Economica*, New Series, Vol.38, No.149, 1971, pp.1–27.

36. Komiya presented his theory as early as in 1967 in Japanese ("Ekonomisuto" July 25, 1967, later included as Chapter 7 of his book: *Gendai Nihon-Keizai Kenkyu*, Tokyo: Tokyo Daigaku Shuppankai, 1975). Its much fuller and latest version by him is "Japan's Foreign Direct Investments: Facts and Theoretical Considerations" in Silvio Borner (ed.), *International Finance and Trade in a Polycentric World*, Macmillan, London, 1990.

37. Edith T. Penrose, "Foreign Investment and the Growth of Firm," *Economic Journal*, Vol. 66, June 1956, pp.220–35.

38. A challenging discussion on this subject can be found in Stephen Gill & David Law, *The Global Political Economy: Perspectives, Problems, and Policies*, Hertfordshire: Harvester–Wheatsheaf, 1988.

39. A few days before the first session of the Commission, Toshio Dokō, 85-year-old chairman of the Commission, called in other commission members to his office and showed them a confidential memorandum which he had exchanged with Prime Minister Suzuki, where it was clearly stated that the privatizing reforms were mandatory on the Commission (cf. Yasuo Maruyama, *Shōgen-·Daini-Rinchō*, Shinji Shobō, Tokyo, 1984, p.24).

40. The sizable amount of the cash-sales intake of the Corporation could have been

invested in the call market to earn some interest income; but all the station offices had to transport the entire notes and coins every day to the specified banks. There were other disallowances, such as the Corporation's inability to make a reduced-rate long-term contract with shippers and to resort to flexible use of the budgeted aggregate payroll fund for the merit system.

41. The ratio of the state assistance (other than the compensatory payment) to the current revenue of the nationally operated railroad in 1984 was: 54.6 percent for the British Railway Public Corporation, 74.3 percent for the German Federal Railroad, and 87.5 percent for the French Nationalized Railroad, as reported in *The 1985 Audit Report on the Japan National Railroad*, annual series.

42. Only in 1977, the law was revised in such a way that the question of rates and fares became a matter of Ministerial authorization rather than that of Diet approval.

43. Cf., in particular, Tatsujirō Ishikawa, *Kokutetsu – Kinō to Zaisei no Kōzu* (The National Railroad – Its Function and the Structure of its Finance), Kōtsūnihon Sha, Tokyo, 1975, Chapter 2.

44. Quoted in the column of "Vox Populi, Vox Dei" of the *Asahi Shimbun*, August 11, 1986.

8 Whither Japan?

1. Lincoln Steffens, *The Autobiography of Lincoln Steffens*, New York: Harcourt, Brace and Company, 1931, p.872.

2. Joseph Schumpeter, "The Instability of Capitalism," *Economic Journal*, Vol. 38, September 1928 (pp. 361–68), p.368.

3. Joseph A. Schumpeter, *Capitalism, Socialism, and Democracy*, 3rd edn, Harper & Brothers Publishers, New York 1950, p.162. Actually, the last paper he presented before his death (January 8, 1950) was "The March into Socialism" delivered before the American Economic Association on December 30, 1949, in which he gave a much fuller account of "the reasons for believing that the capitalist order tends to destroy itself and that centralist socialism is [with some qualifications] a likely heir apparent" (*Ibid.*, p.417).

4. Oskar Lange and Fred M. Taylor, *On the Economic Theory of Socialism*, Minneapolis: University of Minnesota Press, 1938.

5. *Ibid.*, p.83.

6. Published in English in an abridged form in *Science and Society*, Spring 1944 (pp. 115–25) as L.A. Leontiev and Others, "Political Economy in the Soviet Union."

7. Paul M. Sweezy, *The Theory of Capitalist Development*, New York: Monthly Review Press, 1956 (the first printing, 1942), pp.52–3.

8. Karl Marx, *Capital*, Charles H. Kerr & Company, Chicago, Vol.I, 1909, p.1026 (italics added).

9. *The New York Times* was quick to seize this opportunity to write an editorial suggesting a turnaround of official Soviet philosophy; and the *American Economic Review* opened its pages to a discussion of the pros and cons by experts in the field, including Raya Dunayevskaya, Oskar Lange, Paul Baran,

M.M. Bober and others (from March 1944 issue to June 1946 issue). Dunayevskaya, in particular, was vehement in criticizing the new position on the grounds that "the law of value" was essentially a concept summarizing the exploitative relation of capitalism.

10. Oskar Lange, "Marxian Economics in the Soviet Union," *American Economic Review*, March 1944, Vol.35, pp.127–33.
11. Karl Marx, *Capital*, Vol. III, p.992. Italics added.
12. In the December 1944 issue, pp.44–60. The English translation of the full text was printed with the title of "Basic Laws of Development of Socialist Economy" in *Science & Society*, Summer 1945, pp.232-51.
13. Such as (1) the social ownership of the means of production; (2) the non-existence of exploitative class relations; (3) the precedence of the planning principle; and (4) the new type of incentives for productive efforts replacing the profit motive.
14. Cf. *Science & Society*, Summer 1945, p.250.
15. P.A. Samuelson, *Economics*, McGraw-Hill, Inc., New York, 11th edn, pp.817–18.
16. See his "The Theory of Optimum Regime" in *Selected Papers*, Amsterdam, North Holland, 1959, pp.264–304.
17. Quoted in Steve H. Hanke (ed.), *Privatization and Development,* Institute of Contemporary Studies, San Francisco, California, 1987, pp.17–18. Italics added.
18. John Vickers and George Yarrow, *Privatization – An Economic Analysis*, Cambridge, Mass.: The MIT Press, 1988, p.425.
19. Heilbroner in *New Yorker*, January 23, 1989. Incidentally, he is a political economist who has been regarded as left-of-center by US standards.
20. John Naisbitt and Patricia Aburdene, *Megatrends 2000 – Ten New Directions for the 1990s,* William Morrow and Company, Inc., New York, 1990, pp.154–77.
21. Steve H. Hanke, *Privatization and Development*, p.216.
22. Assar Lindbeck, "The Efficiency of Competition and Planning," in *Planning and Market Relations*, edited by Michael Kaser and Richard Portes, Macmillan, London, 1971 (pp.83–113), pp.102–3. Italics in original.
23. Vickers and Yarrow, *Privatization*, p.426.
24. J.K. Galbraith, *The New Industrial State*, Houghton Mifflin, Boston, 1967, p.32.
25. *Ibid.*, pp.13–16.
26. K. Marx, *Grundrisse der Kritik der Politischen Oekonomie*, Dietz Verlag, Berlin, 1953, pp.592, 596, translated into English by Herbert Marcuse in his *One Dimensional Man*, London: Routledge & Kegan Paul Ltd., 1964, pp.35–6.
27. *Ibid.*
28. Paul A. Samuelson and William D. Nordhaus, *Economics*, McGraw-Hill Book Company, New York, 13th edn, 1989, p.977.
29. Lester Thurow, *The Zero-Sum Society*, New York: Basic Books, Inc., Publishers, 1980, p.95.

30. J.S. Mill, *Principles of Political Economy*, p.751.
31. Ryūtaro Komiya, "Ureubeki Migisenkai" (The Lamentable Shift to the Right), *Gendai Keizai*, Spring 1979.
32. Kenneth E. Boulding, *IHJ Bulletin*, p.7.
33. In *Yomiuri Shimbun*, April 28, 1965.
34. Using NATO's definition of "military expenditures," which includes pension payments for armed forces. Cf. *Asahi Shimbun*, October 19, 1988, where comparison was made for the fiscal year 1988.
35. "Not to have nuclear weapons brought in" was the phrase which did not allow confirmation inasmuch as the US policy of nuclear deterrence (on which Japan relied) required secrecy on the deployment of such weapons. Thus the Japanese government acquiesced in the "transit" sojourn of nuclear-deployed US warships, claiming that it was different from "introduction." The "1 percent of GNP" ceiling came to be exceeded since the fiscal year 1987.
36. In *Asahi Journal*, March 6, 1962.
37. In *Bungei Shunjū*, September 1979.
38. Article 3 of the Special Measures Act for the Protection of the Environment of the Inland Sea of Seto.
39. Today's Japan, overgrown into material affluence and financial euphoria, may no longer impress foreign visitors as she did Lincoln Steffens on his first visit to Japan on his way back from Russia to the United States (1917). But it may be worth quoting a passage from him which described his arriving from Vladivostok to a port city in Japan. "We arrived at Sakai late at night, and I saw dimly a common sight – the unloading of a boat at a dock – that was beautiful. Just columns of tiny Japanese women, all clean and each marked, daintily, with the letters of her owner or renter, carrying out our cargo. The special train we boarded looked small, but neat, clean, and beautiful, and early the next morning, when I lifted the curtain of my window to look out, I saw – beauty. Rice fields, with mountains in the distance behind them, a familiar picture. And so at Tokio: beauty, taste – Japan is a thing of beauty. I had never imagined that any civilized country, any civilization, could be so lovely as Japan, and I corrected my picture of Greece, old Greece, which may have been something like Japan. That, I thought, is the way all civilized countries will look when every detail of their life is brought up into harmony with their culture" (Lincoln Steffens, *Autobiography*, p.768). Still, I believe that potentialities do remain.
40. Based on a report in *Mainichi Shimbun*, evening edition, April 9, 1980.
41. See *SIPRI Yearbook 1989*, Oxford University Press, New York, 1989, p.188.
42. Defined as "concessional in character to avoid severe burden on developing countries and conveys a grant element of at least 25 percent."
43. *Japan's ODA 1989*, Ministry of Foreign Affairs, 1990, p.55.
44. A critical analysis of Japan's ODA, citing empirically a number of representative cases, is given in Kazuo Sumi, *ODA Enjo no Genjitsu* (The Actual Record of the ODA Aid), Iwanami Shoten, Tokyo, 1989. The author complains of the deliberate hiding of information by the Japanese authorities on many of the critical aspects of the problem.

45. Morishima wrote in *Bungei Shunjū*, September 1979: "Nations are now protected by 'software' such as diplomacy, economics or cultural exchange – not by 'hardware' like tanks and missiles."
46. J.M. Keynes, "Economic Possibilities for our Grandchildren," in *Essays in Persuasion*, Macmillan and Co., Ltd, London, 1931, pp.369, 372.

Bibliography

A. Basic materials relevant to postwar Japan

Ackerman, E.A., *Japan's Natural Resources and Their Relation to Japan's Economic Future*, University of Chicago Press, Chicago, 1953.

Bronfenbrenner, M. and Kogiku, Kiichiro, "The Aftermath of the Shoup Tax Reforms," *National Tax Journal*, Vol. 10, No.3 (September 1957), pp.236–54 and Vol. 10, No.4 (December 1957), pp.345–60.

The Cambridge History of Japan, The Twentieth Century, edited by Peter Duus, Cambridge University Press, New York, 1988.

Cohen, Jerome B., *Japan's Economy in War and Reconstruction*, University of Minnesota Press, Minneapolis, 1949.

Cohen, Theodore, *Remaking Japan: The American Occupation as New Deal*, The Free Press, New York, 1987.

Dore, R.P., *Land Reform in Japan*, Oxford University Press, London, 1959.

Dunn, Frederick S., *Peace-Making and the Settlement with Japan*, Princeton University Press, Princeton, 1963.

Fearey, Robert A., *The Occupation of Japan, Second Phase: 1948–50*, Macmillan, New York, 1950.

Fodella, Gianni (ed.), *Social Structures and Economic Dynamics in Japan up to 1980*, Università Bocconi, Milano, 1975.

Japan's Economy: In a Comparative Perspective, Paul Norbury Publications, Ltd, Tenterden, Kent, 1983.

Goldsmith, R.W., *The Financial Development of Japan, 1868–1977*, Yale University Press, New Haven, 1983.

Goodman, Grant K. (ed.), *The American Occupation of Japan: A Retrospective View*, Center for East Asian Studies, University of Kansas, Lawrence, Kansas, 1968.

Grad, Andrew J., *Land and Peasant in Japan: An Introductory Survey*, Institute of Pacific Relations, New York, 1952.

Hall, Robert K., *Education for a New Japan*, Yale University Press, New Haven, 1949.

Harvard-Yenching Institute, *A Selected List of Books and Articles on Japan in English, French and German* (compiled by Hugh Borton, Serge Elisséeff,

William W. Lockwood and John C. Pelzel), Harvard-Yenching Institute, Cambridge, Mass., 1954.

Iijima, Nobuko (ed.), *Pollution Japan: Historical Chronology*, Asahi Evening News, Tokyo, 1979.

Japan Resources Association, *A Key to Japan's Recovery – Natural Resources Policy and the Occupation* (edited by Shun'ichi Uchida, et al.), Japan Resources Association, Tokyo, 1986 (bilingual).

Kahn, Herman *The Emerging Japanese Superstate: Challenge and Response*, Prentice-Hall, Englewood Cliffs, N.J., 1970.

Kōdansha, *Encyclopedia of Japan*, 9 volumes (Editor-in-chief: Gen Itasaka), Kōdansha, Tokyo, 1983.

MacArthur, Douglas, *Reminiscences*, McGraw-Hill, New York, 1964.

Martin, Edwin M., *The Allied Occupation of Japan*, Stanford University Press, Stanford, 1948.

Mitsubishi Economic Research Institute, *Mitsui-Mitsubishi-Sumitomo: Present Status of the Former Zaibatsu Enterprises*, Mitsubishi Economic Research Institute, Tokyo, 1955.

Okimoto, Daniel I., *Between MITI and the Market*, Stanford University Press, Stanford, 1989.

Passin, Herbert, *Society and Education in Japan*, Columbia University Teachers College Press, New York, 1965.

Patrick, Hugh and Rosovsky, Henry (eds.), *Asia's New Giant – How the Japanese Economy Works*, The Brookings Institution, Washington, D.C., 1976.

Patrick, Hugh and Tachi, Ryūichiro (eds.), *Japan and the United States Today: Exchange Rates, Macroeconomic Policies, and Financial Market Innovations*, Center of Japanese Economy and Business, Columbia University, New York, 1986.

Samuels, Richard J., *The Business of the Japanese State*, Cornel University Press, Ithaca, N.Y., 1987.

SCAP Government Section, *Political Reorientation of Japan, September 1945 to September 1948*; *Report*, 2 vols., 1949, Government Printing Office, Washington D.C., 1949.

SEKAI (Editorial Staff of), *Three Statements for World Peace*, Iwanami Shoten, Tokyo, April 1950.

Shinohara, Miyohei, *Industrial Growth, Trade, and Dynamic Patterns in the Japanese Economy*, University of Tokyo Press, Tokyo, 1982.

U.S. Department of State, *Occupation of Japan: Policy and Progress*, Government Printing Office, Washington, D.C., 1946. (Reprint, 1969, Greenwood Press, New York.)

Vogel, Ezra F., *Japan as Number One – Lessons for America*, Harvard University Press, Cambridge, Mass., 1979.

Ward, Robert E. and Shulman, F.J. (eds.), *The Allied Occupation of Japan: 1945–1952: An Annotated Bibliography of Western-Language Materials*, American Library Association, Chicago, 1974.

Yamamura, Kōzō and Yasuba, Yasukichi (eds.), *The Political Economy of Japan: Vol. 1. The Domestic Transformation*, Stanford University Press, Stanford.

1987, Vol. 2. *The Changing International Context* (edited by Inoguchi, Takashi and Okimoto, D.I.), Stanford University Press, Stanford, 1988.

B. Other materials of special relevance

Balassa, Bela and Noland, Marcus, *Japan in the World Economy*, Institute for International Economics, Washington, D.C., 1988.

Blakeslee, George H., *A History of the Far Eastern Commission*, Government Printing Office, Washington, DC, 1953

Bronfenbrenner, Martin, "Inflation Theories of the SCAP Period," *HOPE*, Vol. 7, 1975, No.2, pp.137–55.

Caves, Richard E., "Export-led Growth and the New Economic History," in Jagdish N. Bhagwati, et al. (eds.), *Trade, Balance of Payments and Growth*, 1971, Amsterdam: North Holland, pp.403–42.

"International Corporations: The Industrial Economics of Foreign Investment," *Economica*, New Series, Vol. 38, No.149, 1971, pp.1–27.

David, Abe and Wheelwright, Ted, *The Third Wave: Australia and Asian Capitalism*, 1989, Sutherland, NSW, Australia: Left Book Club Co-operative, Ltd.

Fukutake, Tadashi, *Japanese Society Today*, 1974, Tokyo: University of Tokyo Press.

Gibney, Frank, *Japan: The Fragile Super Power*, New York: W.W. Norton & Co., 1975

Gunther, John, *The Riddle of MacArthur: Japan, Korea and the Far East*, Harper & Brothers, New York, 1951.

Hadley, Eleanor, "Trust Busting in Japan," *Harvard Business Review*, Vol. 26 (July 1948), pp.425–40.

Hanke, Steve H. (ed.), *Privatization and Development*, Institute of Contemporary Studies, San Francisco, 1987.

Hymer, Stephen, *The International Operations of National Firms: Study of Direct Foreign Investment*, MIT Press, Cambridge, Mass. 1976.

Jansen, Marius, *Japan and the West*, Princeton University Press, Princeton, 1980.

Kojima, Kiyoshi, *Direct Foreign Investment: A Japanese Model of Multinational Business Operations*, Croom Helm Ltd, London, 1978.

Komiya, Ryūtaro, Okuno, Masahiro and Suzumura, Kōtaro (eds.), *Industrial Policy of Japan*, Academic Press Japan, Inc., Tokyo, 1988.

Lange, Oskar and Taylor, Fred M., *On the Economic Theory of Socialism*, University of Minnesota Press, Minneapolis, 1938.

Lincoln, Edward J., *Japan: Facing Economic Maturity*, The Brookings Institution, Washington D.C., 1988.

Lindbeck, Assar, "The Efficiency of Competition and Planning" in *Planning and Market Relations*, edited by Michael Kaser and Richard Portes, Macmillan, London, 1971, pp.83–113.

Minami, Ryōshin, *The Turning Point in Economic Development: Japan's Experience*, Kinokuniya Bookstore Co., Tokyo, 1973.

Odaka, Kōnosuke, Ono, Keinosuke and Adachi, Fumihiko, *The Automobile*

Industry in Japan: A Study of Ancillary Firm Development, Kinokuniya Company Ltd, Tokyo, 1988.

Okimoto, D.I. and Rohlen, T.P., *Inside the Japanese System: Readings on Contemporary Society and Political Economy*, Stanford: Stanford University Press, 1988.

Packard, George, R., III, *Protest in Tokyo: The Security Treaty Crisis of Tokyo*, Princeton University Press, Princeton, 1966.

Patrick, Hugh (ed.), *Japan's High Technology Industries – Lessons and Limitations of Industrial Policy*, University of Tokyo Press, Tokyo, 1986.

Penrose, Edith T., "Foreign Investment and the Growth of Firm," *Economic Journal*, Vol. 66 (June 1956), pp.220–35.

Pugel, T.A., "Limits of Trade Policy toward High Technology Industries: the Case of Semiconductors" in R. Sato and P. Wachtel (eds.), *Trade Friction and Economic Policy*, Cambridge University Press, Cambridge 1987.

Sax, Joseph L. and Conner, Roger L., "Michigan's Environmental Protection Act of 1970: A Progress Report," *Michigan Law Review*, Vol. 70, No.6 (May 1972), pp.1003–106.

Schumpeter, Joseph A., "The Instability of Capitalism," *Economic Journal*, Vol. 38 (September 1928), pp.361–86.

Tamagna, F.M., "The Fixing of Foreign Exchange Rates," *Journal of Political Economy*, March 1945, pp.57–72.

Tsuru, Shigeto, *Towards a New Political Economy* (Vol. 13 of *Collected Works of Shigeto Tsuru*), Kōdansha, Tokyo, 1976.

The Mainsprings of Japanese Growth: A Turning Point?, Atlantic Institute, Paris, 1976.

Vernon, Raymond, "International Investment and International Trade in the Product Cycle," *Quarterly Journal of Economics*, Vol. 80 (May 1966), pp.190–207.

Vickers, John and Yarrow, George, *Privatization – An Economic Analysis*, The MIT Press, Cambridge, Mass., 1988.

C. Selected list of publications in Japanese

(a) Official publications

Special Survey Committee of Ministry of Foreign Affairs, *Basic Problems for Postwar Reconstruction of Japanese Economy* (Nihon Keizai Saiken no Kihon Mondai), September 1946 (Japanese Original), 1977 (English edition), Japan Economic Research Center, Tokyo.

Economic Stabilization Board, *Comprehensive Report on Damages to Japan from the Pacific War* (Taiheiyō Sensō niyoru Wagakuni no Higai Sōgō Hōkokusho), April 1949.

Economic White Paper, No.1 (Keizai Jissō Hōkokusho), July 1947.

International Enterprise Section, Ministry of International Trade and Industry, *Business Activities of Japanese Firms in Foreign Countries* (Wagakuni Kigyō no Kaizai Jigyō Katsudō), 1990.

(b) Statistical materials

Ohkawa, K., Shinohara, M. and Umemura, M. (eds.), *Estimates of Long-term Economic Statistics of Japan since 1868*, Vols.1–14 (Chōki Keizai Tōkei – Suikei to Bunseki), Tōyō Keizai Shimpōsha, Tokyo, 1965–88.

The Bank of Japan, Research and Statistics Department, *Economic Statistics Annual* (Keizai Tōkei Nempō), Annual Series (bilingual).

Comparative Economic and Financial Statistics: Japan and Other Major Countries (Nihon Keizai o Chūshin tosuru Kokusai Hikaku Tōkei), Annual Series (bilingual).

Analysis of Business Conditions of Major Enterprises (Shuyō Kigyō Keiei Bunseki), Annual Series.

(c) Other important works cited

Arisawa, Hiromi (ed.), *History of the Showa Era Economy* (Shōwa Keizai Shi), 1976, Tokyo: Nihon Keizai Shimbun Sha.

Hayashi, Yūjirō, *Economic Planning in Japan* (Nihon no Keizai Keikaku), Tōyō Keizai Shimpōsha, Tokyo, 1957.

Ishikawa, Tatsujirō, *The National Railroad – Its Function and the Structure of its Finance* (Kokutetsu – Kinō to Zaisei no Kōzu), Kōtsū Nihon Sha, Tokyo, 1975.

Komiya, Ryūtaro, *Studies on the Present-day Japanese Economy* (Gendai Nihon Keizai Kenkyū), Tokyo Daigaku Shuppankai, Tokyo, 1975.

The Japanese Economy Today (Gendai Nihon Keizai), Tokyo Daigaku Shuppankai, Tokyo, 1988.

Miyazaki, Yoshikazu, *Gendai Kigyō-ron Nyūmon* (Introduction to the Theory of the Firm in the Present-day), Yūhikaku, Tokyo, 1985.

Business Groups in the Postwar Japan, 1960–1970 (Sengo Nihon no Kigyō Shūdan – Kigyō Shūdanhyō niyoru Bunseki: 1960–1970), Nihon Keizai Shimbun Sha, Tokyo, 1976.

The Structure and Performance of the Japanese Economy (Nihon Keizai no Kōzō to Kōdō), in 2 volumes, Chikuma Shobō, Tokyo, 1985.

Nihon Sangyō Kōzō Kenkyūsho (ed.), *An Analysis of Japanese Heavy and Chemical Industries on the Basis of the 1961 Input-Output Table* (Shōwa 36-nen Sangyō-Renkanhyō no Sakusei niyoru Wagakuni Jūkagaku Kōgyō no Bunseki), Nihon Sangyō Kōzō Kenkyūsho, Tokyo, 1964.

Nihon Sozei Kenkyū Kyōkai, *The Shoup Recommendations and the Japanese Tax System* (Shoup Kankoku to Wagakuni Zaisei), Nihon Sozei Kenkyū Kyōkai, Tokyo, 1983.

Okamoto, Yasuo, "Multinational Firms and the Multinationalization of Japanese Firms" (Takokuseki Kigyō to Nihon Kigyō no Takokusekika), Nos.1–4, *Keizaigaku Ronshū*, Vol. 53, no.1 (April 1987), pp.2–37, Vol. 54, No.3 (October 1988), pp.67–92, Vol. 55, No.2 (July 1989), pp.43–76, and Vol. 56, No.1 (April 1990), pp.53–100.

Shinohara, Miyohei, *A Treatise on Industrial Structure* (Sangyō Kōzō Ron),

Chikuma Shobō, Tokyo, 1976.

Sumi, Kazuo, *The Actual Record of the ODA Aid* (ODA Enjo no Genjitsu), Iwanami Shoten, Tokyo, 1989.

Takemae, Eiji, *Postwar Labor Reforms in Japan* (Sengo Rōdō Kaikaku), Tokyo Daigaku Shuppankai, Tokyo, 1982.

Tanaka, Kakuei, *The Plan for Remodeling the Japanese Archipelago* (Nihon Rettō Kaizō Ron), Nikkan Kōgyō Shimbunsha, Tokyo, 1972.

Tsuru, Shigeto, *Reflections on the Price of Land* (Chika o Kangaeru), Iwanami Shoten, Tokyo, 1990.

Uekusa, Masu, "How Is the Corporate Tax System Working Actually?" (Hōjin Zeisei no Jittai o Tsuku), *Tōyō Keizai,* August 4, 1973, pp.52–59.

Series editor's note

MARK PERLMAN

Widely honoured for his scholarship (including the Presidency of the International Economic Association and several honorary degrees, including one of two ever given to Japanese by Harvard), well-recognized as a principal intellectual leader and influence in Japan itself, Professor Shigeto Tsuru is known to many in the West for his extensive, if seemingly unorthodox, work in macroeconomic theory. Among the earliest of these are his classic comparisons of Quesnay's *Tableau* with Leontief's Input–Output analysis (in 1942) and Marx's *Tableau* with "Underconsumption (including some Harrodian) Theory" in 1953, his 1938 essay, "Mr Dobb and Marx's Theory of Value," and to his aficionados his very youthful (1934) "Dialogue between Denis Diderot and Karl Marx." But along with these theoretical essays are many works trying to explain Japanese economic insitutions not only to the Western world, but, needless to say, to the Japanese. This volume is but the latest of many such efforts.

For many, certain facts of Professor Tsuru's professional life are likely unknown. He is a man of strong intellectual views, individually arrived at and continuously subject to empirical testing and revision. He was wont to quote Quesnay's admonition to the effect that "Ceux deux parties, je veux dire la Théorie et l'expérience, que se concilient parfaitment bien, lorsqu'ellesse trouvent réünies dans une même personne, se sont de tout tems mais envain, livré une guerre continuelle, lorsqu'ellesse trouvent séparées." Secondly, by birth and by marriage he has had access not only to what some call the "corridors of power," which makes his insights particularly sophisticated, but also because of his integrity he has been able to play a regular role in the mainline socialistic opposition camp in Japan, while at the same time having continued contact with thinkers in other camps. Thirdly, he is a literary stylist – early on he became an indefatigable scholar/writer of originality, sophistication and wit. His formal economics education was largely in pre-Second World War America, but his professional career, as both a theorist and as a policy analyst, largely flowered in war-time and post-Second World War Japan.

Born in 1912, the son of a Nagoya engineer-industrialist, Tsuru, while still in higher school, became politically involved in 1929–30 as one of the student leaders in "Anti-Imperialist League" activities against the Japanese military, then in the early stage of aggression towards China. For his troubles, he was arrested and detained for several months. Afterwards, having been expelled from his high school, he was sent by a wise (if exasperated) father abroad to America to complete his education.

His undergraduate work was at an excellent, if small, college (Lawrence) in Wisconsin as well as at the University of Wisconsin in Madison during the summer sessions. At that time, his major academic interest centred around the fields of social psychology and philosophy; and his first publication in a professional journal was on the subject of "The Meaning of Meaning" in 1932. In his junior year he transferred to Harvard where he took his baccalaureate degree (1935) and his doctorate (1940). In Cambridge, Massachusetts, he became one of the recognized leading intellectual leaders of the graduate student elite of the time – an elite including Paul A. Samuelson, Richard M. Goodwin, Robert Bryce, Robert Triffin, Abram Bergson, John Kenneth Galbraith, Alan and Paul Sweezy, Wolfgang Stolper, and Richard A. Musgrave, to say nothing of such "youngsters" as Evsey Domar, James Tobin, Joe S. Bain, and Robert M. Solow.

His pre-Second World War published works in Marxian economic theory were regarded as particularly original and important, an example being "On Reproduction Schemes" written earlier but appearing as an appendix to Paul Sweezy's *The Theory of Capitalist Development*, 1942. Schumpeter, to whose guidance Tsuru owed a great deal, discussed, in his *History of Economic Analysis*, the relation between Marx and Quesnay and wrote that on this subject "the interested reader finds all he needs in ... [the appendix to Sweezy's volume] by Shigeto Tsuru." Tsuru was actually one of the leaders in the founding of *Science & Society – A Marxian Quarterly*, on account of which he was to suffer McArthyite persecution in 1950s.

Another important fact of his life was that in June 1939 he married Miss Masako Wada, daughter of Dr Koroku Wada (later to become President of the Tokyo Institute of Technology), himself a brother of Marquis Kido, the Lord Keeper of the Privy Seal, the Kido family being the descendants of the so-called "Three Architects of the Meiji Restoration." Tsuru and his wife remained in the United States for several months after the Pearl Harbour attack by Japan before they were repatriated as enemy aliens, during which time, however, Tsuru was able to conduct a fruitful academic life at Harvard, assisting Gottfried Haberler in the research on quantitative import control and Wassily Leontief on the treatment of government sector in the input–output analysis.

It can be surmised that given his political views, Tsuru was not immediately called to Japanese government service; instead, he established some ties with a business college, the one antecedent to what is now Hitotsubashi University (of which ultimately he became President). In 1944, he was drafted into the Japanese army as an infantry private, but after three months he was discharged and was invited to join the Japanese Foreign Office. What role he was to play there is not known; and Tsuru himself has spoken little about it. But the record shows that he was sent to the Soviet Union in March 1945 and returned to Tokyo at the end of May just after the heaviest American air-raid on that city. Train services stopped short of the terminus, and he walked the last miles in the midst of devastation only to discover *miracolo miracoli* that, except for his library, his home (part of the Kido family complex in Minato-ku) had been virtually uniquely spared.

The painstaking role of his wife's uncle, the Marquis Kido, in attempting to end the war is well-known; what is not as well-realized is that Tsuru learned most of the action directly at second hand, so to speak, partly because the Marquis was living in the same house as Tsuru after the May air-raid. Thus, from 1944 until the present, Tsuru has observed all major Japanese developments more or less "at nose length." During the Occupation, Tsuru served first as an economic advisor to the Economic and Scientific Section of the Supreme Commander of the Allied Powers. Then, during the brief Socialist (coalition) Administration of Prime Minister Katayama, Tsuru was made a vice-minister with the Economic Stabilization Board (1947) at the age of thirty-five. His work there is best known for his almost one-man endeavour in the drafting of the *Economic White Paper of 1947*.

After the fall of that government, he rejoined the faculty of Hitotsubashi, where he built up the well-known Institute of Economic Research. In reviewing his intellectual development, Tsuru has noted the influence of a variant American pragmatism on the eventual flowering of his thinking.

Accordingly, his erstwhile Marxism, generally idiosyncratic and rarely doctrinaire, developed gradually into a blended Fabian form, but also in part into a concentration on applied rather than only on theoretical problems. In particular, his work on the relationship of the measurement of all aspects of national income, including externalities and other environmental considerations, to real welfare-orientated national development, is worth close attention. It was quite appropriate that Harvard University, when conferring an honorary degree to Tsuru in 1985, referred to him as "one of Japan's most highly esteemed economists and a founder of the Japanese environmental movement."

He has written prolifically; indeed, when he eventually retired from

Hitotsubashi University (1975) and published his *selected* works in collection, there were twelve volumes in Japanese and one volume containing but one-third of his many English essays. To these should be added, of course, seven books originally published in English as well as his Australian Dyason Lectures and his forthcoming Italian Mattioli Lectures.

After retirement from Hitotsubashi, Tsuru joined the *Asahi Shimbun*, a major newspaper in Japan, as an editorial advisor where he remained for ten years, after which he became professor in the faculty of international studies of the Meiji Gakuin University. He retired from this in 1990 and now serves as Chairman of the Village Shonan Incorporated, a newly established scientific and cultural center for international exchange in the process of construction at present.

He is a member of the prestigious Japan Academy today.

Index